# THE NEW RULES

## OF

# REAL ESTATE INVESTING

## 24 LEADING EXPERTS REVEAL THEIR
## REAL ESTATE SECRETS

BY

## Chris Prefontaine

ALONG WITH

## Nick Prefontaine & Zach Beach

SMART
Real Estate
COACH

D1554193

Published by Chris Prefontaine

ISBN: 978-1-7338606-0-4

Contact us at support@smartrealestatecoach.com

Printed in The United States of America

This publication is designed to provide accurate and authoritative information in regard to the subject matter covered. It is sold with the understanding that the publisher is not engaged in rendering legal, accounting, or other professional services. If legal advice or other expert assistance is required, the services of a competent professional person should be sought.

# YOUR FREE BONUS

We've loaded this book up with advice and insights from the 24 leading experts we interviewed and from our own team members. But we didn't want to stop there, so we created a **resources page** including everything referenced in this book—links, PDFs, videos, and more—to accommodate your learning style and help you put the advice from this book into action.

The great news is that you can access this site completely free of charge. Just fill out our simple form and we'll give you access to the entire vault of resources—and you might even find a few free gifts in your mailbox!

You can find it at

## TheNewRulesBook.com

And if you have any questions, you can always contact our team at

## Support@SmartRealEstateCoach.com

Please note that Chris Prefontaine or Chew Publishing, Inc. DBA / SmartRealEstateCoach.com earnings are in no way average and that any examples provided should not be considered typical as your results will vary due to many factors. If you think you can get rich by simply clicking a button or allowing others to do all the work, then we recommend you do not invest your money in any educational program or business tool, as it will not be a good investment. Our team is here to support you and we hope that you make buying decisions because you are also dedicated to success.

From time to time we send emails promoting other company's products or services and may earn commission for doing so. It is important to realize that while we only send products that we believe will help your business, we do not recommend investing in anything without doing your own due diligence. As with anything in life, in order to succeed you will need to put forth effort and be persistent. And finally, any information provided is educational and cannot be taken as legal or financial advice.

We are not attorneys. Laws change in every state from time to time. Always check with your attorney before buying and/or selling real estate for the applicable laws, etc. These laws may or may not affect some of the techniques we teach. There are no laws to our knowledge that can STOP you from profiting in real estate, but you'll need to seek a qualified local real estate attorney.

As of the posting of this disclosure, we are aware of laws in the following areas that are different from other states. This is not all inclusive and only those that we are aware of:

Texas: Lease/purchase restrictions unless you comply with local changes. We have JV Partners in Texas currently.

Maryland: Foreclosure laws within 20 days of foreclosure. We don't teach foreclosure for many reasons. Some restrictions with buying subject to existing mortgages.

North Carolina: Comply with 3-day right of rescission as well as recording agreements when doing lease/purchase.

California: Foreclosure property laws. We don't teach foreclosure.

Obviously if you are outside of the US, your laws will vary, and we are not familiar with them.

This book is dedicated to all of our associates around the country and to all aspiring real estate entrepreneurs...

May our paths cross before we fill all states!

# CONTENTS

# FOREWORD

## Dr. Joe Vitale

Too many books these days are fluff. They're smoke and mirrors. They don't have much substance. They sell the sizzle and not the steak. That's not what I want, and I doubt it's what you want. What you and I want is material that works: ideas and methods we can implement—proven strategies we can take to the bank.

The good news is that this book delivers exactly what you want. It's got techniques, hacks, shortcuts, and more, all straight from the minds of the people living and breathing success. I loved thumbing through the pages, stopping anywhere, and finding golden nuggets of practical wisdom. This is the kind of vault of knowledge worth hundreds of thousands of dollars in real-world experience. You are going to love it.

I also know Chris personally. He's got an amazing track record of success. He's always learning, stretching, trying new ideas, and helping others with his tested wisdom. He's gathered experts he knows and picked their brains for their street-smart insights, secrets, tips, and more. These people are living this business, and they're openly sharing their discoveries with you.

If you're serious about wanting to be successful in this business, you've picked up the right book at the right time. It's a how-to manual for your expanded success. Read it. Implement it. And keep referring back to it. It's going to be your best friend on your road to more sales and more success. Expect miracles.

**Dr. Joe Vitale** is the author of way too many books to list here. Find out more about him at MrFire.com.

# INTRODUCTION

In 1991, after my father sold his company, I was employed by the new owners. The independent, entrepreneurial thinking that I was so used to didn't last long. I was called into my managers' office after three short months and told I was being fired. I didn't know it then (at the age of 25), but this was a serious turning point—and the best thing that could have happened to me.

I had been dabbling in real estate for the past two years with a builder friend and partner. We would tie up pieces of land with no money down, package a "to-be-built" home on it, and once it was sold to a buyer, we would build it with all the subcontractors and suppliers waiting until the end of funding to get their money.

In 1994, I got my real estate license and became a real estate agent at ReMax. In 1995, I bought a Realty Executives franchise. My territory was Central Massachusetts. With an office of 15 agents, we were operating at much higher than the per agent homes sold nationally (I believe the national average is still between one and four, which is pathetic; our agents had a minimum of 12 or they were asked to leave). I had a small team: one assistant and one part-time runner who put up signs, took pictures, and ran personal errands. We were doing 100 homes yearly.

One day in 2000, I was in my office prospecting—alone—and a gentleman walked in. We'll call him Tim. He said he was with Coldwell Banker and told me they were interested in moving my team to their offices. Long story short, after two months of negotiations, they agreed to pay approximately $250,000 to have me and all my agents. But before I could take the offer, I had to first structure some kind of deal to be released from my franchise, which we ended up doing for a small cost.

At Coldwell Banker, I continued my new construction activities and did some land flipping. I'm a big advocate of constant education, and in one of the high-end programs I was in ($1,000 per month back then was certainly "high end"), I met a gentleman who broke off on his own to start speaking, coaching, and training.

He asked if I would work as a coach with his team, and I agreed to do it a couple days a week. I ended up coaching 48 clients for a couple years, all high-end real estate agents and investors earning over $1 million each.

In the years before the 2008 real estate debacle, we completed numerous rehab projects, new construction homes, condominium conversions (multi-unit buildings turned into individual condos after the legal work, engineering, and local permitting were done), and other investments. My post-2008 experience is covered in my first bestseller, *Real Estate on Your Terms: Create Continuous Cash Flow Now, Without Using Your Cash or Credit*—and alluded to throughout this book—but the lessons that process taught me were invaluable, and I'm thankful for them now. At the time, the 1991 firing and the 2008 crash seemed like rotten experiences, but in reality, they were amazingly timely. And I now know that for sure.

I want to help the struggling investor who is looking to take their business to the next level. I want to help the corporate person wishing they didn't have to go to their job on a daily basis.

Coaching investors over the last six years or so, I've noticed an enormous gap: it's the difference between buying a course or going to a seminar and confidently completing a deal. Most courses or seminars are built to give you enough—*but not all*—of the skill sets and resources necessary for a successful, fun, and profitable real estate business.

Along with my kids and our amazing team, I coach and train investors on how to actually go out and get deals done. Every week, we do free strategy calls for people who have seen our webinar or purchased our video program, the **Quantum Leap System (QLS)**, and on almost every call, we hear the same two things:

1  "Yeah, but is this course going to give me everything A-Z, or just upsell me to something else?"

2  "I've already spent thousands [or "tens of thousands," or "over $100,000"] on education, and I haven't done any deals."

All I can say to this is "wow"—but we've acted on it. It drove us to take things further than just our **Quantum Leap System (QLS)** course. We did two very important things:

First, we created a community of what we call "associates" around the country who can literally do deals with us. Second, to further our efforts to close the gap and help you—yes, *you*—do deals and design a lifestyle you deserve, I decided to write this book along with my son Nick and my son-in-law Zach.

Nick was in the same office as me for several years as I worked through the 2008 mess with banks, suppliers, the IRS, credit card companies, and more. He is now our buyer specialist in our own buying and selling entities and a coach to many of our associates and students.

Zach went from bartender and personal trainer to our seller specialist in our buying and selling entities. He also coaches many of our associates and students. They are both amazingly effective and efficient.

With over 100 episodes behind us on our top-rated **The Smart Real Estate Coach Podcast**, we decided to take 24 of the episodes that we feel will best help you to close that gap, summarize them for you in an easy-to-read format, and add our personal touch—in the form of notes, comments, and "takeaways"—since we know all of the interviewees and the techniques and subject matter we've discussed with them.

We encourage you to make notes on each chapter and list some of your own takeaways. This book is not meant to make you an expert in every area it covers, but to give you resources, references, and a place to go as you encounter opportunities and challenges in your own business.

We buy primarily with lease purchase, owner financing, or subject to existing financing because it allows us to do deals without using our money, credit, or signing personally on anything. We do, however, come across other deals and other challenges that require us to utilize the strategies offered by experts in these chapters. We want you to be able to do the same, becoming the "master transaction engineer" I wrote about in *Real Estate on Your Terms.*

Set up a schedule: finish just one chapter every _____ (go ahead and fill in "day," "week," or whatever works for you), and when you've finished the book, I invite you to email Nick, Zach, and me. We'll be happy to offer you a free strategy call. Just email support@ smartrealestatecoach.com and include New Rules strategy call in the subject line.

**Happy studying!**

Chris

**P.S.** If you haven't read my first book, *Real Estate on Your Terms: Create Continuous Cash Flow Now, Without Using Your Cash or Credit,* I'd like to send you a copy *for free*. Seriously! I'll even pay for the shipping costs. You can find more info on our free *New Rules* **resources page** at TheNewRulesBook.com

# BE THE FIRST PENGUIN

## On Mentors, Bravery, and Daily Disciplines

### Catapulting with the Right Coach

I was reminded recently of Tim, one of my coaches who was incredibly effective for me way back in 1995–2000. Tim always pushed me hard in March: he pushed me to prospect, network, and generally work hard. Why in March? Because I was a real estate broker, and all of that work in the spring set up my entire summer season of earning—if I did it properly.

I do the same thing with our associates around the country (**Associate Level** with **Smart Real Estate Coach** is by application only; learn more at smartrealestatecoach.com/associate). From January to May, I push them very hard. Then I do it again from June through October. It truly sets up the whole next year. I'll call up one of our associates and say, "Look, don't worry about your results this month. It's irrelevant to what you're doing this month. *Do* worry about sticking with the game plan we put in place that said if you do A, B, and C, you'll get the results you want. Just stick with that and, over time, the average will go up and down, but it will happen." What we do is very predictable when properly executed.

This past month, for example, we took one property and sold one property. On a surface level, you might think, "That's dismal! You guys have been in business for a while!" It doesn't matter. This month, we'll probably sell four and take five or six new homes under contract. Why? We just keep doing the same activities. The end result will be the same, over time—on average. We know this because we track our numbers, which enables us to predict and project with certainty.

I want to paraphrase for you a great article that Denis Waitley wrote called "The Power of the Right Coach." I hope you'll also grab onto this idea of hiring your own coach or mentor and creating the lifestyle that you deserve.

## The Value of a Mentor

You always hear me talk about designing your lifestyle. This is what it's all about. It's really a very simple concept: you find someone who is where you want to be or has been there, someone who has traveled the path you want to travel. You connect with them and ask them to mentor you. *Bam*. That's it.

I'll give you a good example. For years, Bill Gates used to speak with Warren Buffett. I don't know if they still talk—I'm assuming they do—but Gates used to speak with Buffett every single day. A coach not only gives you the strength you need to succeed—we all need and want that—but is also in your face in a positive way with the feedback that you need to adjust your path as you go.

I'm a big advocate of getting on a plane or getting in a car and going to see your mentor. That's why we allow our associates to come to our office and interact with me, with my son-in-law, Zach, my daughter, Kayla, my son, Nick, my wife, Kim, and the rest of our team; it's super-important.

Let me tell you a story about Tim. I was out at Tim's house once in Big Bear, California, where he lived on the lake. Tim's probably a good 15–18 years older than me. We were going for a jog (at the time, we both did a lot of running). I was talking to him about how I was going to expand my brokerage and open other branches, and he just stopped. He put his arm out, stopped me dead in my tracks, and said, "Why do you want to do that?" Standing in the middle of the road, he went on to tell me why that was going to be a waste and an energy drain and would create more headaches. Wow. If I hadn't listened to Tim, I would never have sold several years later like I did. I would still have been in the trenches, probably creating a bunch of overhead with very little net return on investment.

Let me give you a different example. We always do **ACAA** with our associates. What does it mean? It means we get them into **action**. That's the first **A**. Then we **critique** their action—that's the **C**. Then we **adjust** based on that critique—that's the next **A**. Then we take **action**—the last **A**. So it's **action, critique, adjust, action**. Notice I didn't say "action, critique, I quit." It's **action**: a phone call, for example. **Critique** the phone call live. **Adjust** the script based on the critique and go take **action** again. This is a constant, never-ending process, and if you practice **ACAA** with us, you won't get off track over time. Just a simple but effective "Chris-ism" I've utilized since around 2001.

Outstanding achievements and incredible comebacks are the results of a motivation to persist under any and all circumstances that is often instilled by a coach or mentor. Coaches and mentors provide corrective devices to keep you on task. I use **ACAA** as my acronym, but they all do this, consciously or not. Picture yourself as a missile in flight; you need some adjustments here and there in order to hit your target.

Since 1995, I've never been without a coach—sometimes two or three at a time. I'm talking business, personal, physical, nutritional, marketing, you name it. Coaching fees from the 1990s until now have ranged anywhere from $200 to $2,000 a month for generic programs. Then there's the mastermind groups and other higher-level organizations, which brings us to a whole other level.

In 2015, I was part of a mastermind group that cost $25,000 to be a member of. Do you think there's probably some really cool people in that group if they had to pay $25,000? Sure, they had to write that check before they could even show up in the room. Some people might call this crazy, but the reality is that our team is going to *learn* directly from that mastermind. We are going to profit—and already have—multi-millions from this association, from direct takeaways, indirect takeaways, contacts made there. I could bullet point a list as long as my arm.

So who are you associating with? Who is mentoring you? And what are you willing to pay in order to achieve all your goals? "Well, I would do that *after* I earn more," you're thinking. Nope, wrong order. Get resourceful and find a way to get it done *now.*

This year we're looking into next year's mastermind groups, education, and the things that we want to be involved in, so I'm interviewing leaders of two different groups: one is a "seven-figure" mastermind. You have to be doing seven figures to get in; then they have to interview you and vice versa. I want to interview them to see if it's a fit. Recently, I paid to get on a plane and take two and a half days, counting travel, to spend an afternoon and a night with Joe Vitale. Everybody reading this book probably knows Joe Vitale. Since that private dinner, many cool things have come as a result, including him speaking at our **QLS Live** annual event, amazing contacts, JV opportunities, and more. These are things we consciously do here as a group, as a team—and after reading this chapter, I hope that you do them too.

Forget the costs for a second. What if the return on investment was absolutely, literally *infinite*? I can trace half a million bucks, plus more, to the different mentors I've had. That leads to the next question.

## How Do You Choose a Mentor?

Make sure they have a history of success. This sounds obvious, but let me say something that's probably not going to be as obvious, and some people may have an issue with: I have looked back at my coaches, and many of them have had some failures that significantly strengthened their ability to succeed, and thus their ability to coach *me* to succeed.

In addition to picking coaches based on their ability to achieve goals similar to yours, choose mentors who in the process have overcome some of the same obstacles that you're facing or that you think you may face. Denis Waitley says, "Seeing your mentors today is like seeing what you intend to be." Make sure you're watching out for that in your potential mentor.

My 2008 Amazon best-selling book *Real Estate on Your Terms* has stories about the challenges and struggles I went through. If you're listening to someone who says they've never failed, it's highly likely that they are absolutely 100% full of crap, if you'll pardon my French. Why do I say that? Because if you've got the axe against the grindstone and you push hard, sparks are flying. Things are happening. You're going to have some failures. It's not about *whether* you're going to fail; it's about *how you react* to failure.

## Challenges Turned into Successes

In 2008, during the national real estate market crash, I remember reading one book in particular. Now, don't take this as a political statement in any shape or form (remember, this was 2008), but Donald Trump's *Never Give Up: How I Turned My Biggest Challenges into Success* is absolutely a cool book to read. I enjoyed it, probably because he went through many lessons over his years in business. Again, I'm not talking about anything remotely related to politics. It was especially timely for me to read back in '08, in a real estate market that most people will agree was dismal. There are so many opportunities out there now that it's absolutely ridiculous, but there were certainly opportunities in 2008 too. I didn't see them because I was knee-deep in crap, but now I see them, and now I'm ready to be even better positioned for the next downturn. There will be one. It's not *if*, it's *when*.

If you're in real estate, you have to change your focus and stop hanging onto what the media says about how the markets are doing. Yes, I got beat up in 2008, but I can tell you now, my entire business (the way we run it, the financials, the refusal to sign personally and get bank loans, the complete re-engineering of the business) is totally different. And it's all because of 2008. That's why I emphasize that challenges can be turned into successes and we all can be better because of them.

Anyway, Trump's book has an appendix that lists 10 success tips absolutely worth sharing with you here. I'm not going to share all of them, but in no particular order, let me give you a few:

## Never Give Up

First, never give up. Don't settle for remaining in your comfort zone. Complacency is a sure-fire way to get absolutely...nowhere.

What *is* your comfort zone? Give it some thought. Whatever zone you've defined in your mind with that question, that's going to be your ceiling. That's a scary thought, so expand your thinking.

## Expand Your Thinking: Read, Read, Read!

How can you expand your thinking? Well, how about reading books that get you thinking outside your box? I look around my office here, and I see *Showboats Magazine*: big, expensive multi-million dollar boats. Do I want to go out and buy a sailboat tomorrow? No. I have no interest in going for a boring (in my opinion) sail. I do, however, have an interest in knowing how these people think, and how and why they do what they do. *Robb Report* is another one.

A book called *The Magic of Thinking Big*, which I read for the first time on my honeymoon—I'm going to date myself here—in 1986, and which I've read several times since. You can't read these things (or a whole bunch of other things that I'm not mentioning here) without thinking bigger; you just can't. How about joining us for one of our upcoming **QLS Live** events? How about grabbing my book *Real Estate on Your Terms*? Expand your mind. It's critical.

I'm about 20 pages away from finishing *McDonald's: Behind the Arches*. Now, if you want to read a book that *can* and *should* expand your mind, that's a great one. I don't care if you're selling popcorn or you're out buying one home every quarter—that book will get you thinking. Ray Kroc started with absolutely nothing, struggled through two, three, four, maybe more failures and then he built an empire. Read the book. You have to read the book.

## Be Passionate

Another point Trump makes in his appendix to *Never Give Up* is to be passionate. My thoughts on this are very simple: if you love what you're doing, it won't seem like work. I don't say I'm *going to work*; I say I'm *going down to the office*. I just love doing what we do. I recently refocused a lot of my energy, for example, on the coaching side of our business. My team, which is our kids, is now 100% running the buying and selling side, except for the financial aspect: they're doing all the prospecting, they're going on appointments, they're handling the buyers, the paperwork—everything. As for the coaching, I can do it anywhere in the world, and I can do it in my sleep—meaning it comes easy to me. I get up pumped to do it. I'm good at it. I love helping associates create deals (of course, the profit sharing that we do with associates doesn't hurt, either). It's not work for me. It energizes me.

Are you doing what you want to do right now? If you want to latch onto our energy, apply for our **Associates Program** and start profiting this year—let's go crank out some deals together. If your area is not taken and we accept your application, we'll be on the phone soon and we'll go after it together.

Let me just bullet a few other points I invite you to think about, in no particular order.

## Be Focused

Ask yourself this: *What should I be thinking about right now?* Shut out the interference and think about it. In this age of multitasking, this is a valuable technique to get good at: being focused, refocusing, and time blocking. For example, I don't take incoming calls if I'm sitting here doing outgoing. Why? I have no idea who's calling. I'm not in control. It messes up my time. Jumping every time the phone rings or every time an email comes in is absolutely insane.

Make sure you focus. Put a sticky note or an index card on your computer that says, "Is what I am doing right now moving me closer to my goals?" That'll get you thinking. That'll keep you focused. Keep your momentum. Don't procrastinate. Did you ever notice a few good things happening in your life or your business, and then find that it keeps snowballing? Scary. Scary good. Did you ever experience that going in the opposite direction? Let's build upon your successes. In other words, see yourself as victorious. If you see yourself as victorious, it's going to focus you in the right direction.

Read every single book you can get your hands on about the law of attraction—that is, using visualization and affirmation to change your life. I love Joe Vitale's *Zero Limits*, and the entire series of books that came after it. One of the reasons I got on a plane to go see him this month is because of that book. In it you'll also find your way to other authors and speakers who are within the same realm. Here's a takeaway for you. Subscribe to tut.com. I'm not going to tell you what it is. Just go subscribe to tut.com for a daily message, and practice focusing your mind.

## Be Lucky

Be lucky. I know that sounds wacky, but this was in the back of Trump's book, and the old saying, "The harder I work, the luckier I get," is absolutely right. Ron Legrand, one of my past mentors from 2000 and a friend to this day, says "The less I work, the more I make."

## Look at the Solution, Not the Problem

"Look at the solution, not the problem." Trump put a similar one in the back of his book, and then he wrote, "Never give up." He keeps saying that. This thought deserves to be reviewed, remembered, and applied over and over and over again. It's extremely important.

We had plenty of challenges in real estate in 2008, and we learned as we moved forward. If we'd sat and whined and listened to others and listened to the media, we'd be whining for years to come. Instead, we refocused on solutions, new ideas, and moving forward.

Since starting our terms and investment business in the real estate world back at the beginning of 2013 (even though we'd been working in real estate for 21 or 22 years already), we've made mistakes. What do we do with them? We say, *How much did that cost us? How did that happen? What can we do to fix it so it doesn't happen again? Do we have to change any of our forms internally, our checklists, our agreements with the attorneys? What is it that we have to do to only focus on solutions?* And as a result, our businesses is rock-solid. We're able to share that with our associates so they don't have to go through the same mistakes. I'm not saying they're never going to make a single mistake, but if and when they do, they have the answers at their fingertips.

## Be the First Penguin

"Experience is what you get when you didn't get what you wanted." I read that in Randy Pausch's *The Last Lecture*, and it stuck with me, so I've been repeating it over and over again. It's a phrase worth considering, in particular when you're pitched a curveball—when you hit a brick wall or a challenge. With every disappointment and at every roadblock, this "experience" thing is what creates breakthrough industries, breakthrough ideas, breakthrough movements, and in my case, breakthrough re-engineering of our business. I'd even say that some breakthrough professions have been made this way in the real estate world, because it's constantly changing. I think this idea is super-important to keep at the forefront. Maybe put this on another index card or a sticky note for your computer. It's also a reminder for us all that *failure is not just acceptable, it's absolutely essential.*

Because of my failure, we're helping hundreds of other investors have a blast and create a lifestyle for their families that they couldn't even imagine before. In *The Last Lecture,* there's a story about this professor who gave his students a "first penguin" award. The award went to the student or the team that took the biggest gamble in trying new ideas or new technology—and failed to achieve their goals. Think about that: an award for taking the chance, taking the gamble, and *failing.* It enabled them to celebrate that out-of-the-box thinking I always refer to. These students used their imagination in a daring, thought-provoking way.

When penguins are about to jump into water that's likely to be full of predators, one of them has to be the first penguin in, right? The first student who failed at their project for this class got that award. Now they know how to avoid future failures. What can someone who knows only success do? They're more oblivious to all the pitfalls. This brings us back to my point that you should be careful when you pick your mentors.

Can I attest to this personally? Yes, I can. After being in the real estate business in some shape or form since 1991, I was still able to make about 15 or 20 large mistakes in 2005, and some of them made my 2007–8 quite miserable. Then I spent three and a half years trying to fix all of that. As a result, by the end of 2012 (and for the foreseeable future), my wife, Kim, and I were in a position not just to experience our best years ever, but also to *have the best experiences.* We are simply amazed at the healthy, productive, profitable, and *fun* culture that we're currently aligned with—by choice—with our family and everything we do in our business.

I'm not bummed about the 2008 market, in hindsight. With the millions of dollars we lost, the costly things we went through, and the subsequent lessons, I'm ecstatic beyond belief that some of my partners and investors stuck with us. Those who did are all reaping enormous benefits. Those of you who didn't? Well, your loss.

Now, if you'd like to rub elbows with those who've overcome some amazing odds and gone on to great success (not just our team), join us for any of our upcoming **QLS Live** events. Rub elbows with some of these other associates and students. I'm not going to give you names, but there's some really cool stories in there. You're going to learn about them. You're going to meet them. You're going to talk eye-to-eye. You're going to shake hands, and you're going to get an awful lot out of it. If you were to come to an event for the private associate mastermind day and then just go home—I don't want you to, but if you did— you'd get tens of thousands of dollars' worth of lessons and experiences just from that. If you don't recognize the penguin in this situation, you'll have to watch from the sidelines. I don't know how else to put it; I'm always blunt. For those who come to our events, you will experience breakthroughs—in your business, in your income, in your bank balance, and in your personal life.

## Daily Disciplines

I always told our kids when they were growing up that with the right discipline, you can be outstanding at anything. Here's a question for you: What new disciplines could you start acting on tomorrow? Today? Which discipline do you know will improve your business and/ or your life, but you just haven't done it yet? What new disciplines could you start acting on right now? You fill in the blanks here:

**I know if I just did** _____, _____,

**and** _____, **I'd get** _____.

I often combine my thoughts on discipline with the simple concept of "making today a better tomorrow," meaning *improve* every day. Think about just improving $1/10$ of 1% each day; you would have a 368% improvement for the year. Make *today* a better tomorrow because what we do today has a direct relationship to the results we get tomorrow. What we do today, every day, is just what?

*Discipline*. It's about the disciplines that we practice. What is discipline to you? I hope at least one or two words or definitions come to mind, but think about it for one quick second before I give you my thoughts. What is discipline to you?

Dictionary.com says it's "an activity, exercise, or regimen that develops or improves a skill; training." That's their definition. Here's mine: "Doing the things daily that you know you should even when you don't feel like it and even when you don't see immediate results." I'm going to add a third part to that: "...and even when no one's watching." That's my definition.

The common denominator of all the successful people I've been talking about, the ones you should rub elbows with, is that they *form habits*. They form disciplines that failures just don't like to do. If you observed my workday, for example, you might see a very pointed effort to meditate, practice yoga, or work out on any given day. This morning, it happened to be yoga and meditation. Yesterday, it happened to be working out at 4 AM.

You might also see that we track numbers. We track everything. I don't care what position you're in or what you track; when you track and monitor something, it will improve and grow. You might also see some quiet time to journal and think. Those are all pointed disciplines that I've learned to do over the years.

They didn't come easy at first. As you may have read before, it might take you 21 days. It might take you 30. Whatever it takes for you to form that new discipline, start somewhere. People say, "How do you get it all done? How do you do all this discipline stuff? Sounds like a lot of work." Actually, it's a lot of work if you *don't* practice discipline in all that you do.

Let's assume you're brand-new today. Instead of getting caught up in the minutiae and baggage of before, here are some thoughts to consider adding to your day:

## Make Three Calls a Day

I don't care what business you're in; you can do three calls. You can call three new people, three new businesses, three new prospects who can add potential new business for you. For us, that's 10 or 15 a week. That works perfectly. You might want to adjust the numbers for yourself. Now, how about also adding in a few minutes of reading in your area of expertise? How about a daily or a weekly accountability process? If you don't know what that is, let's talk about it. Email me at chris@smartrealestatecoach.com.

## Substitute a Good Discipline for an Unproductive Habit

How about substitution? What does that mean? Take a habit that you currently don't like or currently is not productive and substitute it with something else. Let me give you a really simple, watered-down example: if you currently wake up and go to breakfast or grab coffee, how about substituting a workout, like I do, and following it with something healthy to eat? I love it. I mentioned earlier that I go to the gym at 4 AM. I switched gyms because I found Anytime Fitness, which is open 24/7. That's a gold mine—you can go anytime you want to. No pressure, but why don't you start that? Get up an hour earlier and go to Anytime Fitness. No plug for them. I don't know the owners, but it's the coolest concept.

## Read Daily

What if you started reading? This time I don't mean in your area of expertise, but just to work on your mind. This shouldn't be "I'm going to read *more*." It should be "I'm going to read *10 minutes every single night*" (if you're not already there). If you haven't started that daily habit, don't say "I'm going to read a book a month" or something crazy. Just raise the bar a teeny bit—I don't know, five minutes will do it. Start somewhere. I love the Audible app; I can get more "reading" in by listening at the gym while working out or by listening in the car.

## Journal Daily

You can write in your journal every night. You can answer these questions in your journal. If you don't have a journal, start one. Answer these three questions in your journal every night and you'll be ahead of most people:

- **What was the best thing that happened today?**
- **What was the most challenging thing that happened today?**
- **How can I improve tomorrow?**

Isn't that simple? Write in your journal every single day.

## Start Small

Start with small steps, but *start*. What can you tackle today? Short steps. If you've never done any of these things, don't kill yourself:

don't say, "I'm going to call 20 people starting today. I've got to raise the bar." That's too much. If you've never called anyone before, you're not going to do 20. Do one every third day, maybe, then one every day, then two every day. Constantly raise that bar. Don't say, "I'm going to read a book a week, starting right now." That's not going to happen. Start small and increase by small amounts. These disciplines will eventually become very, very easy, and very, very rewarding.

It was like that when I started writing my first book in August of 2016. To many people, that could seem like a daunting task. It could seem overwhelming. We just took it one step at a time as a team. I'll give you another personal example: my daughter Kayla started riding horses at age seven. I got her started on that. She went from having her horse walk, walk, and step over fence posts that were lying flat on the ground, to jumping five-foot hurdles in national competitions seven years later. That was accomplished with small steps. Nick, when he had his head injury and was in a coma in 2003, had a goal to *run* out of the hospital, but could that happen right then? He started with small steps: therapy, small movements, exercise. Small steps—you get the point.

## Set Your Goals

What else can you do starting today? Regardless of what position you're in, there's an activity. There's a person you can call. There's something that'll make a major impact on your business if you act on it today. What is it for you? Or *who* is it for you? Decide.

**Finish the statement. Get a pen out right now and finish the one that applies to your business:**

If I could get _____ to do business with us, our business would totally change.

If I could get _____ (a prospect) to join with me, it would catapult our business.

If I could get _____ (type of deal), our business would skyrocket.

You get the point here. Those who succeed in any business (and at life in general) have simply decided to do some things that others are not willing to do. Don't be left behind. Very few people realize that success is within their reach. *Your* success is within *your* reach.

## Take Action

Is the word "by" in your daily agenda? Why do I say that? Life goals, the big picture goals, are reached **by** annual goals, which are reached **by** monthly goals, which are reached **by** weekly, and then daily, which are reached **by** what? Your daily disciplines. That's it.

I know people say, "Aw, man, all this sounds like a lot of work. Daily disciplines are going to take all this time, and I don't know if I can do it." No, they're actually easy. What's hard is accumulating all kinds of things on your list that you *don't* do and then trying to tackle them all at once. *That's* hard work. After months and months of not putting in the time on your disciplines and dealing with that heavy workload, you'll say, "I wish I had, I wish I had…" Don't get caught in that wish syndrome. I love what Tony Robbins says: "Don't get caught up *shoulding* all over yourself." Don't "should" all over yourself. That's it!

I want to wrap up with this thought: you'll never, never, never, never change your business or your life until you change something that you do *today*—so what one thing will you start today? Write it down.

You can reread this over and over again. You're probably the type who'll *want to* read this over and over again, but in order to experience a quantum leap in your business, your finances, or your life, you have to *take action*. As I say when I wrap up literally every episode of our podcast (smartrealestatecoachpodcast.com), grab one, two, or three of these action items that I've tossed out—and take action!

## TAKEAWAYS FROM THIS CHAPTER

1 Find a coach who is where you want to be, or has been there.

2 Never give up.

3 Expand your thinking: read, read, read!

4 Subscribe to tut.com.

5 Infuse your day with disciplines like exercise, journaling, and reading.

6 Decide to call three new prospects a day.

7 Whatever your goals, start small and increase gradually.

# ALL IN THE FAMILY

## Nick Prefontaine and Zach Beach

One of the main things we do differently in the training and mentoring space is that we are, first and foremost, a family company. In our opinion, this is a huge differentiator. We buy and sell every month, so our fingers are always on the pulse of the market. We then go out and coach, mentor, and train students around the country to do exactly the same thing, and some of them become what we call our "associates." These are people who actually do deals with us. They are out in the field doing deals on a consistent basis, and we help all along the way, or at particular points. That could mean calling their sellers, their buyers, helping with deal structure—whatever it takes. This is super-important, because people are out there buying courses and attempting deals on their own, and some are making costly mistakes. Others are just not able to pull the trigger out of fear, lack of confidence, or whatever else stops them. We lock arms with them and get the deals done.

We're not about selling another product. *We want to do deals.* The market is missing this important piece: it's all about implementation. Also, the market changes. Major changes can take place in as little as one week, and they can affect your business and cost some dollars if you're not working with someone who is still in the trenches. Unfortunately, there are many, many speakers, educators, and "gurus" who teach and sell products, but haven't done a deal themselves in months or even years.

I'm not aware of a support system anywhere else in the industry—in this country—that allows you, the student, the investor, the corporate person looking to be an investor, to actually speak with and have access to four or five different people like we have on our team, depending upon what you need help with. The kind of support we can provide simply doesn't exist. In fact, one of our company's **Six Core Values** (see page 63) is that *we empower individuals and families.* We happen to do that through real estate, but when you're out there in the trenches, I promise you that there will be challenges—personal challenges, financial challenges, mental and emotional challenges—so the coaching does go beyond real estate.

I've asked two people on the team to contribute here. I want you to get to know them. I want you to see how they can help you personally. I've asked my son-in-law Zach to share with you. He has more or less replaced me on the buying side of our family business. On the coaching side, he helps the students and the associates who are working with sellers in their businesses. I've also asked my son Nick to contribute. He is our buyer specialist, who has basically replaced me on that side of our family buying and selling business. He also works with students around the country when they go to sell their properties, and this includes everything from speaking with their buyers, maximizing their three paydays, getting the deal closed, and more. Since Nick started with me in 2014, our average **Payday #1** grew from $10,400 to over $25,000.

The biggest question I hear is, "OK, I've got property. Now what am I going to do to get it sold?" Everyone panics about that. It's a rather important step because it's going to pay you quite well when done properly. Enjoy this chapter and learn from some of our team members— what their strengths are, and how they can help you.

In contrast to most of the other chapters, this one is kept in the form of the conversation it is based on. You get to "peer in," so to speak, while Nick, Zach, and I have our chat.

## Nick: Born to Do Real Estate Deal-Making

NICK: First, I should mention that, growing up in this business, I was doing cold doors to pre-foreclosures back in high school— when I was 16. My dad first started *this* terms and coaching business around 2013, and already by the end of 2014, he was getting overwhelmed trying to market all of the properties he kept getting, so he asked me to help him out. At the time, I was going full-bore as a real estate agent, so I was hesitant to start helping him. Once I did, I realized it's the best thing I ever did, because it evolved into working with some of the buyers and not just helping with marketing, which is how I started. Dabbling with that more and more led to me becoming the buyer specialist that I am today.

CHRIS: I remember at the end of '14 when we made this move, I was overwhelmed, as Nick said, with buyers. That brings up a very important point. I want readers to know that *we know* what steps you're going to hit. Each week one of our associates calls us and says, "Here's what I'm wrestling with," and we say, "I *knew* that's exactly where you'd be right now." When you start getting four, five, six—certainly when you're up to seven or eight properties—you can sometimes feel overwhelmed. So we're going to walk you through the exact process to scale or create a system or a virtual assistant or another in-house person like Nick or whatever it takes. We've been there, and we're going to help you with the benefit of hindsight.

NICK: When I was a real estate agent and used to call buyers back, I remember always getting very defensive people: "Well, what did you call me for? Are you a real estate agent?" And as soon as I mentioned that I was a real estate agent, they'd hang up on me. These were buyers who had inquired about a property. But when I was returning calls on the rent-to-own side as an investor, it was just so different—so much healthier, because these people didn't know where else to turn. They had experienced a recent life event, perhaps, or maybe were just looking for a better solution and couldn't get conventional financing, so they needed a program like ours.

CHRIS: **I want readers, especially those who are real estate agents, to know that Nick was licensed for the better part of eight years, and I was licensed for the better part of 18 years. We do understand both sides, and we have a huge amount of respect for real estate agents. We're merely pointing out the differences. And I'd also like to say to real estate agents that you are leaving an inordinate amount of money on the table by not understanding or learning these strategies.**

**We have a video as part of program that is called The Path, which outlines for you the day I started in the terms business all the way until the end of 2017. You see what that path is and you can make plans based on what we went through, because you're going to go through the same things. On the *New Rules* resources page at TheNewRulesBook.com, we have a 3 Year Plan to build a $1 million yearly business for you. This is not guesswork. This is what we created, and we're certain you can too. You can probably do it even**

more quickly now that everything is in place, and now that technology and tools have improved. Be sure to download it today.

## Zach: From Bartender/Personal Trainer to Real Estate Investor and Coach

ZACH: I never thought I was going to be involved in real estate. I've been dating Chris's daughter since I was in middle school, so I've always seen real estate from an outside view. The closest I got to it was doing physical labor when I was 13 or 14 years old on one of their "raise the roof" projects, where they would buy a single-level ranch and add a second floor, making it more of a colonial-style home. I needed some extra cash, and physical labor was up my alley, so I didn't mind getting my hands dirty.

So we grew up and I went off to school, and then we decided to move down to Newport, Rhode Island to enjoy the rest of the family down here. I was a bartender and a personal trainer, so I would wake up early in the morning and train people to become fit and healthier (although that gets a little frustrating, because no matter what you tell people to do, some of them don't do any of it). I was bartending late at night, so my schedule was a little crazy.

I was always in the background watching this business develop with Chris and Nick. Eventually, we got the invitation to join the family business. So on the side, I added another project to my day. I started making a few phone calls from home to sellers. That was back in December of 2015 and into the beginning of 2016, when I first started dipping my toes into the water. I started to enjoy it and started to get a little bit better at it.

Kayla and I decided to join the family team full-time in the spring of 2016. My last bartending shift was April 1, 2016— that's when I called it quits. I had a goal in mind that I was going to be done bartending by the time I was 25; I didn't want to make it a life career.

I've been full-time at real estate for just over two years now. So if anyone is reading this who is completely green and has no idea how to get involved with real estate or how to approach it, I would love to help you. I've been there. I simply did what we teach our students: I followed the path and got properly trained. You can too.

CHRIS:   **As part of our free webinar, you get a free strategy call so that you can chat with Nick or Zach or me. You can be specific with your question when you schedule it and say you want to talk to Zach or you want to talk to Nick. Whatever you need help with, we get on the phone with you. That's part of what we do as a family support structure and part of what we offer with our webinar. If you can handle listening to me for 60+ minutes, I encourage you to register for that today. You can go to smartrealestatecoach.com/webinar.**

**Did you notice that Zach said he called from home, for just a few hours a week at first? That's exactly how I started. There was a closet on the second floor of one of our attorneys' offices where Nick and I had an office, and I would go in there a couple of mornings a week for one or two hours and call FSBOs (For Sale by Owners) and expireds (homes that didn't sell with a real estate agent). So if you're reading this and thinking, "I'm in a corporate job, I'm limited by my income and schedule," well, it's the nature of a corporate job that you are limited. But you can make the transition. If I started with just a few hours a week in a closet, you can carve out a few hours a week somewhere and start. We have systems in place that will guide you.**

**On the buyer side, it's a little more automated. Nick is always chatting with people who want to chat with him. So**

unlike the real estate agents of the old days, you're not cold-calling, and you're usually not getting people who will hang up on you. (You might get people *to hang up on*; you can't help that.) But for the most part, you're talking to people who want to talk to you.

---

**Zach:** "No matter where you are in life—in a corporate job, working as a teacher, a police officer, or even a bartender like I was—you can put together a plan of action to accomplish your goals. I have spoken with many of our associates about this, as they are typically not full-time real estate investors. I want you to stop and think to yourself, *Am I truly satisfied where I am in life right now?* If the answer is no, then it's time to evaluate your life and take action. I know it's scary, but there is nothing scarier in life than regret."

## Nick's Niche

NICK: When a buyer has already looked at the property and has returned a form to me saying that they're interested, I call them to review it with them. That's one of my high-payoff activities right now. Just asking a few simple questions, making a few suggestions, I'm able to get their down payment up from, say, $2–5,000 all the way up to $20–30,000 just by asking a few questions. I ask them in a simple, matter-of-fact way, not pressuring them at all.

We'll structure additional down payments to coincide with tax refunds and work bonuses. We'll work out other creative ways to drive up our **Payday #1** and drive up their likelihood of not only being financed eventually, which is their end goal, but also putting them in a position to get the lowest rate and maybe even avoid PMI (private mortgage insurance, which adds cost to the buyer's monthly mortgage payment). That is definitely my high-payoff activity at the moment.

Remember, this isn't just better for us; it's better for the buyer. We try to structure all of our deals so that when the buyer is ready to get their own mortgage, they don't have to come up with more money.

CHRIS: Nick does a fantastic job. He's mastered his script in order to get those down payments up. For those who are looking to improve on getting more money and driving up **Payday #1**, that's all it is—time on the phone helping buyers. If you can increase your **Payday #1** by even $2,500 per deal, for example, look at what that does for your yearly income. It's a game changer.

NICK: It's really the same for the buyer and me. It's just a few simple distinctions and a few tweaks in language and tone that make the conversation flow more easily. There's not a person reading this now who *shouldn't* get the special training that John Martinez offers at a special rate just for our students. I urge you to go pick that up now on the ***New Rules* resources page** at TheNewRulesBook.com.

CHRIS: We provide the scripts you need, and John's training is simply amazing. We only suggest things to our students and our community of associate that we do ourselves. Nick and Zach have gone through John's online course and attended his boot camp. If you're willing to put in the time, the scripts and related training are the easy part. Just like an athlete or professional actor, you're going to spend some time studying.

Now, you're going to have a learning curve, but we're going to help you. How cool would it be to be able to pick up the phone and say "Nick, I'm having a challenge with this," or "My conversions are not the same as you guys are saying it should be"? That's what we're here for; Nick and Zach will role-play with you and help critique your live calls. Your learning curve, your time to master the scripts, will shorten considerably.

Nick mentioned the importance of increasing the down payment. Whether you're in the terms business now or not, you should know that we have the ability to create three paydays per deal. I mentioned earlier about transitioning to this business from the corporate world or whatever it is that you do. Well, what if you could create cash *now*? When I say "now," it could be 30 days or 180 days until your first deal's **Payday** #1. But after that, it's cash over time—cash flow monthly (**Payday** #2). Then you get cash on what we call "the back end," or when you exit the property by getting your tenant-buyer financing (**Payday** #3). That's pretty cool. You create that with every deal. And our average as I'm writing this is around $75,000, give or take $5,000. That's $75,000 created per deal—all three paydays.

I'd like you to pause for a minute or two, close your eyes, and think about what even six new deals this year might look like for your financial picture. The 3 **Year Business Plan** () sketches out 18 deals, but I just want you to think about what 6 × $75,000 might look and feel like.

Now, a word about our mentoring and coaching. I can go all the way back to my college days when I had mentors. I would always try to go see whoever was my mentor at the time. When I was a real estate agent in the 1990s, I remember going to visit a real estate agent who sold 225 homes per year. I had heard him on a CD (probably a cassette at that time), so I went to his office and sat with him. I didn't say a word. I just sat and listened as he prospected. It changed my business forever, and I went off to do 100 homes a year after that.

So how cool would it be for you to come sit with Zach and Nick in what they call their "war room" all day? You'd hear and see them speaking with buyers and sellers. And how cool would it be to spend the next day in the field watching Zach meet with and talk to sellers? Our associates experience a two-day visit as part of their benefits. You have the opportunity to do that!

## Zach's Niche

ZACH: My typical day is calling sellers. Nick must be dealing with really nice people, because I get to deal with the sellers, and I've gotten *plenty* of people hanging up on me. But that comes with the territory, and it's OK. We have a pretty good system set up here with the two virtual assistants I coordinate to make sure we're getting leads from different lead sources. We generally use expireds and For Sale by Owners (FSBOs), but also vacant homes and now, rentals; we're pulling different leads from as many different areas as possible. We don't want to have all of our eggs in one basket. Throughout the day, I'm just trying to generate as many leads as possible. This is clearly one of the key things we teach our students. Without leads, there's no business.

I also take the next step and work on converting those leads into appointments. I go to the house and meet the seller and do a walk-through. This means that I walk through the property, write down some notes, take some pictures, and make sure it's a house I want to purchase through the terms business.

I also make sure that I want to deal with the seller, because if we don't like the seller for whatever reason, we can simply choose not to work with them. Once you understand that there's no shortage of leads in your area, you get to craft your business exactly the way you want to.

After that, I can convert that appointment into a contract. Generally, that's done with a couple of calls to an appointment and then one additional call, in order to plan everything out and make sure that the seller and I are on track with our numbers and our timeframe. The end goal is to get what we call "takens," or getting contracts accepted. (We call them "takens" with our weekly and monthly tracking.) That way, we can get that house over to Nick and let Nick sell it so we all get our three paydays.

## Our Seller Specialist Course

CHRIS:  Thanks to Zach we now have a course that we call the **Seller Specialist** course. Associates can not only go through the training themselves, but they can actually create a business in which they have leverage and can help train another seller specialist for their team. That allows them to start to scale their business like we did, if they choose to. Some of our associates are doing that right now. That's what Zach is working on next, finding another seller specialist so that he can transition into overseeing or coaching him or her. Between our core **QLS (Quantum Leap System)** video program and the **SSP (Seller Specialist Program)**, anyone can run their entire business if they choose not to be an associate and have the hands-on relationship with us.

ZACH:  The **Seller Specialist Program** was definitely a group family effort and we all had to do our part to create it. It took roughly 12 months for me to go from completely green to becoming a seller specialist and being able to generate the leads, go on appointments, and then get contracts accepted. So we created the program that way. Not only do our associates use it, but students around the country use it to become seller specialists themselves, and then to train somebody else. This program is basically walking you through my transition from bartender to handling all the acquisitions for our family company.

I work with associates on their seller scripts. I want them to master their scripts so that eventually they won't need me.

We'll also do a couple of things like role-playing a seller call. That way, I can critique their scripts. We like to be hard on the associates during role-play so that when they get on a call with a seller it's very easy—it's a normal conversation. They can be very nonchalant. Do it enough, and it becomes second nature. The greatest athletes of all time practice hard so that game time is actually easy.

Chris and I also jump on the next-level calls with sellers who are speaking to our associates. Our associates are generally good on the first call even if they're new. The first call is to find out more information—they're dipping their toes in. But, depending on the level that they're at and how long they've been training with us, they may get to a point in the conversation at which they're no longer comfortable. So we have them refer that seller over to us and Chris or I will do that next level of conversation. We can answer some of the more in-depth questions and get the seller to an appointment stage with our associate.

But the number one thing that we help our associates with is deal structuring. It's a huge benefit to have us in their corner. There are just so many ways to structure a deal, from how we buy to how we exit, and everything in between.

Be sure to subscribe to our YouTube channel. We release three videos minimum every week, and one is "Deal Structure Sundays." You'll see all different kinds of deals: youtube.com/smartrealestatecoach.

CHRIS:    **If you're an associate and you're doing deals, you're interacting with us pretty much non-stop. We can safely say that as of this writing, there are two, three, four people a month—maybe that's an understatement—saying to us, "Look, I bought this program and I'm not doing deals," or "I have this mentor, but I only can chat with him or her once a week." That's not what we do.**

One of our **Six Core Values** (see page 63) is to help *complete transactions with the highest integrity* with you as the potential associate anywhere in the country. What does that mean? That means the first two calls might be "starter level"—foundational in nature—but after that it's as needed. *We match effort for effort* (one of our **Six Core Values**; (see page 63)), so if you're actively doing deals, you could be on the phone with us as often as daily—whatever it takes. I spoke with one of our associates three times today. I'm sure that Nick and Zach have spoken with others. We're all hands on deck when you're ready to do deals.

If you're not in the terms business but in a different niche, maybe the mobile home business, we don't coach on that. But find someone that does it, and make sure you're getting that kind of support or mentorship and are in that type of environment.

A great place to hear different experts aside from this book is our podcast at SmartRealEstateCoachPodcast.com.

## Obstacles Associates May Face

NICK: I think the number-one obstacle for people when they first get a property is that they get overwhelmed in spending too much time on the minutiae—stuff that doesn't matter. Part of what I do is to help them pinpoint what's truly important and what to focus on. Once I point it out, it's simpler for them. Without that kind of shepherding, there's the potential for them to get too caught up in the details. A lot of things are not as important as they may think at first, and they benefit from the hurdles, challenges, and mistakes that we've gone through and created systems for.

CHRIS: I remember calling my mentor when I got my first contract. "I got the contract, and I told him I would get it sold for him as part of our deal, because I've got to fill the home before I start making payments—but what the heck am I going to do if I don't?" He chuckled and said, "Look, the last thing you're going to have to worry about is a buyer. When you buy on terms and can offer it on the right terms, you're going to have a flock of buyers. A lot of people are taught in the wholesaling business to build a buyer's list first and then go get a property. We don't concern ourselves with that whatsoever. We get a home and then the buyers flock to us." I remember like it was yesterday when I had 25 or so buyers on my list and I thought that was awesome—we now have several thousand.

NICK: That is a common misbelief amongst investors and in the industry: *I need to build a buyers' list because I don't have anyone to sell the house to.* You'll come to find out, however, that once you get one of these properties and offer it out to the terms market, to the rent-to-own market, it's about five times bigger than the conventional market because it's people who cannot pay cash or get a loan. So buyers are never the problem. In fact, on a national level, about 80% of the buyer pool are in that category: they can't get a loan in their current financial state.

My specialty is helping educate the buyers, and sifting and sorting through them. Once we get a good one, I help them understand the importance of getting their deposit up. Once the buyers let their guard down, they're going to tell you the best they can do. They start to feel like you're part of their team, part of their plan to eventually own their own home instead of renting.

CHRIS: See the *New Rules* **resources page** for information about the free webinar already mentioned. We also have a **Quantum Leap system (QLS)** video program with 10 modules and over 64 videos. In one of the modules, Nick spends a little over an hour telling you all the key points to getting homes sold. Whether you're in our **Associate Program** or not, you have access to that. It also contains the **Buyer Process report** that he wrote, which walks you through our complete buyers' system. We have video training on launching properties properly and a whole bunch more. All that is in there.

ZACH:   Continuing on the topic of the buyers list: when you think about getting a home and building a buyers list, one helps build the other. So you're building a buyers list, and that's from buying a home in a certain area and then simply following Nick's system, which will attract all the buyers you need—and then some. Now you have a giant list ready for when you buy another house in that area. That makes it even easier to sell that second property.

NICK:   Yes, that's a huge point, Zach. Here's an example of how I handle that conversation: "Oh, you don't like this home? Make sure you register on our new property notification list and we'll get you something in the future." What Zach mentioned is important, because we have a buyer coming into the office here shortly who was on our buyers list from before, and we haven't had a property out his way for a while. But as soon as we launched our most recent property to our list (which we do before we advertise it to the public), he called on it. Now he's got an appointment to come talk to us about it. We'll have a new sale today!

ZACH:   The reason we don't have properties out there is because it's a two-and-a-half-hour drive! But I heavily vetted the seller, and it's worth the drive; from my point of view, he's the perfect seller (I have a profile of an ideal seller on my dream board; if you don't have a dream board, make sure you make one and put it up). He's a seller who's easy to work with, flexible, and looking for alternative options. In fact, as soon as I notice those three qualities in a seller, my conversation really kicks up a notch and I try harder to build rapport with them because I know we've got a deal on our hands that will be both fun and profitable.

CHRIS:    **Another point about that two-and-a-half-hour drive, because associates ask about this all the time: if Zach goes out there for two hours, he only goes once; he won't go back. Everything else is automated. Nick doesn't drive two and a half hours to show the house. We don't show homes. We're not real estate agents or tour guides (sometimes they're one and the same—sorry, real estate agents). This is all part of our system. You'll learn how to do this too. What's the average payday? $75,000. So was it worth Zach's trip out there? Who cares if he had to go back two or three times to close it out? It's worth it!**

ZACH:    If I had to pick just one major challenge for someone who's just getting started, it's probably learning the scripts and building confidence. Confidence is the number-one obstacle you need to get over. Nobody's comfortable on the phone, especially speaking about a business that they just started new. It's the hardest part; they're not sure what questions are going to be asked. They've never been there before. So as soon as the seller is on the phone with them, they're not confident, and they're probably scared.

   So I want to get the associates to the point where they're comfortable and it's a normal conversation. I actually just jumped on the phone with an associate last night and said, "You need to role-play the scripts to the point that it's a normal conversation." I remind them that it's just them and the seller on the phone, having a normal conversation. I remind them that they're just explaining to the seller how they can provide a solution. They're not there to try to sell them anything. It's a normal conversation. We don't sell or pitch; we solve challenges by offering solutions.

Now, in that conversation, you're looking for all the signs that point to *We can be a solution for each other. We can be a fit. Our goals are in sync.* If that's the case, we should continue to move forward and move them to the next step, such as an appointment. If it doesn't make sense, get off the phone. You have too many other people to call. You don't want to waste your time, because time is money. Chris mentioned critiquing calls and role-playing earlier—these are two key components to dramatically speed up the rate at which you can learn and be most confident.

CHRIS: **The point is, you're not selling. If you find yourself selling or convincing, the deal's probably going to fall apart. You're doing what Zach said, which is to logically walk through a protocol that he'll teach you. Nick will do the same exact thing with you on the buyer side because if he has to sell someone, guess what? They're going to default or not show up for the buyer appointment. It's not worth it. Just follow the logical, predictable steps we outline: If A, then B; if B, then C—and if that doesn't happen, we close the door and move on.**

### Mistakes to Avoid

ZACH: Go out and get a mentor. The biggest mistake, which is easy to avoid, is *not* getting a mentor. I don't mean a consultant who can speak with you at limited times—I mean a full-on mentor or coach who can work with you. Kayla and I were recently talking about the first deal for which I got the contract signed. This house ended up being a nightmare, unfortunately, because we had to spend tens of thousands of dollars on getting the property deleaded. I said to Kayla, "If we were in this business by ourselves, and this was the first deal that I did, I would probably be out of business. *One and done.*" But if you have a mentor who's already been there, you can avoid losing that money.

If an associate came to me and said, "Zach, I have some questions on whether this property is deleaded or not," or if there's major concerns associated with the property, I've already been there. I can say, "Well, you might want to do X, Y, and Z to make sure that you're covered," or, "Make sure that you switch up the contract and change up the liability side of things and your exposure." Find a mentor who's doing what you want to do and then just copy them.

I mentioned the liability side. Look, Chris and our attorney have spent hundreds of hours on our custom agreements. Every single time we get a curve ball or challenge over the last several years, they tweak the agreements to better protect us and for better deal flow. These forms and agreements are worth thousands (if not tens of thousands) of dollars, and guess what? They're all available in our **QLS Video Program**.

CHRIS: **Every guest I have on my show says, "You've got to have a mentor." Most of them have spent, like me, a quarter million dollars in their career with mentors. I don't know any other way to do it. I hope that our niche and our personalities and our communication style fits for you, but if it doesn't, find someone who does. We're not so naïve as to think that we're the be-all for everyone.**

**This touches on another of our Six Core Values (see page 63): *we're clear, blunt, and to the point—there's no gray area.* Some people will be offended by that. If you are, we're not a fit for you. If you like direct communication, where we're all about results, then we're a great fit for you. If you decide to**

apply for one of our associate levels, we'll ask your permission to communicate bluntly and coach you very directly.

NICK: When it comes to the buyers, it's just as important to know what *not* to say to a buyer as to know what to ask or what to say. There's a particular process to take these guys through, step by step, before they become comfortable with you. First and foremost, you want them to be comfortable with you and understand that you're a legitimate business.

You also want them to be comfortable sharing their information with you, and telling you the most they can do on their down payment. You don't ask that stuff too soon because then they're going to think they're negotiating with you. Then later in the process they find out there's no negotiating with you, the investor. They're really in negotiation or in competition with *other buyers*. Once they understand that, they're not as guarded with you. We also have a number of automated videos that educate and prepare them, and that cuts down our time on the phone.

CHRIS: One associate we've spoken to recently was saying *way, way, way* too much up front to their buyers. Don't try to reinvent the wheel. Follow the system that works. You're not on the phone to give a seminar. Just follow the scripts.

Also, when you hire a mentor, make sure that mentor is really leading the charge and staying ahead of you in every way. With our coaching and mentoring, for example, no matter who we're working with, we try to stay ahead with the latest real estate techniques, forms, processes, our own reading, and attend relevant seminars inside and outside of real estate. In general, we try to stay ahead of the curve so that we have something to offer them. As a family team, we are able to provide this kind of hands-on, high-level support.

I can't think of a company that could possibly get four or five people more driven, more into self-improvement, more into spending money to improve themselves, and then being able to offer that to others.

So if you're going to go hire a mentor who's not in our niche, make sure they do that with you and for you and that they are currently doing what you want to do. Absent that, it would be equivalent to you giving $100,000 to a financial planner to invest *before* asking them what their success rate is, before asking for their tax returns. If their tax return shows $30,000 in yearly income or that they're broke, it would be insane to trust them with $100,000 to invest. But that's what you're doing when you hire a mentor who's out there teaching, but not in the trenches. If they haven't done a deal in two or three or four years... Frankly, even after about nine months, you'd already be outdated.

## Meditate, Work Out, Read:
## Daily Productivity Rituals

NICK: My morning routine is important to me. I meditate anywhere from 30 to 40 minutes, and try to make it a daily practice. After I finish breakfast, I usually have anywhere from 40 minutes to a little over an hour to just work on myself and reflect on my goals. I usually sit with coffee or tea. I don't work out every day, but I do cardio a couple of times a week, and that usually helps keep the energy up.

ZACH: With my personal training background, working out is my meditation. I probably should meditate a little more. I've been trying that Calm app that Chris uses, but it's not yet a daily activity. Working out is my release and definitely my number-one productivity ritual; as soon as I get that done, my energy level is a lot higher.

Second, I'm very goal-oriented and task-driven; I like to accomplish things. So at the beginning of the day, I write down three or four things I would like to accomplish that day. They generally have to do with the number of leads I want to generate, or deals I want to get done before the end of the week, or appointments, or helping the associates get deals done.

Third, when I get home I definitely like to read and then just enjoy the family. When I read, I'm increasing my mental capabilities. Most important, I think, is the gratitude that comes from going home to hang out with the family. That makes me want to get up the next day and take on the world.

## What We're Reading: Trump and Tony Robbins

NICK: I just started Tony Robbins's *Awaken the Giant Within*. I like going back and looking at some of those older books. This my first time going through it.

ZACH: My goal is to listen to Audible, because I do a lot of driving—or when I'm at the gym. I'm listening to *Influence* right now. I like to read a regular book as well. Some people might get mad at me, but I'm reading *The Trump Factor* right now, which has a lot of the deals that he's done. It definitely takes you to a higher level, thinking about what you can accomplish with deals. Then I try to read a financial book or the most recent Tony Robbins book.

CHRIS: **Please, readers, no 40,000 political emails. This is not about politics. *The Trump Factor* wasn't written by Trump, and it's heavily based on deal structuring, accounting, asset growth, and so on. I think we gave it away at our last live event. I don't care if you love him or hate him, it's a great book. Forget who's in it if you don't like it, but do read it for the deal structuring, thinking big, building an asset base, a strong balance sheet, etc.**

### Openness, Honesty, and Boundaries:
### Tips for Families that Work Together

ZACH: First and foremost, I don't want to suggest that every single family should work together. I'm not sure if I could work with some of my cousins, or even my own brothers. I just think that we happen to fit. But if you want to work with your family, I think it's very important that you put together clear boundaries. We make jokes about it because we actually used to live on the same street. Chris, Kayla, Kim, Nick, and I used to wave to each other and say, "How was your day?" at the end of the day.

We all hang out together a lot too. We have our cocktail hour and dinner and things like that, so it's important that you set clear boundaries. It's also important to be as blunt and black and white with everything as possible. When you're working in business, you're dealing with money, and everyone has paradigms about it, and there's jealousy involved. So lay all that out at the beginning. That way, nobody's holding anything in.

CHRIS: **So if the family is not a fit, that's OK. One of our associates got to a point where they needed help at a certain level, scaling their business. But their family member didn't want to do anything or wasn't a good fit for it. So we structured the entire system and protocol with them to be able to hire a virtual assistant for particular duties and say, "Here's the outline. I need a virtual assistant to do these tasks in this manner..." So we'll help you scale it at whatever level makes sense for you, with or without the family component. It's part of the path we set together.**

NICK: I'd like to echo what Zach said—it's not right for everyone. I wouldn't jump right in with two feet and rope the whole family in, but ask questions and see if it's a good fit for everyone.

Maybe even try a personality test. If it's the right fit and everyone's on the same page and everyone's clear and doesn't pull their punches, it can be very rewarding.

CHRIS: Aside from the family component, we're also a bit different from the mentoring and education side of things. You won't find us running around the country doing what are referred to as "preview events," trying to put you into a $10,000 boot camp or some type of upsell. That doesn't exist for us.

We have a very simple path to success: it's the free webinar and the **Quantum Leap System (QLS)** video program that you can do right from your living room. No one is pressuring you—you go as fast or as slow as you want to. It includes calls with us. Then you can decide if you're going to run with this on your own, at your own pace, or join us as an associate—it's that simple. We'll see you once a year at our **QLS Live** event.

That's how we run it, and if you're an associate at the top two levels, you get that for free. At the **Associate High 6 Level** you also meet for a private **High 6 Mastermind** yearly. At the two highest levels (**Immersion** and **High 6**), you're also getting a visit from us in your market to work with you. All our levels get to take advantage of a free two-day office visit where you can actually see us working in the trenches, visit sellers with us, work with us to set up your business properly—and more. That office visit is worth $25,000 minimum, and you get it for free with the associate levels. For more information, check out the free *New Rules* **resources page** at TheNewRulesBook.com

## TAKEAWAYS FROM THIS CHAPTER

1 We know where you are because we've been there ourselves.

2 You can be brand-new to real estate and still succeed as long as long as you follow the system.

3 Learn scripts and the phone calls will come easily.

4 You don't have to sell or pitch. Instead, focus on solving problems and adding value.

5 Find a mentor who's active in the business and willing to be your biggest champion.

6 All work and no play makes us unproductive and miserable: meditate, work out, read, and spend time with your family.

7 Set goals to grow each day, week, month, and year.

8 If you work with your family, keep lines of communication wide open, and establish clear boundaries.

# WHAT'S YOUR EXCUSE?

## (Seriously)

## Nick Prefontaine

In this chapter, I want to tackle the excuses and mental barriers that keep you from reaching your goals and achieving your dreams in business and in life. There are times when we make excuses be-cause—let's be honest—dreams are hard work. My world is the world of real estate: buying, selling, and investing. I love what I do. The rewards are great, but if I don't stay focused, if I let small or large setbacks get me down, I can find every excuse in the book not to push forward.

Whatever we do, there will always be challenges to overcome and obstacles to move past. I want to give you the tools to stop with the excuses and get on with those dreams, real estate and otherwise.

This is the story of a setback that hits really close to home for me—it's my own story! An accident back in 2003 left everyone wondering if I'd ever be able to walk, talk, or eat on my own again. I only know this because that's what the doctors told my parents while I was in a coma.

### My Accident

It was February 5, 2003, the day for ski club. It was 2:00, and we were heading toward Wachusett Mountain. We brought our gear with us on the bus so as not to miss a precious moment once we got to the mountain. When we arrived, we headed straight for the top. On the way, we noticed that it was very icy because it had been raining. People were wiping out everywhere. But I was young and invincible; needless to say, I got to the top and headed straight for the biggest jump with all my speed. Going up to the jump, I caught the edge of my snowboard, which threw me off balance...and that's the last thing I remember.

I was told later that I landed on my head and that I was in a coma for three weeks. The doctors told my parents that I would probably never walk, talk, or eat on my own again. Less than three months later, I *ran* out of Franciscan Children's Hospital in Boston. How did I go from being in a coma, unable to walk, talk, or eat on my own, to running out of the hospital?

---

**Chris:** It's a great story, for sure. I can't tell you how grateful we are as a family for how it all turned out. We'll revisit Nick's story a bit later and you'll find out how he made it out of Franciscan Children's Hospital and how he overcame excuses. Nick's story could have taken a very different turn. When challenges overwhelm us, we can get sucked into that overwhelm. We can make excuses and get stuck in that mode. Or we can choose to move forward and tackle challenges—one at a time.

## What's Your Excuse?

What are your excuses? What are the stories that you tell yourself every day about why you "can't" do something? It probably seems pretty insignificant when you compare it to my story. What's keeping you from pursuing something, whether that something is a thriving real estate business or some other dream?

I try to be as up-front as possible about the huge upsides of our **QLS** video program and our associate programs. Your earning potential in our **3 Paydays** real estate system can be truly phenomenal.

But I try to be just as clear about the challenges. There are always curveballs in any real estate transaction. Challenges arise that you have to address. But these are the times when you have to say to yourself, "I'm not going to stop. I'm going to figure out a way to fix this." Adopt the mindset that challenges and setbacks are completely normal and great learning experiences, rather than feeling thrown off by them in any way.

Whatever you're doing, whether it's real estate or some other large or small undertaking, it takes commitment. For me, commitment is doing whatever it takes for as long as it takes to achieve a goal. Excuses just get in the way of your commitment. It's important to find ways to overcome them, and that's what I did. So what are *your* excuses?

I recently heard from three of our associates. All three had great excuses for why things weren't working for them—so they thought. Two fought back against those excuses and thrived, and one decided the program wasn't for them.

One associate had a buyer fall through, so they had a house with all its expenses looming over them. They strapped in, followed the program, and did what it took to find another buyer. They saved the deal and wound up with money in the bank! In fact, it turned out better than it would have with the previous buyer, as is often the case.

Another associate took a while to get things off the ground—six months without a first transaction. But they stuck with it and followed the program. Now they are one of the top-producing associates in our whole program, achieving $1 million in all three paydays in just 18 months.

I'm often reminded of my recovery: How do you think I learned how to walk, talk, swallow, speak, write, and take care of myself again? Right—one at a time. When you're starting a seemingly-insurmountable task, take a step back before you dive in. Once it's underway, tackle one thing—one obstacle—at a time.

## The Steps You Need to Take

OK, so how do you actually get yourself beyond potential excuses? At our most recent annual **QLS Live** event, retired staff sergeant talked about the **STEPS** he uses to get himself unstuck from excuses.

**STEPS** is a handy acronym to help you keep excuses in their place: S stands for **smart goals. T** is for your **tribe. E** stands for **exploring new options. P** is for **positive outlook**, and the final **S** is for **self-discovery.** Let's take a closer look at how these **STEPS** can keep you committed to your goals for the long haul:

- **Smart goals – Smart goals are specific, measurable, achievable, and realistic.**

- **Tribe – Surround yourself with the right people—those who will challenge you and help you to grow. Find a mentor.**

- **Exploring new options – Educate yourself by reading, listening, attending seminars, and, of course, following that mentor.**

- **Positive Outlook – Stay positive. If your day starts out poorly, or takes a bad turn, learn how to recalibrate.**

- **Self-discovery – This is a lifetime practice of understanding who you are and why you matter.**

These **STEPS** can help get you beyond the challenges and the excuses.

With that in mind, let me share with you how I took steps to move past my challenges. How did I go from being in a coma, unable to walk, talk, or eat on my own, to running out of the hospital? First and foremost, I set goals, and I *always* had the goal to run out of the hospital. That was a pretty big goal, considering my challenges. Along the way, I had several smaller goals, or checkpoints, to help me get there.

I want to close with another story, this one from Shilo Harris. Shilo has used the **STEPS** and other tools to stop excuses from getting in the way of his dreams. (When he spoke at this year's **QLS Live** event and shared his remarkable story, you could hear a pin drop; there wasn't a dry eye in the audience. We hope you can join us at our next annual **QLS Live** event.)

On his second deployment with the 10th Mountain Division, Shilo was assigned and worked near southern Baghdad. On February 19, 2007, Shilo's armored vehicle was struck by an improvised explosive device (IED). The explosion injured the driver and ended the lives of three of his fellow soldiers. Shilo survived but with severe third-degree burns to 35% of his body. The severity of the burns meant that Shilo lost his ears, the tip of his nose, and three fingers. The crushing explosion fractured his left collarbone and C7 vertebra.

Shilo spent 48 days in a medically-induced coma. Waking up from the coma and realizing the extent of his injuries was the challenge of his life. One counselor in particular helped him see beyond his current condition. "If I am going to get better," he realized, "it's totally up to me. I've got to be willing to do the work."

So that's what he did. He literally put one foot in front of the other, turning a few steps into 10 steps and 10 steps into 50. He now travels all over as a motivational speaker. Shilo delivers the motivation because he's lived those highs and lows, and has decided not to let excuses get in his way.

Now, my story and my accident pale in comparison to Shilo's (he was in a coma for over twice as long as I was! Pretty amazing when you think of it), but even so, I can relate to Shilo like no one else. Earlier, when I talked about handling one challenge, one obstacle at a time, that's exactly what Shilo did. There is no other way but forward. Even when faced with a lot of challenges, obstacles, or problems, don't get overwhelmed. Handle one thing at a time, always do your best, and I promise you, you'll come out better for it.

I could go on and on about my admiration for Shilo, and it still really wouldn't do him justice. I have so much respect for what he's endured and who he is as a result. I say this about my accident and coma: if I had to go back and do it all over again, *I would—in a heartbeat*. It made me who I am today, and I wouldn't change that for the world. I hope that I can continue to collaborate with Shilo, and who knows? One day, we may share a stage together, both telling our stories.

**Chris:** We continue to work closely with Shilo and other veterans and appreciate immensely all those who serve and have served.

## TAKEAWAYS FROM THIS CHAPTER

1   Don't let challenges provide you with an excuse to stay stuck where you are.

2   Face your obstacles one at a time.

3   Break down your goals into smaller, more achievable checkpoints.

4   Surround yourself with people who will challenge and encourage you.

5   Stay positive.

6   Believe in yourself.

# 100 DEALS
# IN UNDER 3 YEARS

## Zach Beach

**In this chapter, you'll learn how Zach went from zero real estate experience to completing two to four deals per month, plus helping students around the country do the same. He will expand on how to work with sellers and create six-figure paydays. He also has some don't-miss tips for overcoming personal obstacles to get your life on track and live your dreams.**

I come from a single-mother household in central Massachusetts, which is where I met Chris's daughter—at our middle school. My mom is a wonderful woman and raised me on a cashier's salary, so needless to say, I don't come from money. But I come from a great family and wouldn't have it any other way. Growing up, I was always told that after you graduate high school, you must attend college, so that's what I decided to do. I think I only wound up actually going to college because all of my high school teachers told me I *couldn't*. I thought, "Well, I guess I'm going to college!"

When I graduated college, I didn't have a clear path for what I wanted to do with the rest of my life. I definitely didn't want to be in the corporate world—I'm more of a "free bird." I had started working as a bartender in Newport, Rhode Island while I was in college. I was grinding away, working nights. But I'm also into health and fitness, so

I thought, "I bet I can get paid to train people to work out and teach them how to eat healthy." I started doing that on the side as well.

As you can imagine, those are two completely different schedules: I would bartend until around 2:00 AM, sleep for about three hours, then catch everyone at the gym at about 5:00 AM. That started to take a toll on me, and that's when I started chatting with Chris. I would ask him, "What's going on with this real estate thing?" I figured I might as well throw something else on my plate, because I was starting to get bored with the other stuff. It snowballed from there. I started by making some calls from my house to get my feet wet…and that's the beginning of my real estate story.

I just turned 28, so I've been in real estate for about two and a half years now. I started bartending at 21, and I told myself that I'd be out by the time I was 25. I hit that nail on the head: I started in April when I was 21, and I ended in April four years later. I switched over to personal training, started doing real estate on the side, and was also in network marketing, because I wanted to find ways to build on something that can do better than hourly pay. Just before I turned 26, I came on full-time, and started creating the business we have here with the family. My starting salary was zero, which created the incentive to get right on it and go after deals.

When I first started making calls, I was still doing the bartending and personal training. My first couple of calls were absolutely disastrous. They were probably disastrous up until month three or four. I was recording my calls and asking Chris for critiques, but it's just a completely different language. Even though I watched Chris, but as I always tell people, I had *no background* in real estate. My real estate background was in physical labor, helping Chris and his family do some building projects back when I was 14. As a result, my thoughts about real estate revolved around building: *Let's go hammer some nails together!* Then I dove into the business and I realized it's more about scripts and speaking with people, structuring deals, and understanding the numbers. Numbers don't come easy to me; math was never my subject. It took some time, but I was eventually able to grasp it. Talking to people and learning, on the other hand, came naturally to me. I'm an avid learner; I could do it all day long. The History Channel is my favorite TV channel.

But learning the language of real estate is not 100% like learning Spanish or another language; it took me some time to wrap my head around the different aspects of this business. I always tell people that our business model isn't the easiest to understand. You have to really want to learn, to educate yourself. We're not wholesaling, and this isn't *buy low and sell high and hopefully you'll make a margin.* Really, it's first understanding how to speak with people, and second, learning to recognize a good deal. In Chris's best-selling first book, he calls that becoming a "master transaction engineer."

Deals are typically based on numbers such as mortgage information, comps in the area, the spread that you can create on a monthly basis, and the sales price. You need to be able to understand those numbers and then ask, "Is this a good deal or not?" After you understand the numbers, you still have to pursue the deal and tie it up.

In short, the transition to real estate wasn't easy, especially because nothing was assured. When Kayla and I decided to join the family company, everything was in limbo. Chris was doing deals on terms—he had 65+ of them in the works—and was in need of help. We weren't yet on a path to scale; we didn't yet have the support team set up and everything we needed to scale and build this business. We were the guinea pigs.

---

**Chris:** I remember quite well that what we *did* have was a tiny hole-in-the-wall office. It was an office and a half at best, and we all crammed around a little coffee table to meet. It was a work in progress. We didn't know what each person's role was going to be. I didn't know who was going to be the buyer specialist or the seller specialist; we just fell into our present roles. And those roles now help students around the country, because they're very specific. What Zach accomplished is amazing, but it's also achievable by anyone reading this, and it's being duplicated right now by our associates everywhere.

## My $1 Million Deal

We recently bought a property right on the water in southeastern Massachusetts (worth just under a million dollars), and we did it by structuring owner financing. We made a down payment of approximately $10,000. We don't typically put money down, but we thought it was a good idea to allocate some of our profits from other deals to tie this one up. Once you get the three paydays dialed in, you very quickly start to accumulate scheduled deposits on all your properties. You can put that in your pocket and create nice reserves, or use it for other deals like this.

We were able to come to an agreement on principal-only payments for 48 months at $2,500 a month. There were a couple of other unique nuances to the deal, which are described in our **Deal Structure Sundays** and YouTube videos. In the next four years, it's going to be a deal worth well over $200,000.

I was proud of that because it took roughly six months to speak with the seller, go through different options, and work through the process with both attorneys. It definitely took longer than most deals, but some deals need massaging and constant follow-through. I'm really looking forward to seeing the end results when that $200,000 (and it could be more) comes out the other end.

---

**Chris:** I want to reiterate two of Zach's points: Yes, it can take some time to create a great deal, and no, we don't usually put money down. But here's the punchline: It wasn't *our* money! How do we do that? *It came out of the other deals.* If you follow our three-year $1,000,000 plan, it's outlined there. You'll have **Payday #1s** and **Payday #3s**, just like I detailed in *Real Estate on Your Terms.*

## A Great Deal for Yourself, Even if You Don't Do a Lot of Deals

My wife Kayla and I were able to buy a property for ourselves in an area of Rhode Island where we wanted to live. We put it on our dream board about a year ago. We used to live in downtown Newport with the crowds, but we wanted our own space, so we bought a property with a water view a couple of towns over from Newport. Now we have some space to grow the family; we have a one-year-old who needs to run around, and a dog who likes to join him. We were able to tie up that deal on a lease purchase. It just happened to be great timing, and it's in a beautiful area. Every day I get to go outside on my porch and look at the ocean.

If you think you can't buy nice properties in nice areas, I'm going to have to tell you that you're crazy. If you are persistent, and you continue to hammer the phones, and you continue to work the system, you can find a property in almost any area you want. It just takes time.

---

**Chris:** I know some people rent forever, but it's pretty safe to say that most of our readers are probably going to buy their own homes in the next five to seven years, and they'll probably do it again five to seven years after that. That's just what the statistics say. So why not do that and *also* generate $200,000, $300,000, $500,000 in profit after your third year? Even if you don't want to get into the terms business, you can go through our course and understand how to buy a home for your family. You can do it like Zach did—no banging on the bank's door, no jumping through all those hoops and still not getting any principal pay-down because your mortgage is new.

## Building Relationships

What I really enjoy about real estate is interacting with people, but I also like seeing the physical property. I think it's so cool that we control property in at least 20 different states. If I wanted to, I could drive to Washington, DC or Massachusetts right now and see a property we control, and I love that.

I'm also very pleased about the family ties and the relationships we create. We always say that we empower individuals and families in our coaching program, but we empower individuals and families in our real estate business as well. We're helping sellers in various scenarios accomplish their goal of selling their homes. We're able to help buyers—I can attest to that now that I've bought a property of my own through our programs—get to that next level in life and be homeowners. It's extremely empowering. We actually have a seller client who had a lease purchase cash-out with us, then became a buyer client and bought a home through us, and then became a student of ours!

There's good, bad, and ugly in real estate, but when you get to experience the good in real estate, you realize that it's a business of helping other people and creating lives for them. And the profits are nice too!

---

**Chris:** I want to highlight the word "control" that Zach used. Together with some of our associates, we control about $25 million worth of real estate—and that figure is growing. On all that property, we've put down maybe a total of $10,000. So just know that you can do that too.

## My Role as Seller Specialist

I help the associates do exactly what I do day in, day out for our buying and selling entity. I pride myself on knowing the entire business, but in order for us to be able to streamline and help out as many people as possible, I focus on the sellers. That entails helping people with their scripts (I've now rewritten all of our scripts), crafting emails, completing follow-up calls or jumping on three-way calls, and structuring deals. I help them put together different options for sellers. If the associate is local, I can go on appointments with them. If they are in our top two levels, **Immersion Associate** or **High 6 Associate**, Chris or I will fly out to them and go on appointments with them.

I do anything and everything associated with getting a property "taken," which means under contract with a lease purchase agreement, an option to purchase agreement, or a purchase and sale agreement. We buy our property several different ways, and I help an associate put a property under contract any way I can. As soon as the property is under contract, we market it and get it over to Nick so he can sell it. We do whatever is necessary to help the associate *win*!

---

**Chris:**  You should come see Zach walk through some of these scripts and the steps to getting a contract in hand. You can do that at the annual **QLS Live** event. You can purchase the **QLS** video program and get the ticket for free, or if you're not quite sure you're ready to dip into the video course yet, just come to the event: get your ticket at **smartrealestatecoach.com**. Either way, come check us out. I want you to hear what Zach and Nick—and our amazing speakers and associates—have to say.

I also want you to picture what it would mean to your pocketbook to have me (and Nick and Zach and our whole team) here talking to you in the living room, or talking to your buyer in a room with 25 other associates. You get a massive amount of actionable information.

## Coaching, Another Key to My Success

Being a coach has taken my game to a whole new level. I've had to cram 10 or 15 years' worth of real estate knowledge into about two years, because I have to be on top of my game all the time. To teach the associates, I have to understand each and every part of the business. I make sure that I'm giving them knowledgeable answers and that I'm 100% on my game to help them get the deals done. When I'm speaking to these sellers, I'm essentially a senior associate to them; I have to make sure I have all the next-level questions answered so we can get these deals done.

Coaching has been a phenomenal experience, and I plan to do it for a very long time. It's a natural fit for who I am. I was captain of the football team in high school, and was able to win a Super Bowl and go undefeated that year. That was a long time ago, but I realized then that I enjoy being a leader. I'm constantly working at being the best leader I can be. It's a natural fit for me to be out in front helping others get to where they want to be. It's become a passion of mine.

Being a coach has taken my life to the next level. Whatever I'm doing—in real estate coaching, in my personal life, or in any other pursuit—I've grown exponentially in all of those areas, very quickly.

## The Office Visit

Part of the coaching experience is hands-on, live, with the associates. That's because the associates come to our office for free, for two days, and hang out with each of us, and they also go on the road. They spend a ton of time with me. They listen to me do live calls, and on the second day they hop in the car with me and go wherever the appointments are. We're in the car all day long, hitting multiple appointments; they get to see it done live and be involved in my interactions with sellers.

If you haven't been on any appointments yet—maybe you're just learning—this lets you experience that situation before you do it on your own. If you've already been doing it a while, you'll have some extra experience under your belt, and you'll pick up a couple of things. That time in the car is also perfect for conversations. I get to know the associates very well during that driving time—we have great conversations.

## Biggest Win

My biggest personal win is definitely marrying Chris's daughter and having my first son. I'm always a dad and a husband first. Another huge win is being where I am today in business—I never thought I could even get this far in life. I'm just enjoying life, and enjoying living on the water.

---

**Chris:** On that note, Zach and Kayla's son Remi is in the office for the day at least two to four times a week. How many fathers or mothers are reading this and saying to themselves, "Man, if I could hang out with family all day and not wait until 5:00 PM or later, that would be so good"? It's a big deal to us too. When we talk about being in the family business, we love it. I get it that it's not for everyone, but if that's your goal, it's pretty cool.

## Overcoming Major Stumbling Blocks

When I was growing up, I didn't hang around the best people. I wasn't in the best situation. From the age of 14 until I was 19 or 20, I was either addicted to or using drugs. That was a major speed bump in the road. That's why having an amazing family and experiencing the things I get to do nowadays, like living on the water, is what I think of as my biggest accomplishment. I just didn't think it was possible; I was very depressed. That life nowadays is this beautiful is completely amazing—and as Chris has told me, this is just scratching the surface. I was one of the lucky ones. I didn't pass away like a couple of my friends did. I'm enjoying this dream immensely.

## Getting Unstuck

When I decided I needed to make a change in my life, I did two things: first, I had to fill a void. I needed to fill the time that I had spent using. A good friend got me into CrossFit, and I started filling my time by working out, with the goal of making my body and brain feel good. That's why I'm an advocate of exercise. I work out at least five days a week.

After I made my body feel good, I had to make my brain feel good. That's when I started getting into personal development. I'm a big Bob Proctor fan. I follow Bob Proctor because I like what he says about paradigm shifts. When you don't feel like you can do certain things, it's likely that you need to change your paradigm. I had to change my paradigm and think good thoughts. I started by feeding my mind with good things. Eventually, I got my confidence back, and I started making good decisions. Things snowballed from there. So (a) make your body feel good, and (b) feed your body and your mind. After that, the sky's the limit.

## TAKEAWAYS FROM THIS CHAPTER

1 Feed your body with exercise.

2 Feed your brain with education and training.

3 Learn how to think positively and make good decisions.

4 Expect that a great deal will take some time.

5 Understand that you don't have to put your own money down!

6 Take advantage of our personal touch—our hands-on coaching.

7 Don't let your lack of experience stop you from getting involved in real estate.

# OUR ASSOCIATE SUPPORT SUPERSTARS

## Kayla and Lauren

At **Smart Real Estate Coach**, we've built a unique family culture. That translates to you, the investor, in how we help you get deals done. Our program is not about buying products, going to seminars, and getting zero done; it's about *implementing what you've learned and getting results* with our hands-on help.

This chapter is based on a conversation with my daughter Kayla, general manager of our buying and selling entities and our coaching and mentoring business, and with Lauren Bulk, who manages all support and affiliates for **Smart Real Estate Coach.** When Nick and I hit about two deals a month, that was enough volume to make a move, and our move was to bring in Kayla to reorganize everything. She created internal checklists and set up everything so it could run on autopilot, or so we could have someone else run it.

Later, Lauren came in and helped with admin. When Kayla took maternity leave, Lauren took over some of the buyer and seller packages. Now they work together to support our associates and make sure everything runs smoothly in their businesses, while Kayla still oversees all company activities.

KAYLA: Since I started organizing everything for the buyers and sellers, and until now, processes were a huge part of systematizing that end of our business. I work strictly on keeping all of the buyers organized separately and all of the sellers organized separately, from the time we get each property to when we sell it. We have systems in our office to help us keep track of things like maintenance items or any conversations we've had. We're now working to get everything into Process Street to take automation to the next level.

LAUREN: I started by doing forms, letters of intent (LOIs), and attorney packages. Then once Kayla was out with her first child Remi, I took over doing the seller documents as well as the buyer documents. I was setting up attorney signings, talking to tenant buyers, and focused on getting them into the house as well as communicating when their payments were coming in. As coaching and mentoring got even busier, we brought on a part-timer to handle the buying and selling side so I could focus solely on **Smart Real Estate Coach**.

KAYLA: Lauren also tweaked our systems a little bit as we grew. We have a lot of different processes to follow to keep everything organized, and Lauren has helped with that.

LAUREN: We set up files in front of the tenant buyers so it's easy for them. They have a checklist to follow. Kayla organized and fine-tuned the systems we had.

CHRIS: **All of those things like attorney packages and systems are what you have access to in our Quantum Leap System (QLS) video program. We have videos on how to fill out those attorney packages. We have the packages themselves, which are worth the 10,000 hours it has taken for our attorney** to put them together, because we are very well protected and properly set up, as are our students. They're at your fingertips in the **QLS** program.

## The Quantum Leap System

LAUREN:  The most common questions I get about the **Quantum Leap System (QLS)** are about how things work. If it's a seller question, I ask Zach. If it's a buyer question, I ask Nick. If it's a big question, I ask Chris. I have a bunch of questions and the answers to them in one large document so I'm prepared for any associate question, and that database has grown and grown. We now have a bot on the website that is "learning" all our Q&As and is already able to answer many questions. One of our **Six Core Values** (see page 63) is that we *constantly innovate and improve*, and this is one huge example.

CHRIS:  Each time Lauren gets a question, that question is also put into a YouTube video, and it comes out on a **Q&A Thursday.** We discuss it on the private mastermind call we hold with our associates every Thursday night. If you want to learn more about that, head on over to smartrealestatecoach.com and there's a free webinar you can dive into. We also get together privately every year as an extra mastermind group with our **High 6 Level** associates.

KAYLA:  Our system helps investors handle just about any issue that comes up: it includes different types of forms, emails, letters, voice-mails, and all those sorts of things for both the buyer and the seller side.

LAUREN:  For example, if a buyer doesn't pay their rent on time, they get a late notice. If they don't pay their deposit on time, they get a 10-day notice. If they still don't pay it, they lose their option to purchase. It's a form letter: I just fill in the blanks for their name, what they owe, and the due date, and send it out. Our students have access to all of that—everything we've learned and adjusted over the years.

KAYLA: We have all these form letters and systems so students and associates don't have to reinvent the wheel. These include simple things like increased taxes that happen during the term of a rent-to-own, "We got a notice that you didn't pay your water bill," and all kinds of other things. We have a series of form letters for sellers as well.

CHRIS: If a deposit hasn't been paid, how does that affect the lease agreement? If a lease agreement is not being paid, how does that affect the deposit portion of the agreement? There are decisions and linked consequences for anything that may come up, and we have the form or form letter for it.

One of the major topics in my book *Real Estate on Your Terms* is what can go wrong; I have a whole chapter on it. If you're doing a strategy call with us (free with the **QLS** course), or if you're just asking questions by email, you'll find that, as a family, we're going to be blunt (it's one of our **Six Core Values**; (see page 63)). We're going to tell you like it is. We're not going to give you a fluffy answer with everything rosy all the time. There will be circumstances that come up in your life and in your business, and we're here to help you.

## What's It Like to Work with Family?

KAYLA: I have either my son Remi or my dog Panda in the office—or both at the same time. I'm always juggling either a four-legged or two-legged creature. It makes sense, then, that a lot of what I do is time management and time sheets. I work on how to fit the most into your day and how to be productive throughout your day without pulling your hair out and going crazy.

CHRIS:   On the issue of time management, I can't recommend Dan Kennedy's *No B.S. Time Management* highly enough. I tend to read it once to twice per year. It's not a boring time management book. It's really a life management book.

I know there are readers who have a role like Kayla's, juggling animals and/or kids, and I want you to know that this is another support issue we can help you with. If you email support@smartrealestatecoach.com as part of our associate program or **QLS** program, you'll be talking to Kayla or Lauren. This is one of our main issues. It's a part of our mission statement and it's one of our **Six Core Values** (see page 63). Our purpose is written on the wall, and it's in everything we do: *empowering individuals and families.* It just happens to be that real estate is the vehicle.

LAUREN:  It's easy to work with family because we're compassionate toward each other. We care for each other—it's not just your stinky co-worker that you can't wait to get away from at the end of the day. But at the same time, since we're a family, we don't really have a filter on what we say. We know that we're going to tell each other how it really is, and not take anything personally. We do the same with our associates.

## Our Community of Associates

KAYLA:   We take what we have here in the office and practice it with our associates: when we answer them, we give them the same respect, but also the same bluntness. We treat them like family.

LAUREN:  Just being on the team for about a year, I've noticed the difference between last year's **QLS Live** event and this year's **High 6** mastermind meeting. All of the associates are much more connected: they reach out to each other with questions before they reach out to us. They find out who knows what, who can help with the issue they're having. Maybe another associate has already gone through it. The private associate-only Slack channel has got them really well-connected. It's helped with those questions and built a very strong, close community.

CHRIS: **With the Smart Real Estate coach team, we're here for you, we're on Slack with you, we're on the phone, we're on email. As an associate, you get to jump on there at any point about any challenge you have in your business or your life, and you have a community at your disposal. I've paid $10,000, even $25,000, to be in mastermind groups that offer what we offer as part of the associate levels. That's a huge thing to be connected with, to be able to pick that many brains.**

KAYLA: Because of the community we're developing, we're quite selective about who we work with. That's because our core values are so tight, and because we treat everybody with respect and like to be treated the same way.

CHRIS: **If you decide to go through QLS video program, you'll see that the associate level is by application only. If you apply to be an associate, you're going to speak with each one of us. That's part of our sifting process to make sure you're going to be a great fit. That's good for us, and it's phenomenal for you, because it ensures that you're going to have success. Success is very predictable once you get on the right path.**

# OUR SIX CORE VALUES

1 **We empower individuals and families.**

2 **We constantly innovate and improve.**

---

**Chris:** How important is that in the real estate business? I was talking on the *SharkPreneur Podcast* recently about the number of people who are teaching but not doing deals! Well, in real estate, if it's six months later, you're outdated, because things change in the industry in every way. We're constantly innovating and improving.

3 **We complete all transactions with the highest integrity.**

4 **We match effort for effort.**

---

**Chris:** As I tell students, we're not out there trying to push a wet noodle or a rope. When we start off with a student and we do the first few calls, it's going to be a back-and-forth. It's going to be reciprocal. This is a game of tennis.

5 **We're clear, blunt, and to the point—no gray area.**

6 **"Team over me."**

---

**Chris:** We prioritize the team over ourselves. The Associates Levels include an office visit, where you'll be able to meet the whole team and see everything we've discussed in action. The experience is invaluable.

## TAKEAWAYS FROM THIS CHAPTER

1   Our QLS package gives you all of the organization you need (including every form or form letter you can imagine), so you don't need to reinvent the wheel.

2   Our company fosters a high level of community involvement from our team as well as other associates, so you get all the support you need, in the real estate business and in life.

3   We're choosy about whom we work with so we all get the best experience.

# DON'T BECOME
# A CASUALTY

## On Commitment, Struggles,
## and Managing Expectations

I was speaking with one of our **High 6** associates yesterday. We speak once a week at 6:30 AM because that's when he heads out to work, so he talks with me for a good hour on his commute. So we were chatting, and he said, "Jeez, I've been listening to the mastermind calls, and every week, I notice that some people aren't on. Why would they do that?" We got to talking about commitment. We talked about his initial commitment of three years. When he started, he invested in himself by joining the **High 6 Associate Level** and securing his area, and he said, "Look, I'm in this for three years, and I'm committed, no matter what it takes." Well, that makes sense, doesn't it? It's just like any other business. Can you imagine buying a franchise or starting any other business just to "try it out"?

Last year at our full-day private mastermind group, which meets at **QLS Live** the day before the event starts (access to this full day of mastermind is a benefit of the Associate Levels), "Please understand that I'm okay with this," I said to the 25 of them sitting there, "but it's a bummer that some of you won't be here next year." And what I meant by that was some of them just won't commit to *doing whatever it takes—no matter how long it takes—to accomplish all of their goals*. Is life full of people that do whatever it takes for as long as it takes to accomplish all of their goals? Of course not (unfortunately). So I made that statement. "It's not negative," I told them. "It's not directed at any one of you; I just know it to be a fact." And about six months after I made that observation, some of them have already dropped off the planet. I literally haven't heard from them. They aren't on the calls.

People say, "Well, I tried it," or "I gave it 90 days" or "I gave it 120 days," which is a complete joke. It's a complete waste of time, and it's what's made us super, super-picky about our selection process as a mentoring and education company. Our process now includes an application and a call with each of our team members, who are almost all family. We try to choose only serious and committed applicants who are committed to the program, committed to learning, committed to themselves, committed to their families, and committed to creating something amazing.

How do I know that some people have a problem with commitment? Why do I identify this as a "commitment" issue? And by the way, whether you picked up this book because you're an associate, a student, a follower of ours, or just because you like our podcast or our YouTube channel, if your knee-jerk reaction right now is a defensive one (*I don't have a problem with commitment!*), well, don't take this personally, but you probably do. I know it's a problem for people because I hear just about every excuse for why they can't do deals. I get the strategy calls after our webinars, and it's unfathomable to me just how many excuses are out there. This isn't brain science. You can make excuses, or you can commit to passionately pursuing something better for yourself—not both.

---

**Zach:**  If you have trouble with commitment or you get a negative gut reaction just hearing the word, it's probably not your fault. It's the way you have been programmed, the paradigms embedded in your subconscious. You probably aren't the first generation in your family to have this reaction. Take a minute and do a self-evaluation. Ask yourself: Why do I have trouble committing? Why do I react negatively to the word "commitment"? Why, every time I get some momentum going in my life or business, do I stop trying or find that my energy is gone? Apply self-evaluation to every aspect of your life.

Now, when I said that your problem with commitment probably wasn't your fault, that was because you probably weren't aware of it. It *is* your fault, however, if this paradigm continues to affect your life in a negative way. Now that you're aware, take action to change your life for the better!

---

**Nick:**    As long as you keep moving forward and taking that next step, there's no stopping you. We've had associates in the past who were proverbial flashes in the pan, busy doing all the right things one minute, and the next minute, they fall off the map. The top associates, the ones who achieve the most success, are the ones who never ever give up. There is only success waiting for you if you continue, no matter what, to strive for your goals.

## Committed or Casualty

Let me give you some examples of commitment from our own associates. I'll also give you an example of someone who didn't stay the course (and who isn't around anymore, which is a shame).

Person A is one of our associates, currently a **High 6**. When he got his first deal, he wasn't getting buyers right away. Now, whether you're doing what we're doing, or wholesaling, or something else in another niche, I know this: If you get all the way through the first deal and you don't have a buyer or a viable exit plan, you're bummed about it. Your reaction may even be to doubt whether any of this works.

If, on the other hand, your reaction is to say to yourself, "I'm not looking left, I'm not looking right, I'm not looking back. I'm committed to this thing, no matter what. I'll find the bottleneck and I'll fix it. I'll get a mentor. I'll do whatever it takes to get it done"—if that's your attitude, you'll get through it. You'll seek answers and you'll find them; success leaves clues and the answer is out there for you. If your reaction is, "Man, I didn't get a buyer! Maybe this doesn't work. Maybe I can't do it. Maybe my market doesn't work for this particular strategy," and on and on with the whining, it's probably going to kill you.

Our High 6 Associate, didn't let it kill him; he barreled through it. The very next two deals he did, he cranked them, and if I'm not mistaken, it was only a matter of weeks before he got a buyer on one of them, which goes to show that what we teach—our way of buying and selling and creating cool deals on a daily basis—*works*, and it works *extremely well*, for those who commit. You get through it; you find a way. I don't care what you have to do.

Person B is another associate, now also a **High 6**. In his first six months, he wasn't doing *any* deals. He was working his butt off. I don't know if it was personal, or if it was the market, or a number of different things—it doesn't matter. What matters is that he persevered. And now, within a week or two, he's probably going to be our highest-earning associate. As I'm writing this book, he's just under his first $1 million in earnings for all three paydays, and he's about 17 months into his business. How's *that* for commitment?

Person C went totally against the grain of what we say to do. She didn't show up for calls, took a four-month sabbatical in the middle of everything—just disappeared—didn't structure the paydays the way we teach, and was generally way off course. (By the way, if you're not familiar with **Paydays #1, #2,** and **#3,** the way we create deals, and bring in $75,000 per deal on average, check out my best-selling *Real Estate on Your Terms,* or visit smartrealestatecoach.com and check out the free webinar. You can be creating three paydays per deal in your area.) Person C wasn't consistent, didn't do as we teach, and decided to go her own way.

Let's say I bake you a cake you enjoy, and you ask me for the recipe. If the recipe has steps A, B, C, D, E, and you do A, C, and half of E, you can't complain when you don't get the same results! It sounds facetious, but it's exactly what some people do in the coaching environment. She didn't put aside **Payday** #1 in case of potential pitfalls, as we teach people to do. She didn't set up lines of credit to make sure that she wouldn't have to stay awake at night worrying if something should happen. I could go on and on. When she lost her buyer on a deal, she became so distraught and frustrated because of the mess she'd made and steps she'd skipped. She's a casualty, doing who knows what now—probably back to her old lifestyle that was making her miserable.

Losing a rent-to-own buyer on a home mid-term, for which you have plenty of time left with the seller, who has a tiny (less than $1,000) mortgage payment, is not a big headache. You use your line of credit for two or three months, because it won't take you longer than that to sell, or you use the cash reserves that you put aside on **Payday** #2, and you get it done. There's a plethora of ways to navigate any of the issues that can come up, and that's not only what we teach, it's what we're here to help with—provided you're coachable.

Well, she forgot all of that. Her word, not mine: she "forgot" to put the reserve away. She also "forgot" to set up lines of credit as we suggested. That she didn't do any of the other things either is par for the course. The downside of that whole story is she's gone. Unlike the first two examples, she's a casualty.

## Getting the Big Picture

The upside of this business is not that you can get $75,000 a deal, or whatever the average ends up being in your market. (We have an associate in Arizona who's closer to $50,000 per deal and one in Washington, DC who's closer to $110,000 per deal—it varies.) What's more important for you to know is the 10,000-foot view: when you enter our program, or leave one of our events, or even when you leave your office visit with us, *you have a game plan*—and it's predictable, profitable, and fun.

Now, I'm not going to tell you what your goals should be, and I'm not going to project ours onto you, or the goals of every associate who comes in here for an office visit. (By the way, that's part of the Associate Program: you come here for a free office visit (if you're not an associate, the normal price is $7,500), you hang out all day with us—in the trenches, watching us do what we do—and then you go out on the road with us for a full day, and you see seller appointments. And when you leave, you have that game plan.

Most people leave here with a game plan with the basic outline we use for a three-year $1 million business plan, meaning that by year three, it's doing $1 million per year with all three paydays). Some will do it in 18 months, and others may take five or six years. Keep in mind that in year one, you're working mostly with **Payday #1s** (up-front deposits). Maybe a **Payday #3** (cash outs) will sneak in there, but it's mostly just **Payday #1s**. After year two and no later than year three, you're working with **Payday #1, #2, #3**, so you can scale that baby up.

You can actually plan your retirement and various points in the business five years out, and get off the treadmill, because you have the predictable paydays all mapped out.

I can go on and on about the big picture, but here's the bottom line: *if you know the big picture, understand the system, and have unwavering commitment, you'll never be a casualty. You'll design a lifestyle that will amaze you and your family.* In fact, we'd like that for everyone in our program. I know it's utopian, but that's what reality *is* for us right now—it's that predictable; it's that simple.

## Struggles Exist. Find a Path Through Them.

I ended the three example cases above with the woman we counted as a casualty. She was pitched a couple of curveballs. Are you going to get curveballs in the business? Yep. You can go to a lot of seminars, a lot of boot camps, listen to a lot of podcasts, and a lot of coaches will give you all the fun and all the fluff. We don't—we tell it like it is. One of the **Six Core Values** we live and operate by (see page 63) is that *we're blunt and to the point and there's no gray area.* Another of our core values is that *we empower individuals and families*—and you can't do that without giving them the whole picture. I have an entire chapter in my last book on what can go wrong. I've been criticized by mentors for doing that. "You're going to scare people away," they said. "If they're scared away by that," I countered, "they shouldn't be in the business, and they shouldn't come in for coaching with us. *It's a business.* There will be curveballs and headaches. I don't know of any business that's entirely free of them. If you find one, let me know.

Are there going to be bottlenecks? Are you going to have challenges that you can't even think about, that weren't mentioned in my previous book? Of course you are. At our 2018 **QLS Live** event, Shilo Harris was the keynote speaker. You can look up his amazing life story, but he went through more challenges than anyone I've ever met or read about—and that includes my son Nick, who had a head injury and was in a coma for a month. That's how many challenges this guy has gone through. The theme of that event was our core value of *empowering individuals and families*, and never giving up.

Here's what I hear sometimes: "Slow market." "Hard market." "My buyer left." I can list thousands of them. Remember, you can't make excuses *and* have success. What can you do if you find yourself thinking or saying these things? Well, for starters, you don't give up. You say, "How can I fix it? How can I get around it? Where's the bottleneck?" If you're part of the Associate program, you reach out on our Slack channel, because we all talk on that almost every day. You can get on there 10 times a day if you want, but we're there almost every day, talking, throwing answers out. That's one thing you can do. If you're one of our students and have our **QLS Video Program**, you can email us; that's part of our support program.

If you're not in our space, if you're in some other niche, call a coach. Call your mentor. If you don't have a mentor that you can pick up the phone and get a hold of, then find somebody whose shirttails you can grab onto. That way, when you're facing the struggles and the curveballs that you knew were coming, you can do something about it.

---

**Zach:** Skills come from struggle. When I read that line for the first time, it hit me like a Mack truck. Everything that I have learned and internalized came from struggle. Struggle is part of the learning process. It's the breaking down and building up of new muscle—the new muscle you need to accomplish the goals you've set. Embrace the struggle, and know that you're getting stronger and acquiring the skills you need to become the person you want to be.

## Don't Start Until You're Ready to Commit

As much as I love onboarding new students to our program, please don't just "give it a shot." Stay at your job until you're ready to absolutely *commit*. Think about it: If you were going to take a company public, or buy a franchise and dump two, three, four hundred thousand, half a million dollars into it, would you seriously say to your family, to your partners, to your kids, or to yourself, "I'm going to give this a shot for three or six months"? Of course you wouldn't. That's silly.

Infusionsoft is the software we use—and have used for years—for our businesses. I am fortunate enough to belong to their Elite Forum group for business owners. Now you can belong to it. They help you scale your business from $1 million on up. It's about building your business from seven to eight figures. When I went to Infusionsoft, they gave me a tour of their company. It's amazing what CEO Clate Mask has done, how they've grown. When I was there, they happened to be in a board meeting. Can you imagine Clate Mask sitting in that board meeting with about 18 investors, partners, board members, and saying, "You know what? Yeah, we kind of gave this a shot, but this 20,000 square foot building we're in, and these 500 employees...I don't know, it's just not working the way I want it to, so let's call it quits." They'd laugh him out of the room.

When you have fire, vision, and unwavering commitment, *there's absolutely nothing that you can't handle* (or find someone to help you handle). Again, I'm not just talking about our niche. If you're in our niche, if you decide to go through our webinar, our home study program, and become an associate, we're here for you. But if not, find someone who can help you in your own niche.

## Discouragement Brings Growth

I don't care what niche you're in, or even what types of deals you're doing—you'll encounter roadblocks and curveballs. I'll give you another example: we once had a lead paint issue that cost $32,000. Would you be discouraged by that? Would you be discouraged if you had a vacant home or two because a buyer defaulted, as in the earlier example?

Would you be discouraged if you couldn't sell a home right away? Maybe the pricing's good (depending on whether you're flipping it or, as in our case, putting a rent-to-own buyer in there), you've just refreshed it, and you can't figure out why it won't sell. We've been there. Well, there are all kinds of options: you can Airbnb it, you can rent it, you can work around it and lower the numbers, you can renegotiate with the seller. There are all kinds of workouts. You don't just throw your arms up. You dig in and find the answers. They're out there.

Would you be discouraged if you had so many properties that it gets hard to manage? As you scale your business, it can get hard to account for things. It's even hard to handle the incoming funds (this is a good problem to have). We hit that roadblock, so we went out recently and found a fantastic software company, onboarded with them, and it solved almost all of our growth headaches at this next level. My daughter dug in, sought a solution, got us on the phone with them, and fixed the challenge.

Would you be discouraged if you didn't get a deal for 60 days and you'd just started? We've been there. We've done all of these things. You work around it and find a way. Maybe you've never run a business, so all of this is new to you. Maybe you're not 100% sure of what you want yet. Get clear on that first, and then we can help you.

Maybe you lack confidence. This is not something most people like to admit. But maybe that's an issue. All of these things are coachable over time. My son Nick and son-in-law Zach and the whole team here are under 30 years old. They've never run a business. So what's the difference between them and you? If you're in your 50s like me, or you're older, or you're under 30 like them and you're doubting yourself, I can tell you what's different: they constantly educate themselves. They constantly seek mentorship in and outside of our office. They constantly ask me and others for advice—and they don't take things personally.

Get out of your own way—don't look left, don't look right, don't look back—and find a mentor. Let your guard down and let that mentor take you to the next level. It's easy to say and harder to do, but you can do it.

---

**Nick:** Anytime there's a challenge to our business, we come out on the other side much better off. We're always developing systems, procedures, and checklists to make sure that negative results doesn't happen again. This is part of growing a business—it's what we expect, and you should too. When you're growing a business, expect challenges, not roses.

## Managing Expectations

You won't fail because of the market. You won't fail because of the systems we teach (this holds true for the systems taught by *any* mentor who's still in the trenches doing deals); we know they work. You won't fail because of your family. You won't fail because of your friends. You won't even fail because of your bank account, because what we do doesn't carry a large overhead on a monthly basis. You fail when you don't properly manage your commitment, your struggles, and your expectations.

In other words, it's all you. If you're not used to hearing about taking responsibility for your actions, you might want to check out Dr. Joe Vitale, and he'll help you get your arms wrapped around the fact that it's all about *you*. And as soon as can do that, you can propel yourself forward and move on to the next level. Incidentally, Joe and I are friends now, and he's speaking at this year's **QLS Live** event—all because I reached out to him, had dinner with him, and worked with him as a mentor for a little while. My family and I only suggest things to our students that we've done ourselves.

Mismanaged expectations are a major frustration for us as coaches, in especially in the real estate training world. Why? It goes hand in hand with commitment. You come in and your expectation is *I need a deal this month or this doesn't work*, or *I need to see* _____ , *or this doesn't work*. You don't need to see *anything*. This stuff has been done for decades and decades and decades. All we did is wrap a system around it and deliver it in a bow so that anyone can follow it, and follow it with some confidence and support behind them. It has nothing to do with all of the minutiae around it. You're managing your expectations and your commitment to say, "I'm sticking with this, no matter what, for three years." And *when*, not *if*, you say that, you'll have success in your first 12 months—but be mentally ready for 36 months.

## TAKEAWAYS FROM THIS CHAPTER

1   Don't start until you're ready to commit for at least three years.

2   Follow the rules—they're there to help you.

3   Expect roadblocks and bottlenecks.

4   Be persistent.

5   Have a game plan.

6   Find a coach who's still in the trenches, and is readily available to you.

# DO YOU WANT TO PLAY AT THE OLYMPIC LEVEL OR HIGH SCHOOL LEVEL?

In this chapter, I want to go over several things that will put you in the best possible position for success. You may already be doing well, but there's always room for improvement. I want you to put yourself in a position where you can increase your success. This is what I like to call playing at Olympic level vs. high school level.

## You Can Choose the People You Do Business With

1   **You don't have to do business with people who waste your time.** This really applies to any business, not just real estate. Have you ever thought about that? *You don't have to do business with people who waste your time!* You know who they are. They're the folks who suck the life right out of you; they drain your energy. Do business only with people who add value, provide increased profitability, and add energy.

2   **You don't have to do business with rude people.** I've gotten off the phone with sellers (my son deals with the buyers) and said, "You know what? I really don't want to talk to that person again. They're just so rude." Or they've been rude on the

phone, and I've actually just hung up! I'd hate to think that I'm being rude myself, but if someone is out of line, and unloads that negative energy on me, I just hang up.

3 **You don't have to do business with people who are impossible to set an appointment with.** If you can't pin a person down, how can you do business with them? I'm sure you've experienced it. If you haven't, you will! You're playing phone tag forever. I've left messages and said, "Please, if you miss me, let me know when I can reach you." So I wait, and the next message they leave, they still don't leave the best times to call them. I just move on.

4 **You don't have to do business with people who are impossibly demanding.**

These kinds of people cost you time and energy, effort, resources... and you don't need that. Ask yourself the following questions:

A   What would the impact be on your business if you spent 80% of your time with people who are a fit for you, and you spent it on what I call **MPAs** (money-producing activities)? (I'm not going to go into them here, but in *Real Estate on Your Terms*, I detail nine secrets to success. If you listen to our podcast, my guests and I bring up plenty of additional money-producing or high-payoff activities, depending on your niche area.)

B   What if you got three great referrals today from each of your sellers? Who would they be from? We've had people we bought homes from with owner financing send us four deals! What if you did that? What impact would that have on your business? How about local real estate agents? How about wholesalers and rehabbers? They send us leads for deals outside of their wheelhouse. One rehabber sent us five leads that were very profitable over the course of a year, so they ended up hiring us to train them to do the deals themselves.

C What impact would it have on your business if you eliminated all the idiots from your database and your daily interactions? I mean it. There are people I've had to cut off. My wife will ask, "Did you talk to so-and-so?" Maybe someone on our team deals with them, but my answer is, "I don't know about them, and I don't even *want* to know." Their energy is wrong for me. Our past landlord is a fantastic example of this. I refuse to interact with him and deal with his childish antics, so someone on the team does.

## Don't Let These Three Things Hold You Back

I find that three main things hold most people back:

1 **We have the wrong priorities; they simply don't match where we want to go.** You need relate your goals directly to your daily disciplines. Everything should match. Everything should mesh. More on this at the end of the chapter.

2 **We let other people control our time.** If you want a great book on time management, I strongly suggest you pick up Dan Kennedy's *No BS Time Management*.

3 **We have a tough time visualizing the end result.** How much time are you personally spending every day on visualizing, thinking about, and planning the end result? Our minds are like parachutes; they only work when they're open. You want to be working *on* your business, not *in* it. I know you've heard it a gazillion times from different people in different contexts, but it holds true in real estate—and in any business.

## Is Your Tree Dying?

I once wrote a piece called "Is Your Tree Dying?." I began by relating a story about a property that Kim and I owned. A small tree we'd planted started to die. This bummed us out, because we loved it—we loved the landscaping, the yard, the tree. We called in the tree specialist, who fertilized it, did whatever it is tree specialists do, but the thing kept dying. Finally, I took the garden hose out, soaked the roots twice a week for over a month, and leaves started to explode from the previously dying branches.

All it needed was *a little more water*. The drip line that carried water to the tree was clogged, and we didn't know it. Today, the tree is flourishing, happy as a clam. All it needed was the right environment to grow in—a *wet* enough environment, in the tree's case.

But the same is true with people, isn't it? Many people don't grow because they're in poor environments. Think of the people you hang out with. What's their income? Yours is probably about the same. Let's explore this idea of environment a little further.

The last 10 or 12 associates who joined us specifically cited the family environment, our family team, as the reason they joined us. It wasn't our special techniques—I think we have some great techniques, but that wasn't why they joined. "Your family team is unique," they told us. "No one else in the industry has it." That insight about our family team is really all about environment.

That's what we foster here: our associates get a chance to come visit us for two days. And at the two highest levels, the **Immersion Level** and the **High 6 Level**, someone on our team gets on a plane and flies out to the associate at our expense. Talk about environment! We lock arms and go at it—we make calls, go on appointments, whatever's necessary.

If you want your wealth to grow, if you want your real estate business to grow, go where people who are growing their real estate businesses go, find someone you can relate to, then watch your business grow. Our two annual events, **QLS Live** and **Business Scaling Secrets**, are good places to start.

## Read Every Day

If you want your intelligence to grow, wouldn't it make sense to read daily in the area of expertise you're looking to expand on? If you read 10 to 30 minutes a day and applied what you learned, you'd be in the top 2% of your industry—some say you'd be in the top 1% if you read for an hour daily. But read at least 15 minutes a day. Jump on Amazon and grab a book every month or subscribe to Audible. If you do both, you can double your reading with a little technology. I listen to Audible books while driving or working out and read physical books on a stationary bike or at home. When I interview businesspeople from around the country for my podcast, one of my questions is, "What book are you reading now?" Most of the time, I buy it—and that pushes me to read even more.

Some students go through our **Quantum Leap System (QLS)** video program, our home study program, and then say, "I don't know if I know enough yet." My response is, "If you went through the program, you know more than 90% of the market right now." I was in real estate for maybe 18 or 20 years before I started doing terms deals like we do now. I thought I knew real estate, but I didn't know *enough*. I just said that to one of my former mentors the other day.

Open up some books, and get yourself into the learning mode. If it's not books, it can be CDs or online courses.

## Improve Your Health and Improve Your Business

I don't care if you go to a gym—in my case, it's Anytime Fitness, because I can go at hours that most people would consider crazy—or you jump on a bike or kayak, or just generally get out. But improve your health and fitness. Since 1995, I've had coaches in real estate, in nutrition, in accountability, whatever it might be. There are plenty of health specialists that can help you in this area.

You may be thinking, "What does this have to do with business?" Because it's all about the environment. It's all about being well rounded, and health is an important piece of the puzzle. You cannot accomplish much with a sluggish energy level or sickly body.

## Improve Your Spiritual Life
## and Improve Your Business

For the same reason, if you want your spirit to grow, go to church, go to synagogue, go to the mosque, find a quiet spot and meditate (as in my case), or pray if that's what you're into. I've been meditating steadily for a few years, and it's something that's helped me tremendously, no question about it. In fact, as recently as this morning it was part of my routine. Years ago, I would never have imagined myself meditating and going to the gym quite so regularly. Now, I can't imagine *not* doing these things.

## Expand Your World and Improve Your Business

If you want to expand your world, go somewhere you've never been before or do things you've always been afraid of doing. If you're willing to go somewhere you've never been before, if you're willing to do things you've never done before, what do you think might happen? You'll probably see success that you've never been before. The real estate profession offers this, and not every business does. It offers you the chance to be anywhere, do anything, and create your own schedule. What I always say is that in Real Estate you can literally *design your lifestyle*.

Sometimes the fastest way to change and improve yourself is simply to change your environment; there's no better way to grow. Then, align yourself with a mentor or group or system.

## Four Criteria for Hiring a Mentor

When doing your due diligence on a mentor you're considering, ask these questions:

1 **Is this mentor doing deals right now**
   **(or, if not in real estate, doing what I want to do)?**

2 **Does this mentor do deals in the niche**
   **in which I want to participate?**

3 **Have they survived at least one real estate cycle (preferably two)?** This question is more or less about making mistakes. You want your mentor to have gone through a few real estate cycles and made some mistakes. I look back at most of my mentors, and most of them have made mistakes—some huge, some small, but every mentor learned from them. I have too. After several cycles in the late 80s, early 90s, 2000s, I can tell you that there are certain specific things that we do every single day in our business that we wouldn't be doing if we hadn't gone through those cycles.

4 **Can you relate to them?** Think about how simple but important that is. I'm not so naïve as to think that everyone can latch onto my style, for example. I'm blessed with a family team who can! It goes both ways, of course—your mentor needs to be able to work with *you*. They may interview *you* while you're interviewing *them*. This is a two-way relationship.

## Take Advantage of New Technologies

Over the last half a decade, what used to be hard got super-easy. Super-easy. It used to be hard to do real estate deals. They're easy now. Before, you had to stay very local, keep your finger on the pulse, be physically located in that geographical area. That's no longer necessary. We teach a new pattern of activities in real estate. We take advantage of the new breakthrough technologies that seem to crop up every one to four weeks. We are evolving non-stop, because we're in the trenches buying and selling three, four, five, sometimes 10 homes a month—sometimes 15 with all the associates around the country. If something new comes up, we're able to share it at lightning speed with everyone so they can all take advantage of it and profit from it. One way we do that is via weekly mastermind calls and another is via our private Slack channel for associates, which serves as a non-stop mastermind group.

You might think it's hard to put technology into place. What's hard is seeking out innovation and—in the face of enormous resistance—leading yourself and your small company or team into new territory. *That's* hard!

So do a little self-inventory. Are you taking advantage of all the systems out there, all the help, all the mentors?

## The *Power of One Daily Discipline* Chart

I was in a mastermind group in the 1990s. (I strongly suggest you join one, whether it's ours or someone else's.) It was around 1992, and there were five of us. We were real estate agents selling 100 homes or more a year each.

One of the members of the group, Mike from Florida, is still selling 200 to 250 homes per year to this day. The average real estate agent nationally might sell four or five. It sounds like a joke, but that's a fact. During a brainstorming session, Mike said, "Look, guys—I figured out how to have a great year this year: if you take your goal for the year and break it down by the quarter, by the month, by the week, by the day, and work it out so you know what steps are necessary every single day in order to achieve those yearly goals, then all you have to do is have a successful *day* every day. Then from day one of the new year to the end of the year, you're guaranteed to achieve your goals."

So we made the **Power of One Daily Discipline** chart, which I've used ever since. On a sheet of paper in landscape orientation, make a column on the far left for all the daily disciplines that you know are necessary. You might not feel like doing them, but you know they're necessary to achieve your yearly goals. Check in with your mentor to make sure they're the money-producing activities and personal habits you need. You might write down *Do a cardio workout* or *Call three people*. It can be anything, personal or business.

Then, in columns running across the chart to the right, you have the days of the month, 1–31. So if it's the second day of the month and you had *Call three people* on the left, you put an × there if you did it. If you didn't do it, you don't put an × there.

You'll find that this accountability to yourself is pretty powerful. Keep doing it for two or three months and you'll find yourself keeping that chart on your desk and checking off the boxes. If you don't do it at the end of the work day, you'll spend the extra 10 minutes when you go home at night or in the morning. You'll want to do whatever it takes to keep yourself accountable on your own chart.

If you want to raise the bar a little bit, get an accountability partner you can check in with every Friday. Here's how it works: let's say it's the end of the day, 4:00 or 5:00 PM on a Friday. You each review your week. You say, "Yes, I accomplished my goals," or "No, I didn't," and then, if you did, what's your goal for next week? If you didn't, do you reset those goals and try it again? Or abandon them and rewrite them because something has changed? It's that simple. Picture it. If you do that every single week, every single Friday or whatever day works for you, you can't get off track, especially if you've given your accountability partner permission to *make* you stay on track.

What are some of the things you haven't been doing that you know would improve your life—your health, your business, social affairs, family—any area of your life you want to work on, but you just haven't done it yet. What if you make just one change every month? (This idea also came out of that 1992 brainstorm.) What if you add just one new discipline every month? If you want to get aggressive, do it every week; if you want to water it down, do it every quarter—but *add one*. How far ahead would you be next year (or three months from now, or three years) with 12 new disciplines, or 12 new ideas? Just think of the potential growth! Play with the chart a little bit.

I encourage you to download the template for the **Power of One Daily Discipline** chart from my website. I include some examples of daily disciplines, but you can brainstorm disciplines that are more relevant to you. You can enroll in our **Quantum Leap System (QLS)** home study program and get some ideas for money-producing activities there. You can add your personal activities. But I want you to take advantage of this chart— there's so much power in using it. I'm constantly working on adding new and better disciplines. It doesn't stop—it's an ongoing process. Make it part of your life and you'll reap the rewards personally and professionally.

## TAKEAWAYS FROM THIS CHAPTER

1  You can choose the people you do business with.
   Work with high earners who contribute positive energy.

2  Get your priorities in order.

3  Make sure your daily activities align with your yearly goals.

4  Visualize the end result.

5  Create the right environment for yourself:
   the right team, the right associates, and the right friends.

6  Take a holistic approach: work on improving yourself mentally,
   physically, and spiritually, and you'll improve your business.

7  Rely on an excellent mentor who meets the right criteria.

8  Take advantage of technology.

9  Use **Power of One Daily Discipline** chart to keep yourself on
   track. Ideally, use it with an accountability partner.

# LEARN SO
# YOU CAN EARN

What is your commitment to learning? Over the years, I've been fortunate to spend time with entrepreneurs and highly successful people. That's by choice. Dan Kennedy's conference in the early 2000s, a Peter Lowe event—if you're old enough to remember those—a Tony Robbins seminar. Those were in-person events, but if I go back further, I remember listening to cassette tapes non-stop in my car, especially commuting to and from college. Yes, cassette tapes were "in" back then.

Back then (and even now), I would be constantly challenged to think about my personal and business plans going forward. And looking back, I've spent hundreds of thousands of dollars over the last few years on education, mentors, programs, and more.

Sometimes I'd walk away feeling like I'd taken a drink from a fire hose. At the same time, I always walked away thinking *huge*—thinking with more clarity. And I found (and continue to find) huge value in learning away from our immediate work environment. *Physically* away from our work environment, I mean—no distractions.

In the summer of 2017, I spent a whole afternoon with the incredible Dr. Joe Vitale, who contributed a chapter to this book. I've pointedly reached out to other successful businesspeople over the last several years, and continue to do so. One reason for that, of course, is that I want to bring more experts on my podcast, but I also want to further my own learning, and I'm super-clear that my own income is *directly influenced* by those experiences, and by those around me.

## Learning Years Create Your Earning Years

I recently finished a book that I really enjoyed. It's one of many that I recommend: *John F. Kennedy on Leadership: The Lessons and Legacy of President*, by John A. Barnes. Chapter 7 references the importance of learning—mostly independent learning and self-teaching. The chapter starts out with a quote from JFK: "There's no school for presidents either. We'll learn together." He said this in response to Robert McNamara, who had told JFK that he didn't feel qualified to be defense secretary. That's pretty major.

This truth has come up many times in conversations about the various businesses that my wife Kim and I have participated in over the years. Those businesses have absolutely nothing to do with what I learned in college or what Kim went to hairdressing school for (during my college days, Kim paid the bills by working as a hairdresser). Now, college does provide some tools, as many of you know—and if you're going to be a doctor or attorney or veterinarian, you obviously need specialized education. But generally speaking, I advise people to avoid getting bogged down in the diploma, the details, all the minutiae. As a general rule, you can never, ever learn too much about your line of work. But that really starts *after* college, for those of you who choose to go to college.

Information and skills are only as good as the uses you put them to. So if you read Barnes's book, you'll learn that JFK wasn't afraid of using new information. He constantly took in new information in order to change his mind about a particular issue or to learn new skills to help him do his job better. (I hate to call it a J-O-B when what we're talking about is being the president of the United States!) He continuously challenged himself with *never-ending improvement*. That's a Tony Robbins phrase that I love: "constant and never-ending improvement."

Being able to learn new facts, to immerse yourself with others who do the same, and to continually step back and work on designing your life and business, is essential for success. Even more essentially, if you're looking to grow your business, you're going to have to grow *yourself*—non-stop. Let me give you an example. Todd Smith is one of my good friends, and he'd always say, "Chris, your income is always going to be directly related to your commitment to personal development, and to evolving and refining the skill sets for any given profession." Notice how he says this holds true for *any* profession?

*Your income is going to be directly related to your commitment to personal development, and to developing and refining the skill sets needed for your given profession.* Think about that. I constantly challenge myself so I can be in a better position to teach others. I need to be able to coach others effectively and generally keep the ball moving forward relative to my own learning curve and to the growth of my businesses. And those businesses now involve my son Nick, my son-in-law Zach, and my daughter Kayla, as well as a phenomenal team that's helping us scale our growth. So it's super-important to me to always be there for our team, our joint venture partners, our associates (students), and our clients across the country.

As Todd used to tell me, by teaching others to do what we do, we ensure constant, never-ending increases in their incomes. And if you're doing that for yourself, you're not just guaranteeing *your own* success. You're guaranteeing the success of the people you hang out with, because they're likely to follow suit. Isn't it awesome to be able to say, "If I go out and learn, learn, learn, learn this year, I know that it's going to increase my income in my pocket next year"?

Let's break that down: your *learning* year might be this year so your *earning* year can be next year. That cycle continues, if you choose. Too often, people let their learning slow down, which slows down their *earning*. Or worse, it could come to a complete stop: when you stop learning, you're actually drifting backwards. Think about it: you're not just stopped. You're drifting backwards as your competition floats right past you on fast-forward.

Back to JFK, who said in 1960, "We all learn from the time we are born until the time we die. Events change. Conditions change. And you'd be extremely unwise to stop." I'm going to amend that and say, "you'd be extremely unwise to stop *immersing yourself in constant, never-ending improvement and learning.*" Make your *learning* the focus of this year so next year can be your *earning* year.

## How Can You Maximize the Learning Years in Order to Grow Personally and in Business?

How can you create the learning experiences that I'm talking about? Let's start from when you get up in the morning. Here are nine things you can do in the morning to jump-start your day. These were essential to my first book, *Real Estate on Your Terms*, right in the first chapter. In 2008, which was a very tough time for us, these key points were pivotal to getting us through all the distractions and challenges:

1 **Meditate and visualize.**

   You can do this before starting your day or week, and/or before going to sleep at night—or even while you're working out. I use a meditation app called Calm on my iPhone. It allows me to pick different meditation focuses, which run as individual meditations or in seven-day increments. You can pick monthly increments as well. There's also some built-in accountability: it posts how many times I meditate and allows me to track it on the built-in calendar.

   Other material I like is by Dr. Joe Vitale, particularly his *Zero Limits* book and *At Zero*. My son Nick likes Mike Dooley (of tut.com), and I know my son-in-law is into Bob Proctor. I find them all helpful for meditation, visualization, and creating a space for good energy.

2 **Work out, exercise, or practice yoga.**

   Do whatever you need to do to get moving in the morning— and do it *daily*, not "when you feel like it." That daily commitment creates some discipline and more energy to accomplish your goals, while lowering your stress. For some of you reading this, that will be key! I find it best to do this in the morning, but for you it might be a different time of day. I do it in the morning because it helps me set up my day. Two or three times a week, I'll be over at Anytime Fitness between

4:00 and 6:00 AM, which is why I joined that gym. And once or twice a week, I do a short yoga session. Figure out what it's going to be for you, track it, and hold yourself accountable.

3  **Review your life plan.**

This is a review of your business plan or goals and the same for personal. You only need to take three to five minutes daily; just do a quick review. For me, it's some index cards I've attached to the life plan I designed. I just take a quick gander at those in the morning. Of course, this requires you to have a life plan and some index cards, so if you don't, that would be a good place to start!

4  **Read something inspirational or motivational.**

There are hundreds of thousands of incredible books out there to keep you motivated and focused. I use one or two of my two or three gym days to nail down this #4. I read something while I'm on one of the machines. (You don't necessarily have to make time to do these nine things all separately; you can do some of them simultaneously. When I'm on a machine that requires me to use my arms, or when I'm driving, I listen to audiobooks on Audible. This has enabled me to double or triple my reading.

When I read, I tend to rotate through self-development, business development, and biographies. But whatever you read, read something every single morning, even if it's for just 10 minutes—you'll be amazed at what happens if you read 10 minutes a day. If you're really disciplined, you can add 10 minutes at night. I believe that if you do this over the next three or four years, you'll get to the top income in your industry. You'll certainly make the top 10%, because most people just don't do it. Get in the habit of *doing* what others aren't willing to do so you can *have* what others won't have.

5 **Listen to something motivational.**

Listen to something motivational, educational, or
inspirational. You can do this on your commute to and from
work or the gym, or while you're on one of the machines at
the gym. You can get a lot of these things done simultaneously.
Your car is a university if you choose to take advantage of it. I
look forward to some to the trips I take on the road just so I
can pop in a bunch of CDs and get caught up. I might listen
to an old boot camp. I can tell you that doing this nets me
hundreds of thousands of dollars a year, no question. I'll keep
my index cards in my console and jot down maybe one or
two ideas on a two-hour trip, or use the voice recorder on my
iPhone. That can be a game changer—and a money changer.

6 **Do affirmations out loud.**

You can take this to the next level and create your own
affirmations recording. Affirmations can be extremely
powerful. All successful people use them in some shape, form,
or fashion. Here are two fabulous books to get you started in
the affirmation space: one is John Alexandrov's *Affirmations
of Wealth: 101 Secrets of Daily Success*. John was a good
friend who happened to live close by me here in Newport,
Rhode Island. We used to frequently golf together and hang
out. He was an amazing attorney, speaker, and author who
contributed a chapter to this book (not to be skipped) before
he passed. But you'll also want to read his *Affirmations of
Wealth: 101 Secrets of Daily Success*. The family has since asked
us to take over all his published works, which we have done,
and we're now in the process of updating them. If you'd like
a free copy, just fill out the form on the ***New Rules* resources
page** and you'll pay only for shipping. The other one is Dr.
Shad Helmstetter's *What to Say When You Talk to Your Self*.
That's an old one, but a very good one, and I checked—you can
find it on Amazon.

7  **Go to lunch at the same time daily.**

When you do, eat something designed to give you energy in the afternoon. So many people I talk to just *drag* in the afternoon, which is avoidable. You can work eating something super-healthy into your daily routine. Get in the habit of doing that at the same time of day, every day.

In the 1990s, when I was a real estate agent running a Realty Executives franchise, I didn't feel 100% in the afternoons, and I couldn't figure out why—between digestion issues and tiredness in the afternoon, I just wasn't 100%. I needed a nutritionist, so I sought one out the way I'd hire any coach. I found Inger Gaar, and I learned a lot from her. This was in the 90s, and to this day, I keep some of the habits that she helped me establish.

8  **Start each day as if you're unemployed.**

Every day, get up and act as if you're unemployed and you've got to start from scratch to earn any income. That'll take care of any complacency! This exercise should do away with any "creative avoidance," as I call it—or anything else you're doing that's not related to income generation. It prompts you to do something productive and not waste the day.

9  **Set your expectations.**

What are your minimum standards? Do you have them written down? Do you have a minimum standard for people that you'll speak with, if that's applicable to your business? Do you have a minimum standard for appointments you'll go on, if applicable? What are your minimum standards that you refuse to go below? Make sure they're in writing.

## Create Learning Experiences at a New Level

Now that we've got you out of bed and on the right track, let's explore creating learning experiences at the macro level so we can predictably create your earning experience. Back in 2013, once I started scaling my business after a total reengineering after the 2008 real estate crash, I made a decision to help others in the real estate education business. So many people were asking me to do just that, to help them out: "Hey, can you coach me? Can you launch me in this business in such-and-such state?"

My very first thought was, "Okay, who's in this business of education, information, and marketing? Who can I best learn from?" There are a whole bunch of people who are phenomenal in this space: Ron LeGrand, Dan Kennedy, Joe Vitale, Wade Cook, just to name a few. I have a list of at least 50, and I'm still seeking out more. I've had interviews, private consulting, and spent other time in a myriad of different ways.

I invite you to do the same thing today: In your field, specialty or industry, whose business do you want to model? Are there several, like I listed for myself? I don't care what business you're in. I don't care if you're a large apartment building investor or a single family rehabber, or if you're into lease purchases and owner financing like we are around the country. I don't care if you're not even in the real estate business. You could be selling popcorn on the corner—it doesn't matter. There's someone out there who can help you. Write down at least six of them right now.

Now what do you do? Contact them! How? I'll give you an example: Ron LeGrand is someone I used to go see at his real estate seminars. I knew he also coached, so I got in touch with his assistant. I asked her, "How much for a private day of consulting?" I had already been to all the events, and I didn't need to attend another unless he came out with something new. I wanted to learn from him on a private basis, and at a much higher level. As individuals, we're totally different from a business, moral, and ethical standpoint, but I knew there were plenty of nuggets I could glean from a private visit. That also happened with Dr. Vitale, Ed Rush, and many others I sought out.

Since then, I've been in two $25,000 mastermind groups, back in 2013 and 2014. I paid $10,000 for a half-day of private consulting,

$7,500 for a dinner, and $2,000 for a one-hour phone call. Now, I can directly attribute well over a half million dollars in income—and more—to the experiences I just outlined for you. I stopped counting how much, actually.

I want you to avoid the mistakes I made, and to avoid saying to yourself, "Well, I can't do that. I can't afford that." Or "Yeah, but..." You've got to start somewhere. Start for free by reading someone's book and then reaching out to them by email or by phone. You'll be amazed how many authors, speakers, coaches, and mentors want to help you. They can interact with you by email or even by phone. Most will do that, at least at a basic level, until you can get yourself in a position to pay. But get that ball rolling. Get yourself in motion.

I attended one of Dan Kennedy's SuperConferences recently (I hadn't been to one in about 10 years) and, as a result, I've been researching many seven- and eight-figure business models and coaching models. I can directly attribute tens of thousands of dollars of income to business coaching and what I learned at Kennedy's conference—not just to the knowledge gained, but to the connections I made or reinforced when I attended. And I've barely scratched the surface: by the time I got on a plane, booked a hotel, and paid for the cost of the event, it was probably, all told, $5–6,000.

But here's what happened: while I was there, I met someone who helped me make adjustments to our YouTube videos, I purchased some courses, I researched other high-level groups. At a certain point, the resulting income isn't even quantifiable. You've got to get yourself out there.

How did I have dinner with Joe Vitale? I reached out to his assistant and booked a private dinner meeting. By the time I got there and back, it was about $12,000 out of pocket. Since then, I've structured joint venture deals with contacts he shared, had him speak at one of my events, and realized over $250,000 in profits so far from that one dinner.

After selling my brokerage business back in 2000 to Coldwell Banker, I took several stock market training workshops, and they were absolutely outstanding. I remember in particular that Wade Cook ran an incredible education business. I was amazed at how he rolled out seminars around the country. I was in awe of how he educated and how he cared about people. I reached out to him, just like I reached out to the other coaches. I had a private Skype call with him and his daughter, and we're currently working on dates to have a visit together in the fall.

You can read about Dan Kennedy and Wade Cook. Wade built a business worth $300–500 million or more in the education world. He even trained Ron LeGrand back in the 1980s and 1990s. He trained a lot of the people you may have studied under or heard about. He's an incredible individual.

So what should you do with all of this? Go seek out the one you feel will be the best to show you the path. No matter what business you're in, support along the way is key. Having someone teach you what challenges or speed bumps to avoid is key. It'll change your life. Just let it happen and trust the coaching system. *Learn* so that you can *earn*.

## TAKEAWAYS FROM THIS CHAPTER

1   Information and skills are only as good as the uses you put them to—you've got to execute.

2   If you're looking to grow your business, you're going to have to grow *yourself*.

3   Your income level is directly related to your commitment to personal development, and to developing and refining the skill sets needed for your profession.

4   Follow my 9 steps for jump-starting your day.

5   Be deliberate about creating learning experiences.

# $180,000 ON 3 DEALS

## IN HIS FIRST 10 MONTHS

## Michael Makredes

In this chapter, we highlight one of our associates: Mike Makredes from Fresno, California, one of our **High 6** associates. He's been in sales all of his professional life, and he's currently in the agriculture industry, working for the largest melon, broccoli, and corn grower in the United States. He handles sales for over 12 million cases, or about $150 million of produce a year.

When I came to **Smart Real Estate Coach**, I had no experience in real estate at all—except for buying my own house, which isn't much. I do have a background in sales and finance: I worked at Wells Fargo for several years while I was at college, and then as a personal banker after college. So I already understood the financing aspect of mortgages and personal loans.

Chris remembers that when we first chatted 9 or 10 months ago, I asked him why his **High 6 Associate Level** was so cheap! That's because once I understood what the program was about, I was all in. I wanted to take advantage of everything he had to offer for my business to succeed. So I went straight to the **High 6** level. If you look at what the **High 6** level offers, it's a no-brainer: you get those 10 deals and for every deal, the averages were at $65–75,000 for all three paydays. Well, looking at that, it's an ROI (return on investment) that simply isn't possible with any other program I looked into—and I looked at everything from coaching programs to franchises to buying existing businesses.

## My First Deal

My first deal that was taken and sold was a sandwich lease. I purchased the property at $365,000 and we ended up selling it for $389,900. This deal was beautiful. Payday #1 was $11,700. It was almost like an owner-financing deal because his loan was a 15-year loan, so the principal pay-down monthly was around $1,080 on a total payment of $1,820. We charge $2,150 for our buyer's monthly payment (rent-to-own) so we have a spread of about $330. The total deal is about $70,000 for **Paydays #1, #2, and #3.** That's the $330 per month spread plus almost $12,000 in that up-front deposit for **Payday #1,** and then on the back end, we're looking at about $35,000. I know that Chris and his team have averages, and have taught averages, in that same range, but it's super-cool to experience it myself and see that what they do and teach every day is so spot-on. This is a great deal—a great first deal. It's only a two-year deal, and it has that much profit in it. September 2019 is when that one will be cashed out. I'm very excited about that. I have great buyers, and it couldn't have been a better first deal for me. You can see why Chris keeps saying that over 18 to 24 months, you can amass several million in payouts down the road.

## Working with **Smart Real Estate Coach**

I never thought it would go so easily. Chris and his team were there every step of the way. It was amazing for me, especially not having any real estate background. Chris's team helped me lock it up under contract with the seller all the way through to getting the buyer, and then closing the buyer out, getting them in the house, and collecting a check. That's the main thing. Once you get that check in hand, it all comes together, and you're even more motivated, because you actually have cash in hand. In the beginning, when you're starting out, you're learning every step, and it's a lot to take in for somebody who's not in the business. But Chris and his team have it all planned out step-by-step, and there's nothing else out there like it.

I used a virtual assistant, the same guy Chris uses. He's had the same virtual assistant for over five years, and the associates get to use him when he has time available. So if there's a waiting list and an associate at the **High 6** level comes in, we get put at the top of his list. This virtual assistant calls a for-sale-by-owner seller, fills out a property information sheet, sends it to me, and then I call. The other benefits they offer **High 6** associates (like the extra mastermind meetings, which alone are worth tens of thousands of dollars, and the learning and networking with other **High 6** associates) are all just amazing.

## Two More Deals

I have two other properties on the market right now. We're really close to closing one—we have a buyer who's deciding. These properties are about 5 or 10 minutes from each other. We have a couple looking at both of them right now, and they're deciding which one they might purchase. They're both pretty close in price, and the couple has already qualified financially.

Both of these came from *expired listings*, listings that had been on with a real estate agent, and for whatever reason, didn't sell. I called both of them about four months ago, and although they weren't really interested at the time, I told them to keep my information. Three, four months later they ended up calling me. They said, "We're interested in selling to you and using your unique program." It's funny, because this is an example of exactly what Chris always says: "You're filling up the funnel when you make your calls every day. This is a numbers game that's very predictable. As long as you stay on track and you hit your numbers every day, you fill that funnel, and these people are going to come back. The ones who really need it are going to reach out to you, so always tell them to keep your information." Just use the follow-up techniques and protocol Chris and his family use and teach us to use. It's totally true: situations change all the time, and I'm getting calls months later.

The first one, he originally had it for sale for $499,000, and he owes about $400,000. I asked him, "What are you looking to get out of this?" (trying to put it on him and see how low I can go with this, and what I can get it for—perhaps in the $489–499,000 range). "I just want to get $50,000 out of it," he says, "and I'll be happy." So we ended up getting it for about $450–$455,000. We put it on the market for $489,000. The buyers I have right now can put down about $14,500 (a little over 3%), and that'll be **Payday #1**. For **Payday #2**, there's a spread of about $300 per month. For Payday #3, we bought it for about $455,000, putting it on sale for $489,000, so that's about $35,000 right there. The principal pay-down on these is about $600 a month, and we have it for four years. That's $7,200 a year for four years—$28,800 total.

Not only that, but for Payday #1, that's just a deposit. Chris taught me how to also capture the first month's check without having to pay the mortgage yet, so we're going to collect the first month's rent ($2,995 in this case). So you're looking at $14,500 plus almost $3,000. That's about $17,500 total for **Payday #1**, all three paydays amount to almost $80,000, and I think Chris talks about his average being about $78,000 right now—so cool.

---

**Chris:**  What Mike is referring to is that he structured his buy—his lease purchase—so that his payments start one month after occupancy. So if someone's taking occupancy December 1, his payments don't start until January 1, but he collected a month. Mike got another $3,000 just from that little technique. We're now teaching a **Payday #4**, which isn't even in my first book, and it's allowing us (and our associates) to capture tens of thousands more *per deal*.

Every deal is not the same; you have to dissect it. I remember in the beginning, when I first started studying Chris's books and going to all the events and learning about everything Chris has to offer. It really came down to what Chris said about needing to be a master at putting together deals. You want to look at the deal and be able to see what you can pull from it. I'm only 10 months into the program and into Chris's coaching, and I can quickly look over a deal now and say, "Hey, we could do this, we could do that." I can see all of the different profit centers that we can pull out of the deal to make a huge profit. Chris's coaching has really opened my mind about how to see things in general on each property, each deal.

For me, it's $180,000 on three deals, and they'll close between one and four years. So in theory, as Chris says, if you put 10 of these together, you'd be somewhere between $600,000 and $1 million. Then you could take six months off, or you could crank it up to retire, or pursue plan B, or whatever. The point is, you have options: really, really *cool and lucrative* options.

## Getting Started

I was a little nervous to make calls at first, because it was all new to me. But you can't look at it that way. There are so many different sellers out there, so many different homes and opportunities. You can't worry about that. The call scripts that **Smart Real Estate Coach** provides made it very easy for me. I kept reading them before I made my calls, even right before my calls, so that I really understood what was in the scripts. If I got a question during my call, I knew how to respond confidently. I knew what I was talking about, so they felt confident in me and in my program, and thought it might have something to offer them.

In the beginning, I was recording my calls and sending them to Chris. He would respond pretty quickly—within a day or two of my call—and I'd read it over and make my critique for the next day. I can't think of a better way to improve on these calls: as Chris says, five or six calls into it, I just felt so comfortable with it. From time to time I sent more recordings to Chris, but I really didn't *need to* after the first few. I still record to this day, just because I'm always looking to critique myself. You can think, "I'm going to change this wording to that" or "I'm going to approach this in a different way."

There's always room to grow—that's my mindset. I'm always going to be a student, always open to learning, because each deal is so profitable, and as they teach us more and hone their way of doing business, it helps us. Just one or two more deals per year, because of some simple adjustments, ends up being so profitable.

It does take effort to fit this real estate program into my schedule. Being in the produce business and on the West Coast, we have to be up at the crack of dawn. I have a one-hour commute to my office, so I'm on the road very early in the morning, and I get home late. I work six days a week, and it's like that about six or seven months out of the year, so I usually do my calls in the car on the way home.

Going into this program, my goals were pretty modest. I knew I needed to learn something totally new, in a field I've never been in. Not only that, but with my work schedule, trying to build up this business was going to take a little time. I've told Chris multiple times that I went into this with a three-year plan, and that's probably way longer than what he would expect anybody to say. I went in with the idea that my first year would be a learning year, and I'd ramp it up in year two and three, but I'm ahead of schedule and ahead of my goals for my first year. This is doable for anybody. It's predictable. As Chris says, if you stay on track with your numbers, you're definitely going to get results, and he and his family team have exactly the tracking and systems that you need daily.

## Don't Make an Offer

One of the things Chris taught me that worked really well on this first deal was *not to make an offer*. A lot of people ask him, "How do I know how much to offer?" When I first started, I had the same question, but he told me to just put it back on them and let them talk. When you let them talk, they tell you more than what you were trying to get out of them. So all I asked is, "What do you want to get out of this?" Once I ask that question, he has a number in their head that he wants. Every seller, of course, is going to want to get the most out of their home, and they think their home is better than everybody else's, but the main thing is to put it back on *them*. These sellers knew what they wanted out of it. I didn't even have to talk them down or anything—I just said OK. But Chris does say that even if they give you that answer, you can often still bring them down even more.

## Finding Deals

My immediate market in Fresno is very tough to get a house in right now. So I decided to take Chris's advice and go a little further out. That's where these two homes are, about an hour and fifteen minutes away. But honestly, that's *nothing*. You go look at the house only after everything else is done by email and over the phone. It's worth it. Would you drive an hour for a profit like that, for $60,000 or $70,000? For these deals, I drove five hours both ways, maybe two or three times. They were expiring. I talked to them back in the summer, about four months ago. They actually went back to the real estate agent because they thought they could probably sell it, but after three or four months, when it still didn't work, they came to me. This just goes to show that deals are out there if and when you put into practice what Chris and his team teach.

## Challenges

These first 10 months have been pretty smooth. The biggest challenge was dealing with my market. That just meant some more dials, more leads per deal. Once I got onto expireds, that number definitely shifted back down, because expireds are a whole other animal, a whole other avenue of leads and opportunities. The bottom line is that you just have to get to know your own numbers, but until you do, Chris and his family team provide averages that you can use to map out your plan.

My other big challenge in the beginning was just *learning* everything. It's not rocket science: it's just learning the lingo, learning the process, a lot of little things here and there. You learn what to do here, the paperwork you need there, and Chris and his team help on all that. But that was definitely the part I was nervous about: I've never dealt with contracts. That learning curve was the biggest challenge. Everything else was pretty smooth, so it was pretty easy.

## Visits with Chris: A Perk of the High 6 Level

Making a visit to Chris's office, and then having him come to me, wasn't something that I thought was going to be important, but when I visited him, seeing how Chris's family runs their businesses totally opened my eyes. They're doing exactly what they teach, from the seller calls that Zach's doing to the buyers that Nick's handling to the tons of things that Kayla's doing in the background with the other team members. It's just amazing how they set it up. It seems so complicated, but it's so simple. Just seeing it shows you that you'd be able to do it wherever you're at. Whatever part of the country you're in, you can emulate exactly what Chris is doing, grow your own business, and be successful. I'm very happy I made that trip.

It was also great to have Chris out here in my territory. I already had my first house under contract, and we had a viewing together to show prospective buyers. Then we were able to write down a plan and go over all the details of how to build a business and scale it from the beginning. It was great to have Chris in person here in my living room and at the kitchen table, mapping it all out and doing calls together. We planned out what to do each day, down to what part of the day I'd do this or that. We mapped out the whole week like that, and I can repeat it every week. It was pretty cool to have someone with experience, who actually does it himself, help me do it right in my own home. That plan is what I've been following ever since. Nothing has changed. It's like he says, the process is predictable—if you stay on track.

I'd also like to highlight that being a **High 6** associate with Chris, I get to share a percentage of others' deals that we mutually agree on for ongoing deals. Another aspect of it is that you get to help coach new members and create another profit center.

## Setting My Goals

Right now, I can go full throttle, and I'm excited to see what's going to happen this next year. My goals for the next 18 months aren't very aggressive—they're very conservative—but the profits coming in will be huge. I feel like I'll hit it easily, tracking where I'm at right now. Even though I'm only 10 months in, I feel like I'm advanced in my understanding of the process and in my dealings with the sellers and others.

My goal for next year is 18 homes taken and sold. That comes out to 1.5 a month, which isn't hard to do if you just stay on top of your numbers and map it out. If I hit that—and I'm very confident I will—it will put me in line for my three-year goal, which is to have 25–30 homes sold. It might sound crazy, but it's definitely doable. I'm going into this with an open mind, with all the information Chris has to offer, which is so valuable: you can never invest enough in yourself, in learning. It's priceless.

My ultimate goal is to do this full-time, which is a matter of having a certain comfort level, knowing where I'm at and what money is coming in. It's going to be huge when I can go full-time with this; I feel like the possibilities are endless. The work I'm doing right now at my full-time job doesn't give me much free time at the moment, but with this, you can predictably plan your time and still hit your numbers. That's the best thing about Chris's coaching and this program.

---

**Chris:** People might see Mike's success and think, *"Wow, that's awesome! How could he do that so quickly and profitably?"*

Look, there's no candy-coating what we do. It's not a get-rich-quick scheme. Unsurprisingly, Mike did 100% of what we suggested that he do:

- He did calls, taped them, and sent them to us for critique.

- He studied his scripts before calls.

- He listened to each and every mastermind call that we do weekly, even if he couldn't make the call live.

- He acquired any book or third-party training program we recommended.

I could go on and on. We now have another **High 6** associate who surpassed $700,000 in total paydays on just 7 deals. What is he doing differently? *Nothing*. He's working our systems precisely the way we teach them. You can too—if you're coachable and you're willing to put the blinders on and work this business the way we teach it.

## TAKEAWAYS FROM THIS CHAPTER

1   Expired real estate listings can be a great source of leads in any market.

2   Make your calls *every day* and fill up your funnel.

3   *Always* tell sellers to keep your information. They may think they're not interested now, but over time, things change.

4   *Don't make an offer*—let your seller tell you what they want.

5   Consider expanding your area: it's worth the drive for $60–70,000 or more per deal.

6   Set goals and work steadily to hit your numbers predictably.

7   Don't stray from what Chris and his team teach.

# AN ASSOCIATE ON THE ROAD TO $3 MILLION

## Bill Reich

**Bill Reich, from Washington, DC, worked in commercial leasing for close to 50 years. After the 2008 crash, he did his due diligence on several companies before coming to be one of our associates.**

I first moved to DC for graduate school, and I wasn't sure what I wanted to do, so I ended up meeting somebody, getting married, and having two kids. Fast-forward 50 years. I've been here in the DC area pretty much all that time except for a year back in New York, where I was born and raised to be a Brooklyn Dodgers fan. I also spent three years in San Francisco and a year in Dallas. But aside from that, I spent a good 50 years here in the DC area.

I spent most of that time in commercial real estate—primarily office sales leasing—and later got into investment sales. I was doing acquisitions in a partnership with an individual out in the Bay Area, in San Francisco. I found myself doing business development in commercial real estate for construction firms or architects. But after 50 years, it got old. It was the same people, the same day, over and over. I felt like I was living in *Groundhog Day*.

Then I got into something very exciting, and I felt that it would be my last step on the path to retirement: in 2006, I came back from Dallas to open up the regional office for a very large real estate investment sales operation. I had six salespeople working for me. Then

2008 happened, as Chris mentioned, and my world was turned up-side down. I lost pretty much everything and had to start over, so I did business development again for a while. I had made the decision to just tuck and roll, whimper in the corner, give up on my dream of being an entrepreneur and just try to make a living. I took various jobs, I worked for various companies, and they were all just jobs. They weren't soul-stirring or exciting. They paid the bills.

For about 10 years, I thought that's the way my life was going to be until it was over. I don't know what it was that changed my mind, exactly. Some reading I was doing led me to look into residential real estate as an investment, and I took the path everybody takes: I went to seminars, listened to webinars, read books, enrolled in courses—spent thousands of dollars on courses—and somehow that windy, twisty road led to Chris Prefontaine and **Smart Real Estate Coach** and his family team. The rest, as they say, is history. That was a little over a year ago.

---

**Zach:**  I remember speaking with Bill for the first time, and he told me that he was going to be our number-one associate. Fast-forward 18 months, and he has a $750,000 business. He's a prime example of someone who was knocked down, but wouldn't stay down. Bill has brought hope to those affected by the 2008 real estate crash.

## The Terms Business is Different

The terms business is totally different from what I was doing: first of all, I was always selling. I was always pushing, whether it was to acquire a building on behalf of a client, sell a client's building, or get some company to commit to the office space I was representing. I was representing office space to landlords. It was always, always selling, especially in the business development field, where I was basically whining and begging and crying for them to allow my client to bid on an opportunity, whether they got the job or not. I did my job if I at least got them into the game.

I'm not selling *anything* in my new terms business with Chris and team. First of all, my posture is that I'm a buyer, not a real estate agent or working for one in any capacity. That completely disarms people who get a phone call from me, because I'm basically here to educate them about a very different option that's available if they have an open mind: "I would like to buy your property; let's explore that together." It's more of a collaborative approach. It's a lot more relaxed, and it's more of a personal engagement with another person. Buying or selling a home is an emotional process for people, and I really enjoy getting to that level. I've missed that my whole career. So this is a brand new thing for me, and it's providing me with a great opportunity for growth as well as a great opportunity to make a lot of money. It's perfect.

---

**Zach:** If you ask the right questions, you'll never have to "sell." We teach you to work toward *disqualifying* each prospect. That way, you only work with qualified people you can truly help.

## Getting in with Chris and His Team

Chris and I have talked about how I spent money on courses before I found him, as many people do. I'm sure some people are reluctant to join up with Chris because they feel they've already spent a lot of money, and it came to nothing. My answer to that is that past failures have very little to do with what you're doing today. Also, it's okay to make a mistake—learn from it.

That last course or that last guru, that so-called "mentor," that teacher that you threw in with who didn't work out for you—were they hands on? Were they with you every step of the way? Are they doing deals today? Do they speak from experience, as opposed to book knowledge? That's critical.

What attracted me to Chris, frankly—and I've told him this a dozen times—is the whole family operation. I also love that he's blunt and to the point; that really speaks to who I am. But it's not just Chris: it's his son Nick and his daughter Kayla and his son-in-law Zach and the rest of their team members who were all there with me from the very beginning, every step of the way. I felt very comfortable that if I was going to make a mistake, I had somebody there to point out the error of my ways and gently put me on the correct path. And that is exactly what's happened. The coaching has been phenomenal, and it comes down to personality. You can mesh with these people and they are truly there to walk by your side as you go on the journey. That was the big thing for me.

I'm very disorganized, so what happens when I come to Chris's team and visit his office? Everything is in order. Everything is organized, everything is peaceful, and everything seems to be on track. That really stuck with me. Also, I get to see how a company operates, and I want to be exactly like that company. I get to take that back with me and it reminds me this is not an impossible task, to become more organized. These people are doing exactly what I want to be doing. It was the same thing when Chris came down to DC and helped me rearrange my office and set up processes and procedures. It was huge for me to have him here. But going up to the mother ship (their office) is the biggest thing. I love these guys, every one of them. The office visit, which is free for associates, is just invaluable.

We have constant dialogue on Slack, which Chris initiated. It's a private group on a private channel for associates only, and it's like having 24/7 access to 30–40 wonderful, like-minded people in a mastermind—amazing. And every now and then, I'll get a call from one of the other associates, or I'll call them. The associates keep up with each other, and I know that I helped some of them get over the finish line and become part of the **Smart Real Estate Coach** community. I have a genuine affection for them and I root for these people constantly. I want success for them, and I also get great advice from them.

---

**Nick:** It's important for you to evaluate whether a mentor or coach is teaching from deals that he did 10 or 20 years ago or if he's still in the market every day, doing deals. Part of what we pride ourselves on at Smart Real Estate Coach is that we continue to be "in the trenches" doing deals alongside our associates. The reason that this is so fundamentally important is that market conditions and tools change *almost every week*, so you need someone who's still in the market and on the cutting edge.

## Six Months of No Deals, Now Going for $3 Million

It took me a while to get my feet under me after I signed up. That's when I made the decision to leave the business development field. I had my own company at the time, so I turned my full attention to building the business. I think it took me five or six months to make my first deal. Since then, I have seven on the books, including the properties that I'm out selling. I think it's conceivable that in one year, we're going to hit a dozen properties acquired and sold, or having done the lease purchase with a tenant buyer. Right now we're slightly under $700,000 earned in all three paydays. I'm pretty confident we're going to hit a million dollars in that first year in business. And that's just the beginning. My goals are ambitious, but within three years, I expect to be doing $2.5–3 million a year.

## Never Quit

You can take heart, knowing that it took me six months to get my first deal and seeing where I am now. Chris has mentioned that other people have quit after six months or even earlier, but what major opportunity cost they left on the table! That's like the story of the miner who's chipping away at the mountain and quits after however many years, and somebody follows up after him and discovers that he was only six inches away from hitting the largest vein of gold that ever existed. It goes to my point: *never quit*. Just don't quit. See the vision of what you're doing. There are times when you'll want to throw up your hands and give up. I've done it in the past, but I'll never be accused of doing that again. Keep on, especially if you've got people around you to help get you across the finish line.

## Avoid Fix-and-Flips; Avoid Wholesaling

For a lot of people, their default position in going into the real estate investing business is that they want to do wholesaling. They're taken with the idea of fix-and-flips. I know there were a lot of people out there who made a lot of money doing this, but it's unbelievably competitive, especially on the wholesale side. It's something you have to do every day. It's a job that becomes a tedious and boring J-O-B, because in order to earn, you literally have to do another deal and *another* deal, versus creating three paydays per deal like I do. We bring in an opportunity with ongoing cash flow because of the **3 Paydays** system. That means you get not only the pops up front, but ongoing cash flow throughout the life of that investment—and that's how you build wealth.

To me, buying and selling on terms is a no-brainer. I can't even imagine doing anything else, so I wouldn't waste a lot of time. If you're thinking about getting into this business, do it. Don't start with "I'm going to try wholesaling." Do what we're doing from day one. Don't make that mistake, and don't wait. It's the most lucrative and wealth-building opportunity I know of in this business. And believe me, at my age, I've looked into pretty much everything.

## The Terms Business for High-End Homes

The smallest house I sold was for something like $499,000. I've got my fingers crossed on wrapping up another house in the not-too-distant future. That one is $1.9 million. I've got four properties right now between $1.5 million and $2 million.

You might be wondering about these higher-end homes. Why would a seller or a buyer enter into a terms contract? There are people on both ends who need a better solution than the usual, conventional deal. That's because the first markets to slow down tend to be for the homes over $1 million, and certainly within the $1.5–2 million range. The DC metro area is a very wealthy area, but some people need help. They need help and they like the idea of saving a 6% commission on a $2 million house. From the buyer's side, typically we're going to get somebody who's self-employed, who needs some seasoning (time to qualify). It's rarely a credit issue. Alternatively, it could be somebody who wants to save more for the down payment so they can get a better rate when they go for their mortgage loan. There are a lot of advantages. It's very gratifying to see people's faces light up when they understand what we do. We really are a great solution.

## Expanding My Company

My goal is to become the go-to company in the Washington-Baltimore area for anybody who wants to entertain selling or buying a house using creative terms, and this is precisely why I went with the **High 6 Associate Level**. My whole focus is on growing the business and growing our brand, and I've got some great people. I'm working with my partner Joanne, whom I owe a tremendous debt. She's become our acquisitions go-to person. She's our director of acquisitions and handles all of our outreach campaigns. She does the prequalification and then she turns them over to me for the next step. Since she lives in Charlotte, North Carolina, I'm the only boots on the ground at this point. I'm all over the territory. I've traveled 200 miles in a day to see sellers. I need to cut back on that and focus on growing the business.

While Joanne is handling the acquisition, she's going to have two more people I'm onboarding right now. One will help us in Maryland, and the other one in Virginia. They both have full-time jobs and are okay with what they do, but they've signed up for Chris's **QLS Live** event and **QLS Video Program**. They love our model. In fact, the lady I'm hiring in Virginia was a seller I did a deal with. I brought her on, I took on her property, and we closed with a great tenant buyer in four weeks. She has since become an acolyte, and her greatest selling point to anybody she talks to is, "I signed up with them as a seller—they're great! They did such a magnificent job for me that I decided to join the company." I can't think of a better proof statement, and she's going to be dynamite, as are Joe and Marilyn. Their intent is to leave their job by the end of this year, and I'm going to get them there. We're going to have a great little organization, and as I mentioned before, I expect to be doing anywhere from 24 to 30 deals a year. That should get us close to $3 million a year by the end of 2020.

## A Constant Student

I've really become a fan of Bob Proctor, largely because of the influence of Chris's son-in-law Zach, who's a big follower. I've enrolled in one of his online courses, which I'm going through right now. I read his books constantly. I listen to his books in the car, driving to appointments. A lot of what he teaches is a synthesis of—and very much based on—Napoleon Hill's *Think and Grow Rich*, which I also read. I continue to go back and read them; I try to read one chapter a day. I also like Joe Vitale, and was excited to meet him at the **QLS Live** event this year—amazing. I love Grant Cardone's energy, and I know Chris has him coming up soon as a guest on his podcast. I get daily videos from Darren Hardy. I'm a constant student. I'm a constant learner. I think when you stop learning, you're dead. I'm a big fan of John Martinez's online course, and Joanne and I are attending his bootcamp in San Diego. I'm enrolled in an Airbnb course, since Chris and I are both involved in Airbnb now by way of one of our properties. I'm really excited to be launching that in the DC area. As a **High 6** associate, I speak with Chris almost daily, and that's really kept me tuned in and focused.

---

**Nick:** There's no wondering, "Gee, I wonder why Bill is having so much success with Chris and **Smart Real Estate Coach**?" It's no mistake; he's a sponge, always looking to learn more. I think every single one of our associates can learn to model his behavior and attitudes about this business. It's also not a mistake that he committed—jumped in with both feet, burned the ships—and did the **High 6 Associate Level**. That helped him become our top associate very quickly.

## Beginning Strategies

Forgive me if I'm saying what Chris always says and it seems repetitive, but I learned a big lesson the hard way. I might have gone in a very different direction if I hadn't listened to myself for 20 or 30 years. It would be much better if I could look back that far and say, "Thank God I made that decision when I *did* get a mentor."

For many years—basically my whole career—I felt I could do it on my own: "I'm clever, I'm creative, I'm smarter than most people," and on and on. I managed to get myself into some very sticky messes and I made a lot of mistakes. But if you're working with the right mentor, you can avoid a lot of those mistakes. You ride on their coattails, you learn from their mistakes. So get involved with somebody who's doing just what you want to be doing, and don't let go of that person.

If you're letting fear stop you, get over it, get past it, get through it. There's too much of life that you *could* have, and that you're *not* having because fear is stopping you. We get caught up in what's safe, we want to operate within our comfort zones all the time, *but that's just going to keep you mediocre.* You've got to try something new. You've got to be willing to make that leap and do it.

---

**Chris:** The 2008 crash was the second time I didn't have at least one (if not two or three) mentors in some area of my life (nutrition, business, etc.). I didn't have a single one during that time, so there was no one to turn to. I didn't realize until it was way too late. I also didn't have one around 1994—another not-so-great time for me. Well, think about the importance of mentors when considering those two major lesson times for me. When times are great, you need a mentor, and when times suck, you need a mentor. I spend an hour once a month with a peer group, and every year I'm in a mastermind group. I spend 15 minutes weekly with an accountability partner, and I'm always seeking education. It's just a necessity; you're not going to grow without it. I'm so proud of Bill and all of the other associates who understand that.

Here's something very important, and sometimes very scary for people to understand: your business and your income will never, ever grow past you. You must constantly challenge yourself (and eventually your team) to grow and learn so you, your business, and your income will grow.

## TAKEAWAYS FROM THIS CHAPTER

1   It's okay to make a mistake—learn from it. Welcome it, as Ray Dalio suggests in his book, *Principles: Life and Work*.

2   Never quit.

3   Avoid real estate wholesaling and "fix-and-flips." Get into the terms business!

4   Be a constant student.

5   Get a mentor.

6   Don't let fear of the unknown or the uncomfortable hold you back.

# AN ENGINEER IN REAL ESTATE

## Don Strickland

Don Strickland, from Dallas, Pennsylvania, is one of our **High 6** associates. He's the "engineer brain" in the group, and one of our most successful associates.

## Getting Started

My professional career started in engineering, and then I got into the telecommunications; I've been in that business for 25+ years, managing and building out networks. That's what I do full-time, professionally.

Many years ago, traveling through different states on business, I started to look for something more. I had always heard about real estate, and in Georgia, I got involved with the Georgia Real Estate Investors Association, with their monthly meetings and with some of the "gurus." I bought a lot of courses, and I guess I made some mistakes. I bought and sold some of my own properties. I'm not sure I did it the right way. I did make some money, but that's how I got started—sort of by accident.

I did a lot that way with the books and courses, then traveling took me away from it. I never really had a good background or a steady mentor or program to sustain me, but because of circumstances and family, I've always wanted to get into real estate. So I bought a lot of the courses, stumbled through them, tinkered, and didn't do deals. But a few years back, I was laid off. The corporate world was changing, and not just in my area of specialty. I had young kids, and I said, "I need to take a different approach to the real estate business: I have to find a mentor to hold my hand and walk me through all of this so I'm not just tinkering."

I did a lot of soul-searching, a lot of internet searches, and some conference calls. I was digging deep, looking for somebody who had a business I wanted to emulate. That's how I found Chris.

About a year and a half ago, I was on the **Smart Real Estate Coach** website tooling around, and I submitted a request for a strategy session call with Chris—just to chat. I wanted to find out what this guy was about, because I liked what he had to say. Chris and I talked about what I wanted to do, my goals, and what he could offer. That was when I said to myself, "I think this is a fit for me. This is what I want to do." It was the mentoring aspect. Unlike past mentors (I won't mention names), this was more of a relationship: a true partnership, a "marriage," so to speak—not just a 30-minute call here and there, or some emails.

Chris and I talk on the phone a lot: early in the mornings, during the day, weekends, nights, whenever I need to talk. If he's tied up, I know he'll get back to me first thing in the morning or whenever. I really enjoy that. That was the kicker for me: the support, the availability of Chris and his team for any question I had, whether I was sitting down with a seller or whatever the situation was. It's just coaching—it's truly a joint-venture type of relationship.

## The Payout

Looking back at how I did in the 20 years before **Smart Real Estate Coach**, just buying and selling my own properties, I was selling to cash buyers, so to speak. In the 20 years I spent tinkering with that business, I can't say I made even $25,000! I was using outdated contracts; I messed up, and I learned some hard lessons. I didn't do things the right way, and a significant part of that was not having somebody by my side—a mentor.

I spent a lot on education in those years: if I add up all the courses, books, CDs, and other materials I've had to purge from my shelves, we're probably talking close to $100,000. Compare that with the last 12 months or so, doing a handful of deals with Chris. What we have on the books right now for just three deals is somewhere in excess of $350,000. That's a huge difference, truly a game changer—a *life* changer. And those aren't even all of my deals.

## Working with the Smart Real Estate Coach Team

The biggest difference between going it alone and working with the team is the support and mentorship: Chris texts me early in the morning, or we chat in the early morning and throughout the day. When I started learning the business, we probably spoke at least 10 times a week. Recently, it's been less and less, but initially, it was a lot of conversations and a lot of support. It's exactly what I needed— the support, the mentorship, the confidence of knowing Chris or someone from the team will always be there. I text Chris or call him, and I know he'll get back to me shortly. Whatever issue I have, I know I'll get an answer or a solution. And now that Zach is such an expert with sellers, plus Nick on the buyer side—it's simply an amazing level of support.

## My Office Visits with Chris and the Gang

I've had two great visits with Chris and his team. When I upgraded to **Associate** from **Consulting**, Chris said, "Hey, you've got to come out and see what we do." Now, it's great being able to talk 10 times a week, and it's nice to be where the action is and meet the players, as I did last year at one of the mastermind meetings. But living and breathing it, watching how it works literally as they do it—that's something else entirely.

My kids were interested too, so I took my family with me. My son wants to do what Zach and Nick are doing. He's ready to go to college next year and then start getting into real estate, so I can model my business after their family business.

The essential takeaway for me was seeing how Chris's business is structured, how it's regimented and systematized between Chris and his family. I took in a lot. I was watching, observing; I went out on the road with Zach, and while I did that, my wife and daughter were sitting with Kayla, learning the entire admin side of the business. Then my son and I sat down with Zach and with Nick. It was neat watching it unfold. Coming home, we had a game plan. From an organizational standpoint, it helped a lot. After our visit, I could say, "Here's what I'm doing (or not doing). Here's what I need to do to get to the next level." The whole experience is unique...and real. In fact, I'll go as far as to say that the visits *alone* are worth the *entire* cost of the **Associate Level**.

---

**Zach:** We get the same reaction from everyone who comes for an office visit: "Wow, you guys actually *do* what you *teach*!" I guess it surprises people because many of the mentors out there aren't in the trenches anymore. The funny thing is that we have a system, and we follow the same steps over and over again—it's not particularly exciting stuff. But our associates tell us that they get their money's worth sitting for hours, listening to us talk on the phone. It really gets me excited when I can see the light bulb go on, and everything clicks.

## Success

After the visit, we put five more under contract, which is about one and a half per month. I've got three more ready to sign. We're dotting i's and crossing t's right now, so I'll probably have a total of eight shortly. I want to have an assistant down the road, to help me scale up. That's what we're looking at next, and when it's time, all we have to do is ask Chris and team about the next few steps.

## QLS Live Annual Event

Being there for a face-to-face, shaking hands and being able to chat one-on-one with Chris and his team, is critical. Talking on the phone or sending an email or text is great, but it's important to put a face to a name and really *get to know* the folks and the business.

When I say this, I'm also talking about the other associates. We talk on the phone a lot because we all mastermind weekly, but again, it's important to put faces to names, get to know personal backgrounds, where everybody came from. We're all there for the same reasons: to do deals, make money, and to help each other, which is a neat concept. It's not about the individual—well, it *is*, but we're all very willing to help each other, which is great. That's what I'd call a true partnership, a team. It was cool. I've been to the office twice, attended two **QLS Live** events, and a private **High 6** Mastermind, open to associates at that level. Just like the office visit, the **High 6** Mastermind is invaluable. Even if I were only to attend that one event, it would be worth the entire cost of the **Associate High 6 Level**—really.

## Avoiding Costly Mistakes

I've made a lot of mistakes, but I'd say the most critical one was probably trying to go it alone. That's a mistake I paid dearly for on one of the properties I had before meeting Chris. I would highly recommend seeking out mentors like Chris and his family. You're not going to find another team that can provide—or would even be willing to *consider* providing—the level of support and service Chris and his team routinely provide. I've spent the money looking for it. I've been through it over the past several years. If you go it alone, you're going to make mistakes, and they're going to be costly. I've found that taking this route with Chris and his team is very profitable. It can happen very quickly or slowly—however you decide to do it. Chris is definitely walking the walk, keeping me (and all the other associates) out of trouble, including legal trouble and expensive headaches down the road.

## One of My Biggest Wins

My biggest win was discovering a model to emulate in Chris's family business. My kids are both interested in it too, which is good, because

I want to keep them out of the corporate world if I can. Now, whether they decide to take that route once they're out of school—that's another story. But we want to be financially free and *get out*. That's one of the biggest wins: finding a support system and having the confidence to make that move.

Another big win, of course, is being able to make a lot of money. This business is highly profitable, over months and years, depending on how you structure it. That's a huge win: finding something that's very profitable and costs very little to run.

I started out with a lot of the virtual assistants and systems in place. My expenses were somewhere around $450 a month, but in the past six months, I've bumped up a couple more services. I built a website through Chris's referral company, for example. Right now, my expenses for everything, soup to nuts, are $650 a month. Think about that: $650 per month, and I've got close to $1 million for all three paydays projected out over the next few years. And I'm still working full-time at my job.

## Daily Routines: *The Power of One Daily Discipline*

Life is busy. I try to juggle my kids' sports, my full-time job, the real estate business, and everything else in life. But being out there and seeing what Chris and his team do propelled me even further. I wake up and ask myself, "What can I do today that's going to be revenue-producing?" I use the **Power of One Daily Discipline** system that Chris taught me.

I try to get up early in the morning, which is when Chris and I usually chat. Then I try to knock out some of the emails or buyer stuff or whatever is going on. I try to make calls to sellers on a daily basis, then work on organization, which is something Chris went over when I was out there. I thought I knew how Chris and his team did things. When I got there, I found out I was wrong! "Don't do that," said Chris. "It's a waste of time." Learning about the time-wasters was key for me as well.

## Mastering the Calls: The Seller Specialist

Talking to Chris and studying the scripts, I learned pretty quickly how to do calls the right way. You can't be afraid to make mistakes. I think that for anybody who's just starting, fear can set in; even now, on some of the bigger properties, the higher-end ones, I feel some fear—and I'm very confident, very comfortable talking to sellers about their property and about how our business works. So I say, "Hey Chris, this is a million-dollar property. What do you think about it?"

What raised my confidence level was studying, jumping in and taking action, and not being afraid to make mistakes. They're just *human beings* on the other end of the line. Worst-case scenario is that they'll say no—that's it. The challenge, initially, was just to wrap my brain around that, then say, "I've got nothing to lose here," and just jump in and *do it*. I sent Chris recordings of a lot of the calls I was doing, and his feedback helped me turn some of the things that I was doing wrong into better scripts and better answers about how we do things, so I was able to improve as I went along. The team spends literally *hours* critiquing associates' calls so that each of us, once properly trained, is a well-oiled machine.

## The Next Challenge

The biggest challenge for me is systematizing and scaling, which I've been chatting about with Chris. I want to go from being, essentially, a one-man show with some assistants to implementing anything that can help me *manage* rather than actually *do*. I want to scale to the next level, and get to two or three deals per month and more—steadily. I've done their new, "next-level" training—the **Seller Specialist Program**, based on Chris's handover of all their buying and selling to Zach. It's really cool, because Zach outlines exactly how he did it— and how we can do the same.

---

**Chris:** This is what our **Seller Specialist Program** is for—to do just what Don is talking about. We saw the need to duplicate the person handling all the seller activity (in this case, Don) so he can run a business. As Don says, he wants to move into the role of running the business. It's exactly what I did between March 2016 and March 2017. We successfully took someone (in this case, my son-in-law, Zach Beach) with no background in real estate, and totally, 100% *duplicated* me so I'm no longer involved in the buying and selling side of our business (as far as actual appointments and calls, at least). Instead, I spend my time focused on helping Nick, Zach, and the team with higher-level deal structuring and anything else they need me for, and helping our associates to do *the exact same thing*.

## Feed the Brain

Right now I'm reading *The Millionaire Next Door*, by Thomas J. Stanley & William D. Danko. I like to listen to audiobooks when I'm traveling without the phone ringing. Finding the time to sit down and read is a bit challenging for me, honestly, because of all of the activities going on. I'm also starting to read Chris's first book to see if I missed anything in all of our time together before the book (I'm sure I did). Already, I'm definitely picking up some nuggets here and there. I highly recommend it.

## More Confidence, More Action

If I could go back 20 years and have a do-over on this business, I'd definitely take action a lot sooner. Experience is 90% of the game, and having access to that is *huge*. I didn't know then what I know now. Back then, I was a little more fearful; I didn't have the confidence I have today. Circumstances are different. Life changes, and so does your mindset. I would be a little more aggressive in my search for what I really wanted to do. It's different timing now, but I'd definitely take action. Mentorship is also key, and I wish I'd had better mentors. If I'd had **Smart Real Estate Coach** even five years ago, I'd have several million dollars more in scheduled paydays. *Several million dollars more*—think about that.

## Don't Sit on Your Hands

Speaking from my own experience, my advice to people looking to get into this business is to just *do it*. If you're already spending money and time, if this is really what you want to do, then *go for it!* A lot of people just kick the tires, which I've done too: I've kicked the tires on some businesses, spent some money, and decided that they weren't for me. That was part of the $100,000 mistake I made. But if you decide you want to do it, make a plan, find a mentor, move forward, and just *do it*—but you have to do it *consistently*. Everybody has challenges. There have been times when I've been frustrated and thought about throwing in the towel. "Nope," I say to myself. "My *why* is much greater than what giving up will bring me." If you're interested in it, and you have a goal you want to achieve, then you *can't* give up—you've got to keep going. I'm happy to talk with anyone who's thinking about coming on board. You can email me at ReachDonS@gmail.com.

---

**Chris:** My wife Kim often asks me which associates are succeeding and why, and my answer is always a series of logical steps: if A, then B; and if B, then C.

In other words, *just follow the system*. Don has been great to work with: he's a sponge, he follows the system, and the numbers don't lie.

If you aren't succeeding, tear down each step and figure out where the bottleneck is: Are you doing calls, but not getting appointments? Are you getting appointments, but not getting contracts signed? It's all very logical.

## TAKEAWAYS FROM THIS CHAPTER

1   If you're interested in this business, don't delay—make a move!

2   Get a mentor.

3   Study the scripts and the calls will come easily.

4   Don't be afraid of the people on the other end of the line—the worst they can do is say no.

5   Be consistent: keep working toward your goal.

# ENTREPRENEUR, ATTORNEY, AUTHOR, COACH AND MENTOR WHO INSPIRED MANY

## John Alexandrov

John Alexandrov was an attorney in Massachusetts for over 30 years. He was best known as a leader, providing business legal services to entrepreneurs and business owners. Simply put, John acted as independent general counsel, overseeing all of a business's legal issues.

If you're not familiar with the term "general counsel," it refers to the highest-ranking corporate officer oversee- ing the legal affairs of a business, but the general counsel to your business should have skills and aptitudes that reach far beyond providing legal services.

A general counsel should be street-smart and have busi- ness savvy and leadership skills. This is where John stood above most advisors. John represented hundreds of business owners and entrepreneurs, and he was as well known for his business skills as he was for his legal skills. John was quite decisive. Capable in all aspects of a business's legal needs, he brought real-life business experience to the table as an entrepreneur and business owner himself. At the same time, John knew how to act decisively, lead, guide, and manage a team of C-level officers in any company to the effective resolution of their legal and business challenges.

John authored three books and audio programs. His book *Affirmations of Wealth: 101 Secrets of Daily Success,* was a bestseller. His audio programs created a wave of financial momentum and wealth in the lives of hundreds of thousands of people worldwide.

John and I met at a mastermind group back in 1991, and a personal friendship and many business relationships ensued. We did this interview in the fall of 2017. After his sudden, unfortunate demise at the end of the year, we wrestled with what to do with the show. Our family listened to it and said, "That is one of the best, if not *the* best episode we've heard—you should let others benefit from it. John was amazing!" With that kind of feedback, I felt compelled to include this chapter in the book.

I've been intrigued by business and entrepreneurs and self-starters my entire life. I started my career as a commercial loan officer at a bank, then went to law school at night. I can remember the first day I walked into a business—it was a small business in Fitchburg, Massachusetts. It was like a mom-and-pop store. I was thrilled that people actually got to run their own businesses. From that moment on, I always felt compelled to work with business owners—either as an attorney or business advisor. I also selectively coach business owners.

I have a deep understanding of both the opportunities and the challenges small business owners face, and what goes on in their heads. I know what challenges them mentally to get to the next level of success.

I like to read people's financial statements—which may sound a little odd, especially because I got a D in accounting when I was in college. But I can read any business's financial statements and tell you within 30 seconds what's going on in that business. I don't care how big or small it is, I don't care what kind of business it is. I just have this natural ability to read financial statements and see, almost immediately, what's going right and wrong in a business.

Something else that comes very naturally to me is interviewing entrepreneurs, because I've done it my entire career. I can sit down with somebody, interview them for half an hour, and pinpoint 80–90% of their issues in business and in life. That can help them to formulate a game plan—primarily a mental game plan—to start addressing those issues.

## Success in Any Endeavor is 98% Mental and 2% Physical

One of the things I've discovered over the years, running my own businesses and coaching high-level people, is that the next level of success, however you define that for yourself, is all mental. Success in business or sports or any endeavor is 98% mental and 2% physical. You have to get up, of course, and do your prospecting calls and mailings, follow up on leads, occasionally knock on doors—and all the physical things you have to do to succeed at whatever career you've chosen. But 98% of the success you'll achieve—or fail to achieve—comes down to *how you mentally condition yourself every day.*

That's why I've been so intrigued by working with entrepreneurs now for 35 years. I've been able to pinpoint why some people implement those mental breakthroughs and go on to live the lives they've always wanted, and others get stuck underneath that glass ceiling. There can be different reasons, depending on your background, culture, training, and belief system, but I'll tell you this: once the walls of Jericho come down—once you shed those stories or beliefs or misunderstandings in your own mind about why you can or can't achieve something—you can make rapid breakthroughs both mentally and financially.

I don't want anyone to take this the wrong way, because I'm a big believer in being very determined and focused on accomplishing your goals, but one of the things that I've discovered over the years is that hard work really *doesn't* equate to financial wealth—most of the time. If you're on task, working hard, and engaged in a career or profession or a project that really inspires you, it's never going to feel like hard work. It's going to feel almost like you're just naturally *evolving* through life, and you'll eventually get where you want to go.

Whenever I've stopped trying to swim upstream, when I've stopped struggling and just allowed things to flow naturally, it's made a huge difference for me. I grew up in a household of struggle. When you're on welfare, you struggle when you can't make your mortgage payment, you struggle when you have to take the bus to the government warehouse to get powdered milk and peanut butter so you can eat for the week. So I grew up with this mentality of struggling and working hard and paying a price for your status. And some of these are virtues—but only if you focus them in the right direction.

## Align Yourself with the Right Question

Hard work for its own sake does nothing but fill time and create *more* hard work for you. Get your mind aligned by asking yourself, "What do I want to do in life?" Why do you want to do it? Is it to make you happy, so you get up every day thinking, "I'm so lucky I get to do this," or are you struggling?

If you can get yourself out of your struggle and more aligned with your purpose and your reason for carrying out that purpose (not just for the sake of money—and don't get me wrong, I love money) you'll find that a lot of things will go your way.

I live in an oceanfront community of about 15 houses. I think the average net worth of the people on my street is over $50 million. I've been observing these people for many years, and one thing I've learned is that they never seem to struggle. Not that they don't have real life issues—a car accident, an employee quitting—but they don't seem to *struggle*. They always seem to find a way to move through life without too much resistance. So I started asking them about it, and most of them said, "Well, why would I worry? That's just a waste of energy."

Worrying *is* just a waste of energy. Faced with the reality of whatever's in front of you, what you have to do is *take care of it to the best of your ability*, and move on.

It's important to *detach from the negative emotions of the past so you're free to focus on what you want to accomplish in the future.* So many people hold on to their emotions, their stories about the past, rather than putting them in their proper place. If you don't let go of negative emotions of the past, you're keeping one foot on the gas pedal and one on the brake all the time: *There's a new home I want—but the last time I tried that, it didn't work, and I lost my $50,000 deposit.* You're never going to get anywhere like that. You'll burn out the transmission and ruin the car. It's the same way with your mentality, your emotions. You want to find a way to have your foot on the gas pedal and *not* be simultaneously stepping on the brake.

## Consider Joining a Mastermind Group

A mastermind group can be extraordinarily helpful, fruitful, and dynamic, and can help you overcome these struggles and get your foot off the brake—if it's the right group. You have to make sure that the people in the group are sincerely committed to it, and that they're striving for things in life that are similar to what you're striving for. I must have read Napoleon Hill's *Think and Grow Rich* and *Grow Rich! With Peace of Mind* 100 times over the years. Napoleon Hill was in the original mastermind group of Thomas Edison, Charles Schwab, and Harvey Firestone. Think about that! They wanted to be the leading industrialists in the world; they got together, and not only did they mastermind *ideas*, they also supported each other in the growth of their businesses. They became personal friends and helped each other flourish in every aspect of their lives. So if you're going to develop or join a mastermind group, make sure that the group has tremendous intention to pursue significant personal and business growth.

## The Boomerang Effect

Napoleon Hill was really big on the idea that your brain is both a transmitter and a receiver: whatever you transmit, that's what you'll receive in return. You can broadcast at any frequency you want, and that's what you'll receive. So why choose a very low-frequency group, individual, property, or business? I like to call it "the boomerang effect": at whatever level your brain is transmitting, imagine a boomerang being thrown. It's a magnetic boomerang, so it picks up everything along the way that's a vibrational match to that thought or idea, and then it comes back to you. Every day, you've got to pay very close attention to *what* you're thinking, *how* you're thinking it, and most importantly, *the environment in which* you're thinking it.

## Place Yourself in an Inspiring Physical and Emotional Environment

Look at your physical environment and ask yourself, "Where is my mental and physical energy going?" Is it going into people and places that reflect what you want your life to be? If you're hanging around with people who are drinking six or seven beers a night, and they're happy to watch the baseball game, go to bed, and get up and go to work the next day, there's nothing wrong with that, but if it's not an accurate reflection of what you want your life to be, you need to change it. It's that simple. I was just at the new home Chris is going to be rehabbing after tearing down the existing one, and it's quite amazing. I was looking out over the Atlantic and seeing boats going by, seagulls flying, people fishing—all kinds of things. He's in a physical environment that inspires him. I surround myself with people who inspire me and even mandate that I elevate my thinking and my actions. So put yourself in the right place with the right people. If you have the choice between dinner at Subway or at the local sushi bar where all the successful people hang out, go to the sushi bar. Put yourself in physical proximity to successful people. It mandates that you elevate your game.

## How Do You Feel About Money?

People have strange relationships with money. Some people love money, some people hate it, some people fear it, some people have anxiety about it. Chris's dad is a great example of someone who knows how to leverage it, how to develop a lifestyle around it, and how to get anything he wants in life by using it properly, but it all starts with his beliefs about money. There are a lot of people who have such negative ideas about money that they're always stepping on the brake and the gas pedal at the same time. They just can't get out of their own way when it comes to their beliefs about and understanding of money.

You may have learned things when you were young—that you were "born on the wrong side of the tracks," that it's "easier for a camel to go through the eye of a needle than for a rich man to enter into the kingdom of God," or that "you can't be spiritual and rich at the same time"—you know, all the nonsense we were taught. It's not true. Some people who are very entrepreneurial hold on to these stories, and that's why they keep running into financial difficulties—not because they're not hard workers, or because they have a business concept that can't work, or because of their customers, or because they don't want to succeed, but because they have a trash relationship with money. They don't understand it. That's honestly how it works. They don't understand the real role it plays in their lives. These people are always chasing after it, but there's always some story of anxiety around it. When I said earlier that success in businesses is 98% mental, a lot of that has to do with our relationship to money.

Back in 1997, I published *Affirmations of Wealth*. It's more than a book: it forces you to take action. It's almost like a workbook. Now, my personal beliefs and paradigms about a few of the things I discussed in that book have changed a bit—especially when it comes to information and how to use it. Some of the examples are a little outdated. Nevertheless, it's been in circulation and selling for over 20 years, so that says something about it. The book is extremely helpful. I hope it changes the way people think about money. The book is distributed for free now to everyone from entrepreneurs to people in prisons and reform schools. It's in homes for unwed mothers, helping them start building lives for themselves and their children. It's in the homes of some of the wealthiest people in the United States. It goes wherever it's supposed to go, and whoever wants a copy of it, I give it away for free. See the **New Rules resources page** at TheNewRulesBook.com for details on how to get it.

## What to Do with Failure

We all have failures. I think my biggest one was not understanding the difference between *complacency* and moving your business forward *without struggle*. You can move a business forward without struggle, without anxiety, guilt, fear, or worry. You do it by implementing great business principles and surrounding yourself with very dedicated, loyal people who are committed to helping you grow your business by developing the right customers. You can do all of that without struggle—and that's the *opposite* of complacency.

There was a point in my career when I had built up a very large, significant title company and real estate appraisal company—and I stopped caring. I was 29 years old and already a millionaire. People were patting me on my back, saying, "Geez, you've done so well. You're great!" It was all nonsense. I was listening to all the B.S. people were telling me, I bought into it, and I became complacent. I took my eye off the ball. I stopped focusing on developing the business. I passed off responsibilities to employees who didn't have the ability to take care of those issues for me. Two years later, the bank was knocking on my door, foreclosing on 23 investment properties, taking my second home away, and telling me if I didn't pay them a quarter of a million dollars, they'd put me out of business. I had to learn to see the difference between *complacency* and being able to develop a business *without struggle*. I'd become complacent and I had to fight my way back. I'll never allow that to happen again.

That was a mistake, but I wouldn't undo it. Getting back on the right track was painful, but what I did 20 years ago put me where I am now—and I *love* where I am right now. I have gratitude for it. Chris and I have talked extensively about this, and about our experiences in general, and we believe that everything really does happen for a reason—but you've got to be open to acting on experience and inspiration.

## Avoiding Complacency

So how do you avoid complacency to begin with? One way is to be in the right mastermind group. The people in the right group are going to tell you to bring your financial statements every quarter or every month, and they'll say, "OK, what's your next goal? How are you going to get there? Fire this person? Hire that person?" I wasn't in the right mastermind group when I was 29, but I know that Chris has masterminds for his different levels of associates around the country, and the nuggets and deals that have come out of those are nothing short of amazing. Everyone should be applying for his associate program, for sure.

The second part is to not take yourself too seriously. Now, it's important to have a strong ego, in the sense of a desire to do and have what you want in life. But if your ego gets out of control and you start thinking you've figured it all out, you'll be afraid to ask the right questions when you *can't* figure it out, the questions that will help you get where you want to go. You'll be dead in the water, going nowhere. So check your ego at the door each day.

The third part is, as I've already mentioned, to inspire yourself by constantly putting yourself in the right physical and emotional environments. When you experience (or see someone else experience) something new, you can say, "I want that too. I want that for my family. I want that for my children. I want that so I can donate $100,000 to that school" (or in Chris's case, to Franciscan Children's Hospital or 3 Angels; I know he's big on that). The mastermind, keeping your ego in check, and putting yourself in places that are inspiring to you—they'll all help you avoid complacency.

## Discipline Equals Freedom

If you want to have a hot dog stand and you have discipline you'll have the very best hot dog stand. I learned this principle many years ago from a coach. He taught me something I never forgot, and I still make use of it today: "The more disciplined you are about anything, the more you'll have of it," he told me. "The more disciplined you are with your money, what do you have? *More money!* The more disciplined you are with your time, what do you have? *More free time!*" It applies to nutrition and health, right on down the line. Discipline equals freedom.

The difficulty is that the word "discipline" is so often misinterpreted. We were "disciplined" as children, so we have a negative gut reaction to the word. But look at what the word really means. The word "disciple" is contained within the word "discipline." A "disciple" is a follower of something. When you're the follower of great business principles and great businesspeople, you're going to be a good businessperson. When you're the follower of a good nutrition routine, you're going to be healthy. When you're the follower of having a great calendar and getting your appointments booked in task lists, you're going to have more time. It's amazing how everything we're talking about is exactly the support structure Chris has built for his **Smart Real Estate Coach** associates and students to benefit from. Chris is a big advocate of discipline; to this day, I use his **Power of One Daily Discipline** chart.

"Discipline" is a very positive and powerful word, not a negative word in any way, shape or form. If you take nothing else away from this chapter, remember that *discipline equals freedom.* The more disciplined you are with anything, the more you'll have of it. Discipline means being the "disciple" of something, the follower of a system, a routine, the follower of business principles.

## Mental Preparation

Mental preparation is extremely important in making sure that you can get to this point of discipline. You have the ability to choose your own thoughts and beliefs. And because you have complete control of your thoughts and beliefs, you're in complete command of your own future. It's vital to take personal responsibility in life so you know you have the ability to be in complete command of your future—and you're willing to do it. In other words, you don't play the victim in any way, shape or form. You don't make excuses, you don't blame things on the economy, you don't blame things on your next-door neighbor or something that happened 30 years ago. Every single day, you have the ability to get up and choose what our thoughts and beliefs are going to be that day. You can choose which thoughts and beliefs to reinforce that day, and *you can choose to live them—or not.*

Mental preparation is extremely important: What do you choose to believe? And how do you reinforce that in your own mind? I do it through visualization and affirmation: I'm constantly visualizing and experiencing. Visualization isn't projecting what's going to happen in the future. Visualization is *living your dreams now.* You have a dream of traveling to Tuscany to go to cooking school. Visualization is closing your eyes now and listening to the sounds, smelling the aromas. Now see the smiling faces of the other people in the group around you. Watch yourself clinking your wine glasses together at dinner. See yourself having fun while you're cooking, throwing flour at your wife or your husband. Visualization is experiencing something *now* to the degree that your belief system says, *It is absolutely mandatory that this happens.* I prepare myself like that every single day.

One of my main challenges is to stay in the mindset that says I can use my brain to leverage my innate abilities to earn more and more money without working any harder. Steve Jobs understood that. He wrote that one of the most influential books he read when he was younger was *Cosmic Consciousness* by Richard Maurice Bucke. I've read the book, and I reread it a couple of times recently since I discovered that Jobs read it. The chief thing I learned is that you can leverage your brain for tremendous results without physical labor. You don't have to work 2,000 hours or 20,000 hours to get 2,000 or 20,000 hours of productivity when you know how to leverage your brain properly. If you know how to throw that magnetic boomerang to pick up the right thoughts and people and ideas and concepts and principles and return them back to you, 19 seconds, 35 seconds, a minute of pure positive focus can help you earn hundreds of thousands if not millions of dollars.

I'm reading *Extreme Ownership* right now, written by former Navy SEALs Jocko Willink and Leif Babin. One of the things they discuss is how to raise your mentality to the point where you take responsibility for everything, never making an excuse, never playing the victim, never *I wish...*, *I hope...*, or *I want* to be different—it's irrelevant. The only thing that's relevant is this: *What are you preparing yourself for in this moment, and what do you want to be doing?* The most important thing for me to do in life is to achieve what I set out to achieve because when I do, hundreds of thousands of other people benefit from it. I really focus on not getting distracted by things on the news, even natural disasters or major events. I feel bad about it, and I'll help or donate however I can, but I'm not going to let it take me away from my focus.

## My Measure of Success

One of my biggest wins is as a parent. I'm extremely proud of the adults my children have become. I have grandchildren now, and it's just phenomenal to be able to have them come to my home and for us to spend time together. We go swimming and golfing, we go to the tennis courts, we go work out, we go out to dinner. I can share that lifestyle with them. I've had ups and downs in my life like everyone else, but I'm extremely proud that my children have turned into the people they are—and I know that I'm taking credit for that. But one thing I have learned over the years is that our children don't do what we tell them to do, they do what we *do*. They observe who we are and they tend to become that themselves. So for me, my biggest success is that my children saw something in me that they wanted to emulate—and they have.

## Gratitude

Wherever you are, *you are where you're supposed to be right now*. You're reading this for a reason. You're doing all the things that you're doing for a reason. Put aside any guilt, fear, anxiety, worry about what's going to happen or not happen in the future. Put all that stuff aside and just follow the system. Be happy with yourself, be appreciative of what you've done for yourself and your family in the past or are doing currently, and have a positive sense about where you're headed in the future. Everything that you've done up to this point has prepared you for where you're going, whether you perceive the past as good or bad, painful or a great experience. If I look at my own debacles, there's not one step, problem, frustration, or worry that wasn't ultimately useful. I'm grateful for them all.

## TAKEAWAYS FROM THIS CHAPTER

1   Detach yourself from the negative emotions of the past so you'll be free to focus on what you want to accomplish in the future.

2   Place yourself in an inspiring physical and emotional environment.

3   Discipline equals freedom.

4   A few seconds or a minute of pure positive focus each day can help you earn millions of dollars if you know how to direct it.

---

**Chris:**   John was different. I remember sitting in the conference room of his law firm in the mid-90s. I was there for a real estate deal, and the first thing he asked me about when he came in was my goals. I'm thinking, "This is refreshing: an attorney who wants to discuss goals!" From that point on, we worked together, had accountability sessions together, socialized together, and had an amazing relationship that I'll miss forever.

# RESPECT THE GRIND

## Stefan Aarnio

Stefan Aarnio is an award-winning real estate investor, award-winning serial entrepreneur, author of multiple books, and very well educated in the real estate space. He built his fortune by purchasing real estate at 40–60 cents on the dollar and became an avid student of negotiation at a young age. The principles you can read about in books—he learned and tested them firsthand on a day-to-day basis in the real world. Stefan travels the world educating businesspeople and entrepreneurs, molding the next generation of successful real estate entrepreneurs.

Stefan is CEO of two multi-million dollar companies. Most people don't even make a million dollars in one business in a whole lifetime. Only 3% of businesses in the United States ever hit $1 million in revenue. At this level, it's a whole different business. He has 10 employees in the office, outsourced contractors, digital contractors, and you can add in the investors. It's a massive group of people to do multi-million-dollar revenue and run multiple businesses.

When I was 16 years old—I'm 31 now—I wanted to be a rock star and be rich and famous. I had a little rock band, and my mother and father told me, "If you want to be a rock star, you have to go to university and get a music degree." This isn't totally wrong, but they were talking about Plan B the whole time: Plan B, get a degree; Plan A, be a rock star. So I focused on Plan B: I dropped out of the business school, dropped out of computer science, dropped out of the music school, and when I graduated in 2008, it was with a major in English and a minor in music—in the States, you call that a liberal arts degree—and there were no jobs for me. I'm a millennial, and the job I got after university was a $10-an-hour call center job selling hotel rooms to rich people in the middle of the night and hardly making any money at all because the commissions weren't very good.

So I told my wife, "I don't want this life. I don't want to be poor. I don't want to be a poor musician anymore." I had a little guitar teaching business, a little rock band, and I read a book called *Rich Dad Poor Dad*—and that book totally changed my life. It said to get into real estate, start making passive income, building a business, raising money—all the things that are good for people to do in business and in life. So then I'm going to seminars, I'm reading books—doing all these things to get out of my situation. Fast forward six and a half years, at 20, I'm a self-made millionaire through real estate.

Now I have two companies: one is real estate and the other is real estate training. I never wanted to be a trainer, but when you start winning in this game, people start phoning you every day and asking for help. So like a good entrepreneur, when people demand, you supply. I've built my business raising capital by acquiring distressed properties at 40–60 cents on the dollar and really building my team. The team is the key to get to those multi-million dollar levels.

## Blue Chip Homes

I focused on "blue chip" homes, meaning median homes, family homes, the middle class dream. These homes are in the middle of the market. Typically, a price up to about 75% of median is the most liquid home. I do a lot of flipping. I'm up in Canada. People don't do as many deals in Canada as they do in the United States. My team does about one house every week, or buys a house, which is great for Canada. I focus on buy-fix-sell single-family homes, "blue chip" homes. That's where we do a lot of our business, either wholesale or flipping those homes.

I have a rental portfolio as well, but I don't talk about it as much because you just "set it and forget it." You buy and do nothing for a long time. I talk a lot about flipping, raising money, and that kind of thing because a lot of investors reading this probably own some rental properties, or have some cash flow, but they need cash to grow their business. So we talk about flipping and wholesaling because the cash side is what so many investors are missing.

## Building the Team

You've got to build your team and you've got to build your systems so that when the people fail, the systems can take over. To do a deal a month or a deal a week or a deal every three days is all about building an acquisition team. My acquisition team is three guys plus me, and we're grinding this market every day, just grinding it like a meat grinder. We grind the private channels, we go to auctions, we do absolutely everything, 17 ways to get deals, but it comes down to three things: networking, marketing, and negotiating.

Building a team like that is all about how well you can train others to do what you do. It comes down to training, management, and leadership. If you have those three things, you can have other people doing your job. Then you don't have to go into these stinky homes anymore; someone else can do that for you.

---

**Zach:**  When you're looking to build your business, focus on Stefan's advice: create systems and processes for a predictable business that you can scale and grow. Once the systems are in place, you can train others to take your place. Now all you have left to do is to manage the people you train and help them maximize their growth. If you have the right people in place, your business will take off like a rocket ship.

---

**Nick:**  Like us, Stefan is still in the trenches everyday, grinding the market and doing deals. This allows him to stay on the cutting edge, just like us. We say that all the time. It doesn't matter which mentor you choose, but choose one who is actively in the business of buying and selling homes, not just teaching. The market changes every single month, if not every week, and you need to align yourself with someone who is actively in the market.

## Fear and Pride

I think there are two major challenges in real estate or training: when you're starting out, it's the fear and uncertainty, not knowing exactly how this stuff works, not having the education. There's a big wall of fear at the beginning. When you start doing a deal a month, the new problem is pride. You think you know everything, you get off your own system, and then you have a problem or a crash.

There are problems coming in, there are problems *staying* in, and there are problems on the way out. It comes down to time, money, fear, and pride—but really, that's all an illusion. It actually comes down to great training—great coaching, mentoring, whatever it is— that can get you through your own psychological problems.

---

**Zach:** Stefan brings up a huge point: if you want to advance and reach the life that you want to live, you have to get out of your own head. You have to let go of the illusions and fears: fear of money, fear of failure, fear of not being good enough. We all grow up with fears, with excuses for why we can't accomplish our goals. It's time to let those thoughts go and focus on how you *can* accomplish your dreams. Then surround yourself with everything you need to accomplish these dreams, including mentors, books, and like-minded people.

## Respect the Grind

I just made a matrix. I call it the "dead patient list." I took the last 100 deals I've done (I've only entered about half of them; it takes a long time to do the data entry, and I've got to do it myself because I'm analyzing it). There are about 50 things that can go wrong on a deal. If there are fewer than 10 things wrong with a deal, it's profitable. If there are 15 things wrong with it, it's probably a break-even. If there are 18 things wrong with it, you're losing 10% of the property's value, and if there are 25 things wrong with it, you might go bankrupt.

So I'm filling out the matrix, going through my "dead patients," cutting up the bodies to see what's inside. In his first book, Chris has a whole chapter about problems, which should give you some indication of how many problems there are in real estate. Dealing with the problems can be fun, and if you have a mentor who doesn't teach the problems and only teaches the fluff, run away.

I like to say real estate isn't "get rich quick," it's "get rich permanently," but it does take a long time: in the first two years you might break even because you're reinvesting in your business. If you survive for five years, you're affluent, and if you make it to 10, you're rich.

That's why I say "respect the grind." That's a little slogan I wear on my wrist. I own the Canadian trademark to "respect the grind," and I sell t-shirts. I say, "Dude, you've really got to respect the grind. It takes 10 years or 10,000 hours or whatever to be a master. You can't just go read one book or go to a two-hour seminar and think you're going to be performing brain surgery. It doesn't work like that."

**Nick:** I was just mentioning this to one of our clients: most people underestimate what they can accomplish in 5–10 years and *overestimate* what they can accomplish in a single year. As Stefan says, you have to "respect the grind," and if you do that for 10 years, you'll be rich. I love what Stefan says here: real estate is "get rich permanently," not "get rich quick."

## When You Hit a Plateau, Get Some Training

I'm a hard-core student. In the last 8 years I've spent $300,000 on training. I've gone to everything. I fly around the world—I fly to the US, I fly to Canada, I fly to Europe—I'll go wherever I've got to go. I've hired several coaches. Right now I have two coaches, two marketing companies working with me, and two marketing consultants. Those are my advisors right now. Tons and tons of advisors.

The best advice I can give people about coaches and mentors and training is to look at yourself honestly and ask, "Where am I plateauing?" If you're plateauing in your marketing, it's time to get marketing training. If you're plateauing in your acquisitions, go get some acquisitions training. In 2016, I was plateauing in my speaking—I wasn't a very good speaker—so I spent $17,000 for a day with a very good speaking coach. Since then, I've made tons of money speaking. If you're stuck or sideways, that's when you need to find someone who's solved that problem and get them to take you through the process firsthand.

## One of My "Dead Patients"

There are two ways to look at failure: you can get emotional, be a victim, cry, "Oh, boo-hoo me, I can't do this!" or you can lay your failure out on the table, dissect it, figure out where things went wrong, and make systems out of that. Right now, I'm cutting up the failures on my "dead patient" list.

I have one doozy of a dead patient—we lost $85,000 on one deal. The city came in five times with massive demands: $85,000 of extra renovations on a property that's only worth about $165,000. Then they came back with another demand: they wanted $95,000 more in renovations. I told them the property wasn't even worth what they were asking. It took four years. I should've just burned it down. That property was a thorn in my side, a nightmare—a major, major nightmare—and it was all because *I deviated from my own business model.*

I had a business model, I deviated from it, and that deal really hurt my company, my brand, and me. Now I've got this "dead patient" list, and I'm creating a new process I'm calling "risk analysis" to analyze the deals that are coming in now in a different way. We want to avoid those off-model deals. At some point every investor wants to go off their model, but I've found that every time I go off the model, that's where the problems are. You pay for it when you deviate from your model—you have to go through a certain number of failures before you can establish a new model.

If you read Ray Dalio's *Principles*, he has a spreadsheet and artificial intelligence to check all the trades for his hedge fund. We're moving to that model now—I've got spreadsheets and models that are going to check every deal. I used to rely on *talent*: I was talented, and I did all the work. Now that I've got four people in acquisition, I need *systems*.

## Think Bigger than You Think You Need To

It always takes longer, costs more, and is a lot harder than you think it is. I was reading Grant Cardone's *The 10X Rule*, and what he's saying is that it's all going to take 10 times longer, 10 times more money than you think. So when you're setting a goal, you've got to set a goal that's 10 times bigger than what you think you need: if you want to be a millionaire, you've got to figure out what it takes to be a 10x millionaire; if you want to be a 10x millionaire, look at what it takes to be a 100x millionaire."

I like the idea that when you set goals, it's so much bigger than you: you have to think geometrically, think beyond your own personal energy and time and effort. So you're thinking bigger than you *think* you need to, and it's always going to cost more and take longer: it's just always going to take *more of everything*. Success takes massive effort.

## Three Books at a Time

I read about 50 books a year. Most CEOs read about 50–60 books a year. I listen to an audiobook in the morning; I'll put it on when I'm getting ready. If you read just a chapter a night in bed, you'll finish a ton of books in a year. Typically, I have three books going at a time: a paperback by my bed that I read at night, an audiobook a week, and probably a third book in my briefcase for a flight or if I'm stuck on a long travel engagement.

I think you've got to be reading at least a book a month. This year, I'm actually *writing* three. I've written three books in the last five years, and now I'm writing three this year. I got two books done last month—that I've written. When you can enrich your mind with knowledge and put that fertile soil in your mind, you can grow some real nice crops. Most people are putting junk food in their brains—TV, the Super Bowl, CNN, Fox News—all that junk. You've got to put good stuff in your brain so your brain can take care of you and your family.

## Pride in Others' Success

The biggest win for me right now is being able to replicate what I've done. I'm sure a lot of readers are thinking, "How can *I* do it?" They're thinking about themselves, but the next level is "How can I get *somebody else* to do it?" Now I can get other people doing what I do, and that's what I'm proudest of today.

First I was coaching and training people on what they were doing in their own niches. Now I've got my own internal team that's able to run this without me, which is pretty cool. It's almost like having a baby: you get to watch that little group grow up. So having the ability to replicate what I used to do on my own with my own talent is, to me, the most exciting thing I've done in my life so far. It's something to be very proud of. I know Chris and I share that feeling; he has his family team and he's been able to scale his businesses with them. Very cool.

## Keep on Top of the Metrics

One thing I've learned, from a book called *Mastering the Rockefeller Habits*, is to do my KPIs (key performance indicators) and look at my key metrics every day. If you're in real estate as an investor, you've got to make a certain number of phone calls every day. I want my acquisition guys making a minimum of 50 phone calls a day. If you're in real estate, you've got to make a certain number of offers every day. Those are really the key things if you're working in the real estate business. If you're growing a bigger business, it's more a question of what transformational things you can do to make your business look different—in a better way—one year from today.

## Sell Vacuums!

I wish I could have dropped out of school at 16 and sold vacuums for a living. That sounds like the craziest thing to say, but I look at my time in high school, and there was nothing left to learn: by the time we got to grade 9 and 10, they had nothing new for us. So if I could, I'd go back in time, drop out of school at 16, and sell vacuums. I'd probably be three or four times richer today if I'd learned how to sell at a young age.

There's also a lot of junk education out there, too much stuff that wastes your time. For me, it was the four-year university degree. That was about six months of content: if I'd had the book list, I could've done it on my own in six months. So don't fill up your life with junk.

Selling is the biggest skill of all. If you can sell, you'll always survive. You'll always thrive. You'll always have money. The last deal I closed was a two-hour toe-to-toe meeting, and she told me four times she didn't want to sell. Then I bought her house for a $112,000—and it's worth $230,000. Before that was a three-hour meeting: they kicked me out three times, they left once, and I just sat in the house. Then I bought their house for $125,000. It's worth $230,000. If you don't know how to sell a vacuum cleaner, you won't sit in that house for three hours with cat pee and a dead cat in the kitchen. You'll leave when they tell you to leave—because you don't know how to sell.

---

**Nick:**  I can definitely relate to what Stefan is talking about here. I turned 16 early in my sophomore year of high school, so by the time school let out, I had my license. One of the jobs that I had was to door-knock pre-foreclosures. All that means is that these people had received a "notice of default" letter from their lender. That could be another book—all of the entertaining stories that came out of that job—but the most important thing was that I learned *how to sell*. When someone is 4 or 5 months behind on their mortgage and you knock on their door, you'd better be able to convey how you can help.

## Real Estate is a Human Nature Business

I'm writing a book right now, so I've got about 50 books on my table. The last one I was going through was Howard Bloom's *The Lucifer Principle*. It's about the darkness of humanity, the darkness of human nature, and the violence of history. It goes through the cycles of history, how humans organize themselves into tribes, how they fight and kill and do all these dark things—which is part of real estate: real estate is a human nature business. I've also been reading Jack Donovan's *The Way of Men*. I'm reading a lot of books about human nature. If you want to be great in business, you've got to study human nature.

---

**Chris:** Stefan talked about building teams. Here's what I'm super-clear on, having been a solopreneur for many years before building a team: there's no way your business or company can possibly outgrow the leadership or the people. In other words, you've got to train and grow your team so the business has room to expand. Absent that, your business will always retract to the skill level and leadership level already in place.

Every year, I seek out trainings, masterminds, and other education to keep that process and scaling moving forward. Our entire team is immersed in the Elite program for bringing seven-figure businesses to eight figures and beyond. You can learn more about Elite on our free **New Rules resources page** at **TheNewRulesBook.com**

Stefan recommends seeking out mentors or groups when you feel you might be stuck, and that's what we do. He also talks about the psychological aspect of the business. Well, that's an entire book or seminar topic unto itself, but suffice it to say that 90% or so of what you need to be successful is between your ears. What are you reading? Who are you hanging out with? While you're working on your real estate skill set, don't forget to work consciously on your mindset, your mental skill sets.

## TAKEAWAYS FROM THIS CHAPTER

1   Respect the grind.

2   Understand that this is a process; accept that it will
    take 10 years and 10,000 hours to become a master.

3   Think bigger than you think you need to.

4   Stick to your model and watch your KPIs.

5   When you start to plateau, get some training.

6   Learn how to sell.

# FUNDING WORRIES... GONE

## Mike Banks

Mike Banks is COO and marketing director of Fund&Grow, and works directly with CEO Ari Page. They've had over 10 years of success and growth. They've been on the Inc. 5000 list for the last two years. They've built a thriving business based on offering exceptional service to all their customers. They boast a dynamic and rewarding work environment for their employees. Mike regularly hosts live webinars, many of which are focused on helping their clientele finance deals and purchases, at 0% in most cases, for up to 12 or 18 months. Connecting and developing lines of credit is something everyone should be doing, so I'm excited for you to learn from him.

We've been growing rapidly over the last five years. We've been steadily growing, helping more and more real estate investors each year access business credit lines that they can use for whatever they want. We've got a ton of clients coming in, and we've been doing this for over 10 years. We've been on the Inc. 5000 List the last two years. We also have an A+ rating with the Better Business Bureau. In order to get an A+ rating, you've got to take care of your clients. You can't just fake it—you have to show your clients that you care, especially in order to avoid any complaints with the BBB. It's very common nowadays for people to go online and complain pretty quickly. The best way to avoid that is to have a very good relationship with your clients. We sincerely care about our clients and about helping them succeed.

We have affiliate relationships with a lot of real estate investing educators like Chris, who refer us clients on a monthly basis, and we do a lot of webinars and podcasts, so a lot of our clients come from real estate investing educators and similar types of organizations. That tends to be our most common industry, and our most common client is a real-estate investor or wholesaler. These are people who are looking to either fix and flip or buy and hold or whatever the exit strategy is. But we do also have a lot of clients in Amazon businesses or other e-commerce, or they have a local business that they're looking to grow or start up. We do work with a wide variety of businesses. We can help anyone, but the majority of our client base tends to be the real estate investors.

## How to Overcome Obstacles to Getting Funding

One of the biggest obstacles to getting business funding—many types of funding, really—is qualifying for the loan. It's typically bad credit that halts or slows things down when you're applying. If you're going to borrow money, you usually need to qualify at some level. This type of funding is business credit lines that are lent by the bank, but it does not show up on your personal credit report. In order to get this type of credit line, you have to have personal credit scores over 700, ideally over 730, to get a decent amount of funding within 30 days.

If you don't have good credit, there's a way for you to repair your credit quickly so you can qualify for this type of funding. We started a credit repair company about six or seven years ago because we were facing this obstacle with our clients; about 30% of them were coming in with bad credit. We'd send them out to other credit repair firms, and we just weren't getting the results that we needed.

So we started Kaydem Credit Help, our sister credit repair company; it services all of our clients who are facing the obstacle of bad credit or derogatory items on their credit reports (things like late payments or bankruptcies). Kaydem can remove all types of derogatory items—in some cases, several years before they were due to fall off. They removed a bankruptcy for a client recently, for example, that was due to fall off four years later. That's our solution for clients facing that particular obstacle. Other than that, it's a straightforward process. If you have a credit score over 700, you can get anywhere between $30,000 to $150,000 in a business credit line that doesn't show up on your personal report. They do need to *look* at your personal report to qualify you, but they don't *report* the business credit line to your personal credit report.

What this means is if you're carrying a $100,000 balance on a business credit line for a recent home purchase that you're going to flip, that balance won't count against your personal score. This is really a big deal when it comes to using credit and keeping your personal credit in good shape. We just had a testimonial come in today: the client got over $40,000, and the biggest thing for them was that their personal credit scores went *up*. This is because we're keeping the debt off their personal report and putting it on the business report where it belongs.

I know a lot of people use their personal credit and finances for business-related expenses; it happens all the time. But with business credit, you can keep your personal credit in better shape. You can also leverage more funding using business credit, because if you put all your debt on your personal report, your scores come down. Then it will be much harder for you to get another loan in the future, even if it's a business loan, because they're going to look at your personal report and see that you're overextended.

The next biggest obstacle is really high debt and maxed-out credit cards. In those situations, we advise a strategic pay-down plan that will get you to a place where you qualify for business credit. We want you to go in that direction because the end goal is to keep your personal credit clear of business expenses. That's why we recommend using business credit lines. Some other companies will just get you a personal credit line because it's easier to get, even though it's going to hamper your personal credit.

## What We Offer: Repeated Applications and Negotiations with the Bank

The size of your business credit line comes down to your existing credit card limits, which dictate what we can get for you. Let's say you have a $10,000 credit card or a couple of $10,000 credit cards. That would usually put you into the $40–60,000 range just in the first few weeks, but then *we repeat that process*. Over the 12 months we work with our clients, we repeat that process four times. So you're going to get anywhere from $30,000 to $100,000, depending on your credit score and your credit limits. When we repeat that process four times, we can get our clients up to $250,000.

So people who have high limits on their credit cards, even $20,000 or $25,000, let's say, are going to end up with higher-end gains. But note that a lot of these gains come from the negotiating process that we carry out for our clients. We follow up with the bank on every application we submit: we reach out directly to the decision-maker at the bank we have a relationship with, and discuss the application on our client's behalf.

If it applies, we'll ask for increases, and I can tell you that it usually does. When we apply for these types of business credit lines, the bank is going to give you only a small amount in the beginning. It's not until you follow through with this negotiation process that you get the larger amounts. In many cases, they're only going to give you $5,000 at the very beginning of your approval. They're going to say, "We need to see six months payment history and blah, blah, blah," but when we call in and speak directly to the underwriter and the decision-maker—the people that we have relationships with—we're able to get our clients increases on these accounts. If it starts out at $5,000, we're able to get them increased up to $25,000, $30,000, sometimes even $50,000.

## Clients with Limited Credit

So to reiterate, it's the credit score, credit history, and credit limits that determine the amount that you're going to get. But if you have really limited credit right now—let's say right now you've only got a

$1,000 and a $2,000 credit card—you need this service even more. What we can do for you is help you build your personal credit report faster. We help you establish an array of accounts on your personal report, bringing you up to anywhere from $20,000 to $40,000. It'll be on your personal report, but this is only for the people who are limited on the personal side. We'll help you build up your foundation with personal credit, and a few months later, you'll be able to qualify for business credit because you've established the foundation and credit history the bank wants. We can help people with limited personal credit accelerate their personal credit building so they qualify more quickly for business credit lines.

We use that same negotiation process to help people who *already* qualify get the largest amount possible—and I can tell you with 100% certainty that we're the only firm that does that. The other firms will ask the client to call in and do it on their own, which just isn't as effective. Chris can tell you this from experience: his rep at Bank of America was only able to get him a $17,000 line on one of his entities and *nothing* on another. We submitted, negotiated, submitted more documentation, confirmed a few things, and were finally able to get a $50,000 line on the same entity for which his representative got nothing. Keep in mind, this representative has a lot of Chris's money in the bank and still couldn't get it approved—we did!

Our credit repair company, Kaydem, is open to working with anyone, even though we developed it specifically to service the Fund&Grow clients. Now we've opened up our doors, we have a sign out front, and we're getting local business. We're doing affiliate marketing. We're doing Facebook ads and a lot more. So if any of Chris's members (or new home buyers, or whoever) know they need credit and want help, they can simply call Kaydem or Fund&Grow and let them know they read about us in Chris's latest book; we'll take great care of them.

## Bring in a Partner for Larger Loans

Our soft maximum is about $250,000. We've gotten people $300,000, $400,000, or $500,000, but it's rarer to get up to those levels. In most cases, it's a lot easier to get over $250,000 when our client brings in a spouse, a family member, or a business partner. We keep that pretty strict: it needs to be a spouse, family member, or a very close business partner. But if a client has that option, we can basically double the amount of funding, and it makes it a lot easier for us to get over the $250,000 mark.

It's usually the people who are starting out with higher credit scores to begin with—or can bring in a credit partner—who are able to clear that $250,000 mark, but it is very possible. If you visit our website, we have tons of testimonials of people who got over $250,000. It's not impossible, but we keep that mark at $250,000 because, realistically, once you get up to $250,000 per person, you can only do so much with this type of credit, and I'd like to set and maintain the proper expectations.

## 0% Interest

There is the possibility of continuing to create new accounts and closing old accounts, year to year, to keep reinstating your 0% interest. You may want to do that, because all of these accounts have 0% interest for 6–15 months. You get an introductory period at 0% interest, so you can do flips or whatever you're going to do, and the money is pretty much free. After that, the interest rate does go up to anywhere from 7% to 16%, based on your credit.

## Flexible Funds

The good thing is that these credit lines are *cash accessible*. We actually show you how to withdraw the cash right off the line. It's very simple. They come in the form of a physical business credit card, but we show you how to cash these accounts out with a 2% fee. You can cash these out and put everything in your account so you'll have proof of funds, or purchase properties and close on them yourself. You can use the funding for marketing money, or to pay for rehabs, or whatever you need.

The flexibility of this type of credit line is one of its biggest selling points. Compare it to other types of loans: a hard-money loan, for example, in which you're stuck with the specific function of the loan. With this type of funding, you can use it for anything you want.

Also, these are revolving accounts, which is helpful: they're always going to be in your pocket, at your disposal for whatever, even an unforeseen expense. Even though the interest rates go up, it's still helpful. As I mentioned before, we have clients who sign up with us two or three years at a time, and we'll apply for more credit lines for them. In some cases, we'll merge accounts with the new ones or we'll close down an old account and set up a new one.

## Free Webinar

Our free webinar on this topic is about an hour and a half or two hours long if you include the Q&A, but it's very informative. We go over our entire process and just hand it over to people. If you want to do this on your own, you can learn about it on the webinar. But we do also have a special offer on the webinar, a discount and bonus package for Chris's students, members, and readers. Everything's on the *New Rules* resources page at TheNewRulesBook.com. Either way, there's some really great content. There's tons of Q&A towards the end: we go live and answer everyone's questions. Then, if you're ready to start getting business credit lines for your real estate investments, you can get started and let us do it for you.

## Pay Down Your Balances

Trying to get your balances paid down before you sign up with us would be helpful, but you don't *have to*. That's the thing: you don't have to do *anything* before you sign up with us, because *we're going to hold your hand.* We'll review your credit with you and give you the absolute best plan of action, but if you're maxed out on your credit cards right now, the best thing to do is to bring those balances down as much as possible. The bank likes to see them at 35%, so if you've got a $10,000 card, you want the balance to be $3,500 or lower.

## Working with Us

We communicate with our clients on a daily to weekly basis. We handle all the legwork. If somebody wants to work with us, or if they want to get business credit lines done for them, they should sign up with us. We handle everything; the best thing that they can do is to just let us take control.

It's pretty straightforward: the client signs up with us, fills out their basic information. We do a consultation call. We go over their credit report and the plan of action. We go over the banks that we plan to target. For some clients, we'll also set up an entity. If you don't have an entity, we'll set one up for you. So if you're one of those investors out there who hasn't set up an entity yet, no worries. We can still get you business credit.

When you work with us, you can let us do our thing and enjoy the benefits. We have a 60-day refund period: if you don't get credit working with us (perhaps it turns out your credit scores were lower than you thought, for example), we give you your money back.

---

**Chris:** No matter your niche, if you think you'll never hit a speed bump or emergency, you're fooling yourself. I have an entire chapter in my bestseller, *Real Estate on Your Terms*, about "what can go wrong." Set up these lines of credit, and when you lay your head on the pillow at night, you'll sleep like a baby!

## TAKEAWAYS FROM THIS CHAPTER

1 Try Fund&Grow's free webinar and learn about their process. Visit the *New Rules* resources page at TheNewRulesBook.com for your special link.

2 Get your credit balances paid down to 35% of potential or less.

3 If your credit needs cleaning up, use Kaydem Credit Help.

4 Remember that your business credit does not affect your personal credit.

5 Sign up and let Fund & Grow do what they do best: get you thousands of dollars in flexible business loans to start your real estate investing.

# KILLING IT
# WITH THE SHIFT TO
# WHOLESALING

## Brad Chandler

Brad Chandler is the CEO of Express Homebuyers and president of Brad Chandler Coaching. In ninth grade, Brad read a book about buying real estate with no money down, and he's been passionate about it ever since. He went from scratch to a seventh-level real estate investing business that does 200-plus deals per year, makes a half a million a month every month in wholesale fees, and operates without his day-to-day involvement.

Since 2003, Brad has compiled over 5,000 real estate transactions. He is dedicated to sharing his experiences and helping others through his podcast, *The Real Estate Investing Hot Seat*, and through coaching and mentoring.

Back in ninth grade, I read a book on how to buy real estate with no money down. I always knew I wanted to do that because of the unlimited earning potential, so I went to school. I came out and worked for an apartment REIT, managing apartments. I'm not a corporate guy—never really wanted to climb the corporate ladder—so I went back to school and got an MBA in real estate. I came out and worked for a developer.

Around 2002, an investor bought my neighbor's house, and I went over and talked to him. He said, "Yeah, I buy houses at 30% below market, fix them up, and resell them." I said, "Gosh, I've got two degrees in real estate, and no one ever taught me how to do that—or even that it was possible." I thought you got rich in real estate by buying a house or a property and putting down the 25% down payment; it would pay off after 30 years, and hopefully appreciate. That's how I thought you got rich in real estate.

After talking to him, I thought, "Oh my gosh, this is exactly what I'm going to do!" I spent eight long, tedious, stressful months working a full-time job, coming home at 6:00 PM, working from 8:00 PM to midnight on weekends, hand-addressing envelopes, pounding the *We Buy Houses* bandit sign—you name it, I did it. In July of 2003, I bought my first house. In July and August, I somehow bought a total of six houses. I quit my full-time job in October 2003, and here we are approaching 2,300 houses, 14 years later.

## Getting in the Right Mindset

I'm terrible at planning—I still struggle with it to this day—so I didn't plan anything. I jumped right in and said, "I'm going to make this work." Each day that went by, I'd show up to these REIA (Real Estate Investment Association) meetings—they didn't call them "meetups" back then, but they were the equivalent of meetups now—and I'd hear all these people doing deals, and every day, I'd think, "If they can do it, I can do it.

I think I was making $60,000 at the time, and I was supporting five people. Living in Northern Virginia, $60,000 isn't a whole lot of money to support five people. One of the first deals I did, I made about $40,000, and I thought, "Oh my gosh, I've made almost as much as I made all year!" When I made the leap, I didn't have a ton of money: when I started out, I had a net worth of *negative* $80,000, and when I made the leap in October, I probably had $20–30,000 in the bank—not a lot of money.

I spent most of my life enthralled by the question of why some people are successful and others aren't. I used to tell people I was going to write a book when I figured it out. Well, in the last six months of building this coaching program, I really did figure it out, and it's basically what Chris says: it's all mindset. 100 people can take Chris's course, my course, any course—it doesn't even matter—they're never going to be successful *unless they have the proper mindset.*

Back then, my mindset was *I am going to succeed. I don't care what it takes* (within legal and ethical bounds, but outside of that, *nothing* was going to stop me). Too many people get in the trenches and a week, a month, six months in, they say, "Hey, this doesn't work. It's too hard!" Imagine if I'd quit in June and said, "I gave it my all, but my wife's been nagging me for too long. I'm just going to stick to my full-time job." I'd still be working for someone else, making a fraction of what I'm making now, and without the freedom and flexibility I now have.

You can read and study and take every course in the world, but without the right mindset, you're never going to be successful. That's why, in our seven-week course, I spend the entire first week on developing the right mindset, because if you don't have that, you're wasting your time.

You've got to give it time. Commit. I think a lot of people just jump from coaching program to coaching program. They'll do it for three weeks, four weeks, and it probably won't work because most people are comfortable where they are: they *say* they want to get better, but most of them just want to go back to their normal, easy routines.

---

**Zach:**   It's important that you digest what Brad just explained in the last couple of paragraphs: it doesn't matter what you do or what coaching program you're involved in—if you don't have the right mindset, *you'll fail every time*—and it will be nobody's fault but yours. If you *do* have the right mindset, though, there's no limit to what you can accomplish.

**Nick:** When we're talking commitment, the same story always comes to mind: in 1519, before his march on Tenochtitlan and conquest of Mexico, Hernán Cortés took over Veracruz. Shortly after he arrived, he ordered his men to burn the ships. Talk about commitment! One of his soldiers laughed, and Cortés promptly stuck him with a sword. Think of that! If you give yourself no way to slide back into your old habits, what could you accomplish?

## Rehabbing vs. Wholesaling

Of 2,300 deals, we've probably rehabbed 1,400–1,500. When I started, and for many years after, I thought what a smart, sophisticated person with a degree, good credit, and money did was to *rehab* houses, while less-sophisticated mom-and-pops who had bad credit and maybe weren't educated did more *wholesaling*. I thought that's how you got into business.

So, for many years, what did we do? We renovated, renovated, renovated. We were killing ourselves, at one point doing 85 renovations at a time—in the DC Metro area, but four hours apart. We got hooked up with three bad contractors over the last three years, and it almost did us in. Last December, I found myself thinking: *There's got to be a better way. What's the hardest part of the business? Construction. So if we could get rid of the construction and rehabbing, what are we really good at? Sales, marketing, and follow-up—we're amazing at that.*

We made the shift in December; now all we do is wholesaling, and we're having one of our best financial years ever. We have a rental portfolio of about 80 houses—we're in the process of selling it because it's a really, really good time to sell a portfolio—and we've dabbled in condo development, but our bread-and-butter is wholesaling 200 houses a year.

"Seventh level" is a term coined by Gary Keller, of Keller Williams; it's the top level you can reach in a business, when your business is actually *running itself*. You're not in the trenches day-to-day operating it, and you could leave for a month, two months, six months, come back, and your business would likely be at the same level or better. That's where we are today, and it's a pretty exciting thing.

## Losing $3 Million on Three Properties... But Still Doing the Right Thing

It's hard for me to say how we came out on top, but I can certainly tell you we've taken a lot of hard knocks over the years. The biggest was in 2005: in the first five months of 2005, we made well over $1 million, and I was young, I was dumb, I thought that I was the smartest guy in the world, so I figured, "Hey, if we can flip houses, we can do development deals." We bought three properties. We probably lost a total of close to $3 million on those three properties—and keep in mind that in 2003, I had a negative $80,000 net worth in 2003, so it's not like I had a lot of money to fall back on.

One of those properties was a house in North Arlington for which we even hired a consulting firm before we "went hard" on the deposit (a non-refundable deposit). We were going to tear down this beautiful house, subdivide the lots, and put up two houses. We projected it to make about $1.5 million. Well, seven months into the permit and subdividing process, they came back and told us, "We made a mistake: it's a corner lot, and you can't subdivide it." We lost about $923,000 on that one deal.

We had a non-recourse loan, which means we didn't have it personally guaranteed. My partner and I could easily have said to our investors, "Hey, we're done. We're not going to pay you." But that's not how I operate, so we did the equivalent of a short sale. We had already spent $400,000 of that $900,000, so we owed them $500,000. They gave us two years to pay it off. We paid it off in 13 months, and since then, we've probably borrowed and returned in excess of $200 million from the same two brothers. I suppose the lesson is that if you do the right thing, you'll usually come out ahead.

I read Chris's story about 2008 and how he treated some of his investors the same way, even if it took him almost five years—and it clearly paid off for him too. We're not attorneys and we're not giving you legal advice, but Chris and I agree that when you do the right thing for people and treat them the way you'd like to be treated, the right things will come your way.

**Zach:** I can attest that navigating a real estate business or any business at a young age is challenging. As a young entrepreneur (young in age *or* experience), you'll be confronted with many lessons—and the word is "lessons," not "failures." Things won't always go smoothly; embrace that uncertainty. If you want to avoid these mistakes or at least limit them, find a mentor to guide you.

If you're looking to get into real estate or to go full time, here's what I did when, 25 years old, I decided to go from bartender and personal trainer to real estate entrepreneur: I found a mentor, studied, took action—and never looked back. I now handle our own deals, buying two to four properties monthly, and help others around the country do another six to eight monthly. If you can follow those simple steps, you're on your way: you *can* and *will* create any success you desire.

**Nick:** From a young age, I've always made a habit of studying success. I've noticed one quality in everyone who's achieved *massive* success: they never give up. They never stop moving forward, even when things look bleak. My dad (Chris) and I shared an office back in 2008, and I remember vividly what his days were like after the market came crashing down. He'd get to the office and be on the phone with lenders, creditors, and investors for much of the day—they were all demanding payment, of course. We'd eat lunch together and he'd jump back on the phone with investors for much of the afternoon. Those days reinforced the lesson for me: *Never give up. Always keep moving forward.*

I say "reinforced," because I'd already learned that life lesson: in 2003, I was in a snowboarding accident. I went off a jump without a helmet, and landed on my head. I was in a coma for 21 days, and the doctors told my parents that I'd probably never walk, talk, or even *swallow* on my own again. Less than three months later, I *ran* out of the hospital.

## Getting to the Next Level in the Wholesale World

The first product I launched was really for the struggling investor just trying to get their business started; they're trying to do their first deal, or maybe they've done a couple of deals and they're just sputtering along. For that class, getting to the next level is simply a question of, "How can I get a first deal under my belt, then maybe do one deal a month so I can quit my job?" I just launched the coaching program, so I plan to work with people at higher levels as I create new programs.

It all comes down to what students want. I'm always trying to help them find their way to freedom, but each student probably has a different notion of what freedom means to them. I sit down and ask them, "What's your *why*? What are you trying to achieve? What are your goals?" and tell them how they can do it wholesaling. Does that always mean doing two or four or six deals a month? No, we build out a program around their goals.

## Do You Really Want to Rehab?

I'm getting away from rehabbing because it's the toughest part of the business. I'm involved in masterminds around the country with some top-level investors, and it's a common theme that I hear over and over again: renovating at scale is very, very difficult. I meet new investors who've been taught by someone that the way you make money in real estate is by renovating houses, and *it's just not true*.

I would stay far away from renovating. If that's your dream—if you like taking a banged-up house and fixing it up—that's great, but learn the business first. Go through two, three, ten wholesale transactions where you work with the title company and start to understand some of the title issues and how you work through them and how the whole process works with the lender. Maybe you can partner with a mentor doing those types of deals, like what Chris and his family do with their associates around the country. That way you don't have to attend the school of hard knocks all by yourself.

There are just so many moving parts to this business. It's not hard, but you have to learn them before you go out and start renovating properties. If you sell a good deal to a buyer, ask the buyer, "Hey, can I pop by this property once a month (or once a week, whatever it is), "just to see how things are going?" You'll learn so much. It was cool to hear Chris had his then-teenage son Nick hang out with one of his maintenance personnel back when he was doing condominium conversions, since that allowed Nick to learn what goes on in the field. This has been a long-winded way for me to say: Don't jump into a rehab—a $40–50,000 rehab—and think it's going to go smoothly. It'll burn you.

Those HGTV rehab shows contributed, to some extent, to the irrational run-up of real estate back in 2006–2008. But here's what's crazy, and this is what most people don't understand: on those shows, they'll say that they're buying a house for $150,000. Then they put in $50,000 and sell it for $250,000, so they're into it for $200,000 and out for $250,000, and they'll put it right up on the screen: "We made a profit of $50,000." Well, you and I *know* they didn't make a profit of $50,000. They'd be lucky if they made $20,000 or $22,000, so let's dial that back and say that they bought it for $150,000, put in $70,000 because their renovation estimate went up, sold it for $250,000, and they claim a profit of $30,000. Well, guess what? There's a good chance they didn't make *any* profit.

They're not figuring in all the transaction costs and the holding costs and the taxes and the investors. They're doing the public a disservice, because it misleads people into thinking, "Oh, this is so easy," and it's *not* easy. As Chris and his family tell all prospective associates, this business, like any business, is *simple*—but *not* easy.

## Killing it with the Shift to Wholesaling

Our biggest, coolest win is what we've done this year. 2018 has been our biggest win of the 14 years we've been in business, because we were really banged up and battered at the end of last year, and we had all this inventory. We had literally tens of millions worth of debt, and in the course of 11 months, we've done a complete about-face, erasing tens of millions of dollars of debt.

We've streamlined our operation even further: we've gotten a lot of bad properties off our books. We're going to have a profitable year. We have 30 team members now; we have the best team in place, and we're ready to launch and scale and take over different markets. Honestly, that's been one of our biggest wins since I've been in business—turning things around, straightening them up, and getting rid of the renovation business.

Our average wholesaling check is $36,000, and that's strong. Most wholesaling gurus tell you you're lucky if you make $5,000 or $10,000, but there are a couple of reasons for that: one, they don't know how to attract the right buyers, and two, they're advocating that you sell to people like I used to be—rehabbers—and rehabbers typically buy at a big discount. So $36,000 is a strong number, and it can be done if you handle things properly.

## Coaching, Teaching, and Helping Others

I started a meetup about 18 months ago. At one of the meetups, I had a "hot seat": I brought up some investors out of the crowd—no preparation—sat them down, and said, "So, what are your goals in investing, and what are your obstacles in reaching your goals?" and I totally broke them down. That was our seventh or eighth meetup, and I got the most incredible feedback: "God, that was awesome!" So I thought, "How can I bring that to the masses?"

I took that same concept and started *The Real Estate Investing Hot Seat Podcast,* and as I'm writing this, the podcast launched two or three months ago. We've gotten incredible results from it: the podcast is like a free 30-minute coaching session. I'll bring on anyone who is struggling and break down every obstacle they might possibly have. Visit the ***New Rules* resources page** at TheNewRulesBook.com if you want to listen to the podcast or apply to be a guest.

The business is now running without me, and I love, love, love teaching, so I started a full-blown seven-week modulated course. Students go through the course, it launches on a Monday, and then on Thursday they get a group coaching call with me personally.

I launched it a couple of weeks ago as of this writing. We're really working up momentum, and people seem to love it. As part of the coaching program, I also developed an ebook called *Wholesaling Secrets: Discover This One Technique We Use to Close Over 200 Wholesale Deals Every Year Consistently*. I have a link to it on my website, or you can get it by sending me a text. You'll find that info on the ***New Rules* resources page**.

## Do the "One Thing"

I'm a huge fan of Gary Keller. I think he's one of the top 50 most influential business people in real estate, maybe in *any* industry. He's written many great books, but *The ONE Thing* is one of my favorite books, so I ask myself every day, "What's the *one thing* I can do so that everything else is easier or unnecessary?" I've got to be vulnerable and admit another character flaw: I've wasted hundreds, probably thousands, of hours over the last 10 years checking my email and doing tasks that weren't related to getting me to my goal. So that's the number-one thing: focus on your dollar-producing activities.

Time blocking: I'm reading more and more about it. High achievers, in business or sports or anything else, block out 30- to 50-minute chunks of time, and are just highly, highly focused on one activity. That one activity has to be without distractions, and it's got to be the activity that you're trying to master and is going to move you toward your goal. I could name a hundred, but that's one thing everyone has to do if they want to be successful. That's how Gary Keller built the world's largest real estate company, by practicing that same principle.

## Growing and Giving Back

My immediate goals are, number one, to grow into multiple markets. Number two, I started this coaching program not to make money—I don't need to make more money—but *to give back*. I want to help change people's lives, and I hope they'll do the same and change other people's lives in turn. Number three, we are in the early stages of creating a lead platform technology that doesn't exist anywhere in the world, that could help us launch our lead platform. We have one of the highest-ranked websites in the industry, so that's a project we're just starting to kick around, to talk to investors. That's a very exciting thing; that's the big thing we're working on, aside from the coaching and expanding the business.

## Read *Deep Work*

Right now, I'm reading *Deep Work*, by Cal Newport. It's all about focusing, taking out chunks of time from your day and getting rid of all the distractions: you need to actually *turn off* your computers, your email, your phone, and sit there with a notepad—whatever it is you need to do to get rid of the distractions and *focus*. It's a really, really great book.

## Hitting the Magic Reset Button

If I could hit a magic reset button, I would never rehab a single house. Had I not rehabbed a single house, *I can't even tell you* how much higher my net worth would be, but scary, scary high, because you'd be eliminating $3 million of mistakes—those three big ones plus millions of dollars of other renovation mistakes. The other change I'd make is in focus. For so many years, I had shiny-object syndrome: we opened markets where we didn't even have our stuff settled in the market where I was going to expand. It's truly about focus—and mindset.

## Set Your Five-Year Goal

This is the one thing I wish I'd done 10 years ago.

Set your five-year goal, then ask yourself:

> What's the one thing I can do *this year*
> to reach my five-year goal?

Then ask yourself:

> What's the one thing I can do *this month*
> to reach that one-year goal?

> What's the one thing I can do *this week*
> to reach that monthly goal?

> What's the one thing that I can do *today*
> to reach that weekly goal?"

And finally:

> What's the one thing I can do *right now,*
> right this second, to reach my daily goal?

Of course, almost no one ever does that—we're always answering emails, going from emergency to emergency, getting caught up in daily life—we're caught on the treadmill, the hamster wheel, where you never make any progress. But if you did it every single day, imagine what you could accomplish.

---

**Chris:** People typically quit too early because of mismanaged expectations. This is one of those things that drives me *crazy.* Get this: if you were to start a business—of any type—and gather a group of investors to fund you, imagine sitting them all down in a conference room and announcing, "I'm going to *try this for a few months.*" Can you friggin' imagine that? They'd laugh at you—and hold on to their wallets. Real estate is not a get-rich-quick scheme. Real estate can create cash flow for you while you build large wealth for you and your family. You've got to manage your expectations and plans and treat it like the big business it is.

We've had associates take six months to do their first deals. Two of them are million-dollar earners. Imagine if they'd quit!

You can watch reality TV shows if it entertains you, but—*man, oh, man!*—don't think for a moment that you're educating yourself. Find a mentor in whatever niche you want to pursue and stick with them for 36 months minimum.

---

**Nick:**   Can you imagine if I'd given up after my first couple of steps trying to walk again? *Nahhh, this whole thing is just too hard. I'm going to go back to my wheelchair to be a vegetable for the rest of my life.* I kept moving, one literal step at a time, and I never gave up, obviously. For more about my story, visit the **New Rules resources page** at TheNewRulesBook.com.

As Chris mentioned, we've had associates take six months to do a deal. I remember it taking upwards of *eight* months for some associates to get their very first deals. But today, those are some of our *top* associates, doing the most deals. It's important to emphasize that this program, like any program that really teaches real estate, isn't a get-rich-quick program—it's a *get-rich-permanently* program. Stick with it, never give up, and keep moving forward. If you do, there's no "*if* I'm successful," only "*when* I'm successful."

## TAKEAWAYS FROM THIS CHAPTER

1   Develop the mindset to succeed—and commit.

2   Focus on what you're good at (or want to be good at),
    but give yourself time to do so.

3   Do the right thing, even when it's hard.

4   If you want to get into rehabbing,
    first learn the business *very well.*

5   Focus on your dollar-producing activities and *stop wasting time.*

6   Set your five-year goal.

7   Do the "one thing" every day to reach your goals.

# ADD VALUE TO OTHERS

## Joe Fairless

Joe Fairless is a full-time real estate investor who started buying multi-family properties in 2013, right around the time we were reengineering our business. He now controls over $160 million in real estate. Prior to that, he was the youngest vice president at an award-winning advertising agency in New York City. He is the host of the extremely popular *Best Real Estate Investing Advice Ever* podcast, where he's interviewed such guests as Barbara Corcoran and Robert Kiyosaki. Joe is also the author of *Best Real Estate Investing Advice Ever: Volumes 1 and 2*, which has been personally endorsed by Barbara Corcoran. All profits from the sale of the book are being donated to Junior Treatment.

## Self-Sacrifice Pays Off: Living Below Your Means

I moved from Texas to New York City and lived there for 10 years after I graduated college. My major was advertising, so I worked at advertising agencies on Madison Avenue. I was making a whopping $30,000 salary—which isn't a lot, especially in New York. Starting out, I didn't have money to invest: my check every two weeks was about $750, and so was my rent, so I certainly didn't have much discretionary income. But as I climbed the corporate ladder in advertising, I was able to save more and more money.

I did that by keeping my fixed expenses the same, so while my friends were getting larger and larger apartments as we all got older, I stayed in the same apartment in the East Village. A lot of my friends made fun of me; I was living like a college kid, but at the same time I started buying houses. I ended up being the youngest vice-president of a New York City advertising agency and after seven years or so, I was making $150,000. That's when I started investing in real estate: I bought my first single-family house in Texas in 2009, and my first apartment community in 2013.

It worked out well for me to keep my expenses low. The only thing I would do differently if I could is to sacrifice *even more* and live in New Jersey or Brooklyn, where I could have bought a duplex—I could have lived on one side and rented out the other. Instead, I was saving up and buying single-family homes in Texas. Hindsight is 20/20—you can't do it perfectly—but that's the only tweak I'd make to what I did, starting out. I've heard Chris suggest on radio shows and podcasts that people live on 50% of what they earn, and that's the same type of plan.

## Value-Add Strategy for Multifamily Deals

My focus now is on value-add multifamily deals. What I mean is that we buy 150+ units built in 1980 or later; our date range is 1980–2000. They are stabilized, but they have value-add components. We usually renovate the interiors of the units, increase rent, forcing appreciation. There are other value-add things we do: build fences, add patios, improve landscaping—but primarily, it's interior renovations.

My business partner and I have nine apartment communities—all in Texas: seven in Dallas-Fort Worth and two in Houston. I'm from Fort Worth, so I know the area very well. The team is my business partner Frank and me. We run the show, and we have an administrative assistant. I have my own assistant for my podcast and similar things. We also have a small team of underwriters who are locked in a windowless basement somewhere, underwriting deal after deal after deal. We have a third-party property management company that oversees each of our deals. Finally, we have a regional manager who oversees the deals in Dallas-Fort Worth, since we have seven of them there, with more to come.

## Tips for Newbies: How to Get Funding and Partnerships

There are certainly obstacles to overcome when you're getting started. You need some kind of experience and knowledge, because the brokers likely won't take you seriously if you don't have a track record in the business. But how do you get the track record without being able to get into the business *because people aren't taking you seriously*? There are some practical things you can do: one is to partner with a property management company in order to get approved for a loan. This is the same type of qualification process you're going to need in order to bring in investors and close on deals. That brings you liquidity, net worth, and experience; credit score is not as important. The lender is not going to lend to you on a large deal if you don't have liquidity, net worth, and experience.

The liquidity and net worth that are required vary depending on the deal, and there are many options. If you partner with a property management company, they bring their track record of experience managing properties in that market. That would qualify you and your team because the management company is now on the general partnership side with you. Check that box for experience.

But perhaps the property management company doesn't have the liquidity or net worth. Neither do you, so you need to find a high net worth individual who will sign on the loan. The loan could be a recourse or a non-recourse loan. If it's a non-recourse loan, then it's a much easier conversation with that high net worth individual. Non-recourse means that there's no personal guarantee unless there's fraud or gross neglect. As long as there's no fraud or gross neglect, the person signing on the loan doesn't have to personally guarantee it.

The flip side is a recourse loan, which your high net worth individual would be personally guaranteeing. That's a more challenging conversation, but it's still possible. The compensation for that high net worth individual could be a percentage of the general partnership, plus some sort of loan guarantee fee that's paid out annually. I've seen a quarter of a percent of the loan balance paid out annually—that's what the property pays. I've also seen 3%, 10%, 15% of the general partnership just for signing on the loan. As you do more deals, you can decrease that. Eventually, you can stand on your own two feet, and you won't need anyone to come in with you on the partnership side. I do partner with my clients. The last deal we closed was a partnership with a client, who helped me with the deal.

## A Failure / A Learning Opportunity

I did pretty well on the first three homes I bought. I used a very conservative model: what I looked for in the house was that it have at least $10,000 worth of equity at closing according to the sales comps. It had to be projected to make me at least $100 a month, and it had to cost less than $1,000 to be move-in ready. Cookie-cutter stuff. Those three homes have since doubled in value since I bought them in 2009, 2010, and 2011 (that's according to Zillow, so take it with a grain of salt).

On the fourth house, I went in a different direction. I departed from my model, and I definitely got my hand slapped. I got an email from a wholesaler saying the house was being offered for $35,000, including his wholesale fee. The wholesaler thought it needed about $5,000 of repairs to get it move-in ready, and the rent was $750 with the current tenant. I just so happened to have a new line of credit from American Airlines Credit Union for $40,000. It couldn't have been more perfect. So I said, "I don't know this area as well as the area where the other three homes are, but the numbers look pretty good, so I'm going to do it."

This did *not* turn out to be a good deal. One, the property ended up needing about $15,000 more in repairs than what was projected.

Two, I hired a family friend (a friend's dad) who had a construction company, and it didn't work out. Apparently, it was the company's only job, and for whatever reason, it didn't work out. So the answer to mistake number one is to make sure you have a trustworthy third party look at the property before you buy it. They need to give you a quote; maybe get multiple quotes. The answer to mistake number two is *don't hire family friends*.

Third, after I had the team fix it up (it took three or four months longer than I expected), it rented for $700. Their tenant had moved out, and I had to find a new one. Remember, it had been renting for $750 before I spent $20,000 on the renovations, so I was getting less rent than I'd been getting before the renovations. The area isn't as desirable as where the first three homes are, so I no longer have that house. I lost about $10,000 or $15,000 when I sold it.

But I learned to stick to my model, keep doing what's been working, and not try to go too fast too soon. The lesson is simple here: as Chris always says, grab onto a mentor who has experience doing what you'd like to do, and stick with them and their teachings 100%.

## Liberation and Financial Freedom

One thing about this business is that you don't even need to know the day of the week. As of right now, it's 11:15 AM, I think it's a Wednesday, and so far, I've had a call with my team at 8:00 AM, gone for a 3.5 mile run, hung out with my fiancée, had breakfast, read a little bit, and handled some investor correspondence. Later in the day, I can ride my bike around the neighborhood. I guarantee that what we're after isn't money—it's *what we do with our time*. When you can choose to do what you want with your time, you're able to accomplish your life's mission—that's my philosophy, and that's why I'm so passionate about multi-family investing. I believe it's an incredibly good way of helping others achieve what they want to achieve financially, so they can do what they want with their time. I think the world would be a better place if we could all do what we want with our time. I think that, ultimately, most people are good, and they would contribute in more meaningful ways if they weren't forced into the nine-to-five as they are right now.

## Focus on Your Strengths

This morning I read *80/20 Sales and Marketing* by Perry Marshall. I took a picture of one section, emailed it to one of my team members, and asked them to include it in something we're doing. It was about how, when you're starting out, you should email five people you know and ask them to name your strengths: What do they think you're really good at? The idea is that ultimately, you have to focus on your special talents, and we all have one or two special talents (two if we're lucky; I think I have one). Once you've identified the special talent(s), you can apply the talent(s) to your business. That means that you set up systems around you to support other aspects of the business so you don't have to try and be a jack-of-all-trades. You can be a master of *one particular area* of your business.

That, I've noticed, is what has grown my business—and it's grown so much! In three or four years, I have $160+ million dollars' worth of apartment communities. My current business partner has certain skill sets and I have certain skill sets, so that allows each of us to focus on our strengths. That's what has grown the company to where it is today.

## Strategies for Success in Multifamily Investing

The first thing you need is a foundation of knowledge, so you'll want to read several books. On my website, I have a list of recommended books to read (joefairless.com/joesrecs/) That's number one: read a bunch of books on multifamily investing. Number two, get active in BiggerPockets, which is a social network for real estate investors. There's a lot of good information in there. Number three, listen to podcasts like Chris's and mine. From both a psychological standpoint and a practical standpoint, you'll learn how to do certain things. Once you have that in place, and you have some knowledge, go find people who are currently doing what you want to do at a very high level, and see how you can add value to their lives.

I have a vision board on my wall, and one of the things on it is a Tony Robbins quote: "The secret of living is giving." As long as you consistently add value to others' lives—you know what kind of value they're looking for, and you give, give, give—it will come back to you tenfold. It's reciprocity: you just have to trust in the process and do it consistently on a daily basis. My podcast is the world's longest-running daily real estate investing podcast. I've done it for *over 1,000 days straight*. For 1,000 days straight, there's been a new podcast up; that's Monday, Tuesday, Wednesday, Thursday, Friday, Saturday, and Sunday. After doing it consistently for over 1,000 days now, and interviewing over 1,000 real estate investors, I see that results come not at the beginning, but toward the middle. Then there's a tipping point, and once you reach a certain level, the floodgates just *open*. As Chris would say, discipline is the key.

## TAKEAWAYS FROM THIS CHAPTER

1  Self-sacrifice pays off.

2  If you're just starting out, partner with a property management company; they'll bring their track record of experience to your first deal.

3  Stay conservative—don't move too big, too fast.

4  Learn what your strengths are and stick with them; then let others on your team do what they do best.

5  Acquire knowledge—read, read, read!

6  Be disciplined in consistently adding value to others. You will reap the benefits!

**Chris:** If you're currently in a job or on a schedule that you hate, change it—and stop making excuses why you can't.

It's true that your income will probably end up within 5% of those you hang out with and/or allow ourselves to be influenced by, so constantly ask yourself, "Who am I hanging out with, who and what am I reading about, who and what am I listening to—and as a result, who am I becoming and how much am I earning?"

Success leaves clues—don't try to reinvent the wheel.

# FROM ALL-COMMISSION INSURANCE SALES TO NATIONALLY-RECOGNIZED SALES EXPERT

## John Martinez

Over the course of the last 20 years, John Martinez has gone from a struggling all-commission insurance sales-person to a nationally-recognized sales expert. Along the way, John has held many sales-related roles. He's completed over 4,000 hours of study on sales and how people make decisions—what really drives them to take action.

John has trained over 200 real estate investment companies, hundreds of salespeople and acquisition agents, and has achieved amazing results in that pool within the real estate world. John is a go-to expert in the real estate world for acquisition and sales training; he works with the best of the best in the industry, the top 5% who do between 50 and 1,000 deals per year.

In my early twenties, I worked for a catering company. I delivered food, making eight bucks an hour, and it was time for me to make some more money, so I put a resume together, and lo and behold, a sales company picked me up. I thought I was special. I didn't know that they hired anyone who willing to work all-commission. That's how I got into sales. Everyone tried to talk me out of it, but I took the leap. I struggled for a while, but I made it my career.

In all-commission work, it's put up or shut up: no one pays you just to show up. You've got to produce actual results—especially in the real estate field. You can call yourself a real estate investor, but you're not getting paid unless you actually make something happen.

## Facilitating a Decision, Not Selling!

Sales has a bad rap. You get this picture of the used car guy trying to talk someone into something they don't need or want, but that's not what sales is about. Chris nails it when he talks about it as communication: when you're in a sales scenario, all you're really trying to do is help someone make a decision. The thing is, it's sometimes tough to have that open, honest line of communication. It's tough to talk about all the things you need to and dive as deep as you need to, because people put walls up. You're a sales guy; they're afraid you're going to take advantage of them, and they won't get the best deal possible.

There are all kinds of fears and anxieties in any type of sales situation, so the real trick to sales is communication: how do you take down those walls and have an incredibly open and honest conversation to determine whether you can help someone or not? How do you convince them to let you help them make that decision? Especially in real estate, perhaps more than in any other field. The decision to sell a house is a complex one; there are a lot of variables, and when there are too many variables, people often freeze up and make no decision at all.

When I look at sales in real estate investment, it's about open, honest communication, and really walking someone down the path so they can make that decision for themselves. You're facilitating the decision, not forcing it.

**Zach:** Buying and selling real estate is a complicated process for most people outside the industry, because there's a lot of emotion involved. The seller's home is usually their biggest asset, something they've worked for their whole life. It's very important that you communicate openly and honestly to find out their needs and determine whether you're the solution to their problem. I've personally spent hours speaking with sellers when I'm *not* the solution, and it always ends the same way—a waste of time. If you can understand that you aren't always the seller's best option and only work with those for whom you are, you'll be a much more successful real estate investor.

## From Sales Scripts to Real Estate

My entry into real estate was completely by accident. We've trained in over 50 industries, mostly in the business-to-business world, high tech and IT, manufacturing, those types of things. I was doing some script training. A company that pulled me in to work with them. They cater to the real estate industry, investors and traditional real estate agents, and they lost traction. They weren't making any progress, so they brought me in to rewrite some of their scripts. They sell leads to real estate agents and investors.

I rewrote their scripts and they started using them. Day one, they happened to call a real estate investor they'd called many times before, and the guy said, "Hey, hold on a second. Something's changed. What's going on?" They started explaining, "You know, we brought in this sales guy, *blah, blah, blah.*" Long story short, we ended up getting connected. I flew down to Texas. He asked me to train his team, and I did. Word spread quickly. Within probably 60 days, I was training 30 different investment teams—it just *blew up.*

Fast-forward a year: I'm part of all the large real estate masterminds, I'm training hundreds and hundreds and hundreds of investors across the country, and it was like snapping your fingers: it took over my business *just like that.*

## Common Obstacles in Real Estate

The biggest challenges I see when people pull me in is that they're producing leads, but most of those sales calls, appointment calls, whatever they are, end up in limbo for some reason. A lot of them end with some form of "Maybe...I'll think about it...I'll think it over... Reach out to me," but no actual deal.

Something else we see with a ton of other people getting into the business is that the new people, if they don't have the right guidance, sometimes over-offer on houses. So the next big challenge we ran into is *How do we win the deals we need to win, even when we're not the highest offer?* Those are probably the two biggest challenges we deal with day in and day out.

## When It Doesn't Come Naturally, Follow the Process

What comes naturally to me is recognizing opportunity; also, recognizing a problem and developing a way to solve that problem. Business is constantly changing and evolving; if it's not, it's dying. You always have to be able to recognize where the next need is, where you have to plug yourself in, and what problem you have to solve.

The next thing I pride myself on is taking action: there are never any guarantees. There's always going to be some doubt, and I think I've gotten pretty darned good at saying, "You know what? I know enough. Let's take some action and see what happens."

Sales, on the other hand, didn't come naturally to me: at first, I absolutely *stunk* at it. I just *hustled*, outworking everyone. But over the years, I developed a process. I want to be clear about that because a lot of people say, right off the bat, "I'm a salesman; I can sell," or "I can't do it"—but that's not what it's about. It's about following the *process*.

Most people, when they think of your classic type of kick-butt salesperson, think of that relationship-building go-getter who can talk to anyone. But when we look at studies, when we look at all the industries with some type of sales component, that's not what we find. If you were to take all those industries and rank all the salespeople so that we can just look at the top 2–3% of salespeople, out of all the top people—depending on the industry—you're going to find that only 2–3% of those top people are "relationship builders." It actually takes something a little bit different to be a superstar salesperson.

## Mentors and Masterminds

Nothing has had a bigger impact on my life or business than mentors. They were important even before I *knew* they were important. My first mentor was a guy named Al Peel. He worked for the insurance company that originally hired me. A year into it, I hustled, got my own insurance agency in St. Louis, Missouri—and that's where I learned that I didn't know how to sell; I just knew how to *work my butt off*.

Whether you're selling the job or selling the product, it's all the same, and Al was the first to introduce me to putting a *process* in place. It changed everything: in 12 months, I went from working as a caterer for eight dollars an hour to making $5,000 a week. I attribute all of that to Al and his process.

I'm from a small town, but we've had some people who made it pretty big, so I've been able to sit down and pick the brains of some influential businesspeople. Peter Herschend, a self-made billionaire who owns entertainment companies, theme parks, and the Harlem Globetrotters, gave me some time. Terry Bowen, CEO of a $300 million company, is still my mentor today. We trade emails and talk all the time.

When I paid for my first mastermind I was thinking, "Is this going to be worth it?" I was shelling out $25,000 to go sit in a room with a bunch of other guys doing business. I questioned that to my core, and I wasn't going to go—until my wife said, "You've got do this." And joining a mastermind, a peer group, probably had the biggest impact on my business and my life. To this day, I'm in multiple masterminds. I love the format. I still have my individual mentors, though, and I think both are absolutely crucial.

## Take the Shortcut: Start with Books

If you can't sit down with someone, at least start reading people's books. "Your net worth is your network." We've all heard that, and I 100% believe it's true, but there are people out there who have *already solved* the problems that you're going to run into. If you can look into their minds by being with them, being with people *like* them, reading their books, listening to their podcasts, you absolutely owe it to yourself to take that shortcut. There's too much out there; there's too much opportunity. It's just silly not to.

**Zach:** The average CEO of a Fortune 500 company reads 60 books a year. We teach our associates and students to begin by reading 10 minutes a day. Start with that and increase your time spent reading over the next year. Reading will change your life—it's changed mine.

## Failures in Partnerships and Markets

You're always going to experience failures, and the more successful you are, the bigger your failures are likely to be. You start playing a bigger and bigger game, and as your chances for success go up, so does the scale of your failures.

I've had a few partnerships. I had one that didn't work out, a huge failure—I lost a lot of money, but I made much better decisions going forward. I learned what partnerships are really about. What does someone else offer that I can't provide? A big lesson here is if you've got two people who know and can do the same things and have the same strengths, it's not going to make for a good partnership. You've got to fill in the gaps. It was a huge lesson, so when I went into my next partnership, it was a tremendous success.

Here's another: we invest in a couple of real estate markets. Our first market tanked. It didn't perform like we thought it would. We picked that apart and learned why. Based on what we learned, we moved into a different market, and had plenty of success there. We've had plenty of failures and plenty of successes, but a lot of today's successes were built on the backs of the failures of yesteryear.

## Effective Sales

Based on what people have written in or recorded for us in testimonials, the biggest thing to know is that you do more deals at a higher margin. That's really superficial, but that's the endgame: doing more deals at a higher margin.

What I think is more important, based on what I've heard from our trainees, is to be confident with that sales conversation. It's vital to understand it's a process, as simple as *They say A, you do B; they do C, you do D.* When you can start to look at with an engineer's eyes, you see that it's just a series of instructions—*if this happens, I do that*—and that starts to relieve a lot of the anxiety people have about sales.

Here's another major point: our sales process is completely aboveboard. You can tell our prospect what you're doing every step of the way: *Here's what I plan to do with you / Here's what we're doing: this step, this step, and this step / Here's what we're going to talk about / Here's why I'm asking these questions.* When there's a process, and it's not only effective, it's aboveboard, it feels *good* to do what you do every day. You don't have that nagging inner voice asking, "Am I tricking him? Am I misleading him? Am I persuading him to make the wrong decision?" It feels good to sell when you can be 100% aboveboard, and confident in everything you say and do.

More money, more deals, higher margins, closing a few deals you wouldn't otherwise have closed—yes. But being able to do that effectively and *feel really good about it* is even better.

---

**Zach:**   It's funny that John describes this as *if A, then B; if C, then D.* The reason it works this way is because he's put systems in place to get prospects from where they *are* to where they *want to be.* If your business has these systems in place, it becomes predictable and profitable. Our business is set up exactly that way: *complete step A, and the result is B.* If you haven't refined your processes to create predictable results, make it a priority today. If you're not sure how to do it, find a mentor and copy them. Your business depends on it.

## Training with the Midwest Revenue Group

We've developed a number of videos addressing a lot of the key topics or challenges that investors wrestle with when it comes to negotiating, renegotiating, cold calling, or handling incoming calls. We put together a video for each topic and made them available to Chris's associates.

We've got free materials, which I highly encourage everyone to take advantage of, because we get really positive feedback on them. Then we've got an online course. It's live—I personally hop on the phone with the group and we go through a sales tactic, strategy, or technique, then talk about it. For example, "Hey, Chris, how are you going to implement that in your business? Do you know when to use it? When would you use it? What does it sound like? Let's role-play that." We go through it like that, to practice and get comfortable with these techniques before using them in the field.

We also have live boot camps a few times a year. Our online course is 8–12 weeks long, depending on when the holidays fall, but the boot camp is all that material over two days in a live setting: 20–40 investors, some just starting out, and about ¾ of them with established businesses doing at least 50 deals a year.

We've also got a "boots on the ground" where every once in a while, I (or someone I've personally trained) will fly in and spend one, two, or three days with the team in the car, actually going on deals. I can say, "I see what you're doing. Now I'm going to sell a deal or buy a house, and you watch what I do. We'll talk about each meeting right afterward and debrief." We have several levels of the training.

**Zach:** I've been to John's bootcamp, purchased his products, and seen the results. I used a couple of his techniques and was able to purchase my own home, a beautiful home on the water—and I got a killer deal on it.

## Satisfaction in Others' Success

My two biggest wins in the sales arena were helping two different companies: we helped one company land a quarter-billion-dollar deal. They were essentially a $20 million company, and within one year, we helped them land a monster $250 million deal. They had to build out their factory and buy out all the land around them—a massive success.

Another one was a telecom company, one of the top four telecom companies in the US. We worked with the sales team in one of the smallest markets in the country, but we locked down the biggest deal in company history, about $1.5 million a month in telephone service. That business was stolen from AT&T, the big bad telecom player, so we were pretty proud of that.

From a financial perspective, those are probably the two biggest deals I've been intimately involved with and helped push through.

The other way I like to look at successes is on a personal level—the impact we can make on someone's life. Greg in New York must tell me once a month, "Man, the training changed my life. It helped me get my business going. We're doing deals." It's like *The Matrix*. Remember how, in *The Matrix* (I know I'm dating myself), the world slowed down for Neo, and he could see everything almost before it happened and knew how to react?

That's what our sales training is like: before, it seems to be almost a dark art—you've got to be a master of this vague sort of magic. But after our training, it becomes crystal-clear how to handle every sales call, no matter what anyone says to you or how they say it, whether they're perfectly calm or upset. Empowering people to feel that way and pull off a great sales call, to close every closeable deal—that, to my mind, is a massive success too. I love the testimonials and feedback we get.

---

**Chris:** Mark Podolsky, "the Land Geek," as he calls himself, had me on his show recently, and he said, "You're doing deals with the family, but now you're teaching. Why?" Among other things, I said what John hits on here: it's beyond rewarding to bring someone, especially someone who's never been in real estate, or who never thought they could be a salesperson, and watch that transformation. Then you get to see the huge success they have because of it. When you look at something like Maslow's hierarchy—exploring why people do what they do and what motivates them—anyone who's achieved even a little bit of success will tell you that you get into most careers or business ventures for the money, but once you have the money, it no longer motivates you. It took a lot less money than I thought it would for me not to care about money. The bills are paid, money's going in the bank, life's taken care of. At that point you can say, "You know what? I can make more money, but it won't change my life at all." Then you've got to ask yourself, "Why am I doing what I'm doing? Do I need to be doing something else?"

## Insights from *SPIN Selling* and Other Books

I like Audible; I listen to a lot of audiobooks. *The Righteous Mind: Why Good People Are Divided by Politics and Religion* is a great one: it's a deep look into decision-making and how people are influenced in those decisions. I just read *Extreme Ownership*, by a couple of Navy SEALs.

I'm rereading *SPIN Selling*, by Neil Rackham; I've probably read that book two dozen times in my lifetime. Rackham examined sales from a very scientific perspective over the course of about a decade. He recorded everything that happened in 30,000 sales calls in various industries, and determined exactly what the top salespeople do that produces success. The crazy thing is, it's not what you think it would be: closing? Absolutely not. They went into the study thinking good closers were the best salespeople. It's actually the opposite. The more times a salesperson tried to close, the less likely they were to get a deal. All kinds of amazing, interesting insights came from that book, and it's what a lot of the higher-end sales trainings are based on today: Sandler Sales, Miller Heiman, *Mastering the Complex Sale*.

## Daily Disciplines

What I do isn't going to be right for everyone, but for me, getting up early and exercising is the first daily discipline. When I start the day before the sun's up and get some good exercise, I always feel better and perform better than on the days I don't. That's the foundation of every day for me.

The second one is to prioritize. I know there are all kinds of books and systems. You've got Dan Sullivan, the Strategic Coach, who has "productive days," "buffer days," and so on. You've got the Keller Williams approach of picking *the ONE thing*. For me, it's as simple as looking at everything I've got to do and picking out one, two, or three of the top things I need to do that day—they're not necessarily things that push revenue, but they do have an impact on my business in the long run. It's not always sales, sales, sales; most of it is, "How do I take care of my current clients in the best way?" because I know that in the long term, word spreads, and I'll get more clients this way.

The third is just trying to be around as many like-minded individuals as possible, even be in my social media groups. Yesterday, I was at a meeting downtown; afterward, I saw a businessperson walking down the street into a coffee shop, so I whipped my car around, went in, and spent 30 minutes chatting with him about his business—just to spend some time with a like-minded individual. That's really important; otherwise, you get trapped in a bubble. You start to think problems are bigger than they are, you start to lose sight. I think you always need to be associating yourself with people of your caliber or higher—the same mindset as you.

## Strategies for Successful Sales

Strategy number one: when you think about selling, there's a tendency to think the spotlight is on you, that it's all about how *you* perform, what *you* share, how *you* interact with someone: *I've got to make this deal happen.* You need to shift that mindset and put the spotlight on the seller or prospect; prospects don't care what *we* have to share with them. The spotlight should always be on them.

As salespeople, *it's never about us.* Looking at tens of thousands of calls by successful salespeople and analyzing what makes for a successful sales call, we find that the salesperson is talking maybe 10–15% percent of the time; it's insane. Make sure the spotlight is on your prospect, not on you—that's where it belongs, illuminating the problem you can solve for them.

That leads into strategy number two: I don't care what product or service you sell, if it's tangible or intangible, we all sell *exactly the same thing*. Every business is in business for exactly the same reason: *to solve other people's problems*. The focus of every conversation should be, "I want to figure out what I'm here to do, what I'm here to help with. First, let's identify that, make sure we're crystal-clear about it; then I'll outline the best way I know to solve it. If you like my solution, we can move forward. If not, no big deal, but let's put one foot in front of the other, because this could end up many different ways. We can structure deals many different ways. Now, what am I actually here for? Let's focus on that problem." *Focus on the problem you're there to solve.*

The third-biggest thing to know is that no is okay. Every salesperson is afraid of getting a no, right? The truth about sales is that *nos don't make or break a sales career or a business*. Nos are actually good: on every sales call, I want either a yes or a no. The true evil that will take down a business or an investor faster than anything are the maybes and think-it-overs.

If you have a no, you know where you're at: either there isn't enough motivation to move forward, or there's still some obstacle or deal-killer you haven't yet addressed. Or it's just a no, and now you know you can stop beating this dead horse. *You know something,* and you can *do something* with knowledge. Maybes and think-it-overs, we don't know. Is it really a no? Is it over? Is there something I could have addressed but didn't that would have turned a no into a yes? What fear or anxiety or obstacle is standing in the way? Is it just a matter of motivation, because you didn't dive deeply enough into it, and if you did, it would turn into a yes?

Yes is good, but no is okay too. Many salespeople don't ask the questions they need to, or take the conversation where they need to, because they're afraid of that no. If you read *Never Split the Difference*, here's Chris Voss, an expert FBI negotiator who goes for no as quickly as possible. Why? Because it's much easier to sell from a no. Once you get a no, tension lessens, the prospect feels safe, and they'll start to share more. *So don't be afraid of no.*

The easiest way to find the Midwest Revenue Group is through Facebook or our website, which is on the **New Rules resources page** at TheNewRulesBook.com.

## TAKEAWAYS FROM THIS CHAPTER

1   When sales doesn't come naturally, follow the process.

2   Sales is about the prospect, *not you.*

3   Sales is helping other people solve problems.

4   No is OK—it's easier to sell from a no than a maybe.

5   Today's successes were built on the
    backs of the failures of yesteryear.

6   Every day, get up early, prioritize your tasks,
    and spend time with like-minded people.

# AMAZING SUCCESS
# AFTER STUNNING LOSS
## And Still On the Journey

## Brian Page

Brian Page made his first million before the age of 30 in the wild world of real estate. He lost it all to the historic crash, as I did. Starting over with no credit or savings to speak of, he built an Airbnb business, and made over six figures in his first six months—all with properties that he *doesn't own*. After automating and outsourcing near-ly every aspect of his business, Brian enjoyed traveling the world and managing that Airbnb empire from his laptop, seeing 20 countries so far. He believes wealth is not merely having money, but also having the time and freedom to enjoy it.

In his BNB Formula Master Class, Brian reveals how he started, how he grew his business so quickly, and how you can do exactly the same thing in any of the 191 coun-tries in which Airbnb operates. The BNB Formula is the only course of its kind: it shows you how to build a six- to seven-figure Airbnb business—again, without having to own a single property. Most importantly, he teaches how to outsource and automate so you can scale the business.

I come from a real estate background, as a lot of you do. Ever since college, I've been a real estate investor. I was flipping homes, doing wholesale deals, rentals—you name it. I did all kinds of real estate projects.

Everything was going great—until it wasn't. I had to start over worse than broke, with no credit. I was looking for a model that would allow me to get into real estate without borrowing, without going into debt. I just wasn't willing to do that.

Airbnb was that opportunity. I had a spare room in my apartment, so I listed it on Airbnb, as lots of people do, and started making money with it. Then I thought, "I could lease properties from owners, turn around, and put them on Airbnb." So that's what I did: I started doing that over and over again, and ended up building up a very healthy income for myself. Eventually, people were asking me to teach *them* how to do it. That's how I ended up becoming the world's leading expert on this business model.

## Learn from Others and Pass It On

Modeling other people is my number-one passion and my number one-skill: I always look for the best, then invest in myself to learn from them. Even today, I spend a lot of my hard-earned money on education, on being coached by the best people. When I started out with Airbnb, there was nobody out there at all, no experts I could turn to who were doing this. I was shocked by that, because I thought, "This is a great idea. It's working for me—why is nobody teaching this?"

I had to learn how to do it on my own, and as I started putting things online and answering people's questions, I *became* that person. I became the authority, the expert on how to build this business with many properties, and that led into what I do today. Essentially, it all came out of necessity, because nobody was teaching it. If you were to google how to do this, I'd be the only result to come up. So I seized that opportunity. As the old adage goes, "See a need, fill a need," so I took action.

I've now been able to teach students in dozens of countries; I have thousands of students around the world. Some of these students have gone on to do things way faster than I did, because they're doing what I teach and learning from all the mistakes I made. It's really encouraging to see that; it gets me jazzed to see people having success themselves.

I believe wholeheartedly in automating and outsourcing business, learning how to systematize business. I learned how to do it with Airbnb and with my home-sharing properties. That allowed me to scale it back to where I was working very few hours a week to manage everything. That's what I teach in my system.

As a result, I had a lot of time on my hands, and I used it to travel. But friends were reaching out to me and saying, "Hey Brian, what are you up to? How are you able to travel so much? You seem to have a lot of time off. You're making good income, obviously—what are you doing?" Then I had strangers reaching out to me asking me questions about how to do this kind of business, and I was answering them. It ended up being a little overwhelming because of the number of people reaching out to me, so I thought, "I'll just charge for my time so I don't have to give up all my time for free." So I started teaching people that way. Eventually I started writing it down. That turned into a course—it just turned into its own business. I'm a businessperson. I've owned lots of different kinds of businesses, and I own several today. I don't believe I have to limit myself to one business. So when I saw this opportunity, I ran with it, and now it's become its own thing. The reason I did it is simply that it presented itself.

Now I'm pursuing new business opportunities. I believe that once you get something systematized, automated, and going on its own, you'll have time to look into something else or build another business. And as I said earlier, when you start out on a new venture, it's important to find somebody who's doing what you want to do. Then you can pay to skip over all the time it would take you to learn it yourself, and you learn through their experience. I would have done that myself with Airbnb if there had been anyone to teach me. Chris and I have that in common.

## My Typical Students

I get a lot of real estate investors who come from a background like mine, a lot of people who own property. You can do this with property you own yourself; that's a great way to massively increase your cash flow with the properties that you own. Other people come to learn from me, and they don't know anything about real estate: they just looking at it as a business opportunity, and that's truly what it is. It's a totally internet-based business that you can build from home, and they come to me to learn how to build it.

I teach all kinds of people, and a lot of people with no experience whatsoever. The thing I love about it is that it doesn't require any kind of highly-technical knowledge. You don't have to be a real estate agent, you don't have to be licensed in any way, you don't even need background or experience with computers or technology. It's pretty simple: if you've ever leased a property before, you can do this. If you've ever used a simple app on your phone like Airbnb or anything like it, you can use this. It's really not that hard. The challenging part is learning how to scale and how to manage all the different listings once you get them—that's really where the challenge is.

You can think of it this way—you're building your own little hotel, but this hotel has rooms all over the place—all over town. That's what I teach: how do you systematize that so you don't pull your hair out and so you have a business you own, rather than a job with crazy hours? That's my specialty.

## Will This Work in My Hometown?

Airbnb is in nearly 200 countries; the only place where they probably don't operate is North Korea. (If you're reading this in North Korea, I'm sorry, but you're out of luck.) I've had so many students now that I've been able to talk to and interview in different countries and cities.

I've interviewed students who have listings in big cities. A lot of students in big cities are doing quite well, but I've also got some students in rural areas. One guy I interviewed recently has five cabins in rural Canada. I asked him how he was doing, and his answer was, "I'm crushing it." How? "I'm the only one in the county with listings on Airbnb, and I've got five cabins." He doesn't even own them, by the way, and he's earning over six figures a year doing that.

I have people in tourist areas and non-tourist areas. This will work in any town that has hotels, that has short-term guests. If there's a hotel anywhere near you, people are paying money to stay there by the night, and that's what we're looking for. We're looking, essentially, to start that on our own.

It doesn't have to be one particular thing: people travel for work, they travel to go to an event space, they travel for tourism, they travel because to hospitals and universities. I have one guy who lives in a university town—we're talking 11,000 people—and he's making tons of money because he has these properties that are right near the school. He's leased them, and students and parents stay there, and he makes gobs of cash flow by putting them on home-sharing sites.

The short answer is that it works in so many different places. But the key is that you've got to know where the most profitable properties are in your particular area. You need to learn how to get those properties—why an owner might allow you to do this—and how you talk to the owner so they're willing to do it if you don't own your own properties. That's what I teach.

## Setting Up a Property

In order to turn your property into a short-term rental or host on these sites, it has to be furnished. What I teach my students is if you're looking to use properties you don't own, focus on furnished places. If you're going to work with a property you *do* own and it's vacant, you'd have to furnish it—I can show you how to furnish it very inexpensively and quickly—and then the goal is to get that money, within the first 30 to 60 days, right back in your pocket. So there *is* a little investment involved to get that going, because you've got to get the place ready for guests. The key is to furnish it with used furniture, not to buy anything new. There are ways to do this very inexpensively and quickly; I can furnish a place in a weekend.

I also tell people to focus on small properties—we're not talking about a three or four-bedroom house, we're talking about studios and one bedrooms and small townhouses. You want to start small with small properties. A lot of people are going to be traveling, but usually it's one or two people. If they're looking at staying in a hotel, that's just a small room—and you're giving them the alternative of staying in your entire one-bedroom condo! It doesn't take much to furnish one of those places. I show my students how to furnish them quickly, get them listed, and get that money right back in their pockets.

## Getting Rental Property Owners to Say Yes

The biggest obstacle for most people is that they don't own properties that are vacant or that are available to do this with. If you're a real estate investor reading this and you do have them, you're one step ahead. But most people don't; they start like I did. I didn't have any property and I couldn't buy any property, so I had to start by approaching owners.

When you go to an owner, if you don't know how to approach them, they're not going to say yes. But I've found some really cool scripts and techniques to be able to work with the owners and present this in such a way that they *do* want to do it, and it's *in their best interest* to do it. Keep in mind, I'm only talking about owners who have rentals. I'm looking for somebody who has a rental and is looking for a tenant. I approach them and say, "Hey, I want to lease your place, but instead of living in it, what I want to do is host short-term guests who come into town. Let me explain to you what I do." Then there's this whole spiel I go into, explaining to them what I do.

Now a lot of owners are going to say no. They're just going to say, "No, I don't get it. I'm not interested." Very few owners will hear the spiel and say, "I'm going to go do that," because if they'd *thought* of it, they would've already *done* it. So I'm looking for the one-in-five or one-in-seven owner who's going to say, "Yeah, I'd consider doing that." And it's not hard to go look at seven rental properties. What does that take—a few hours on a Saturday or a Sunday? I just look at it as a numbers game. I approach people, I tell them what I do, I present it in a non-salesy way, and some of them will say yes. And if they say yes, we're off to the races.

## Setting Up the Agreement

There are two ways to do it: I can sign a lease and then just put that property right on Airbnb, or I can do a month-to-month agreement, which is better. That means I don't have to sign a long-term lease. I can approach the owner and say, "I don't want to sign a year lease, but if you let me sign a month-to-month agreement with you, I'll pay you slightly more than what you're asking." Let's say they're asking $1,500 a month. I could say, "I'm going to give you $1,600 a month for your place," and they're going to ask, "Why would you do that?" I respond, "Because I'm going to make money with your property, and in exchange for letting me go month-to-month, I'll just pay you a little more than market rent. Is that fair?" And you'd be surprised how many owners will say, "Sure, that's fine." It gives you the ability to get into the property without a long-term commitment. I mean, really, think about it—what owner is going to say no to more money? It's a very easy conversation.

So there are many different ways to do it, but essentially, you're taking property and putting it on Airbnb, and the money you make on Airbnb is going to be greater than your costs for the property. I can't guarantee what you'll make, of course, but most students get back two to three times their cost. Is that a good investment? You bet!

So if it's a property that costs $1,500, rent and utilities—the total cost—that property could bring in $3,000, $4,000, or $5,000 a month. It's insane, but that's how it works, because the cash flow is so much greater on a nightly basis than it is on a monthly basis. You're basically playing arbitrage. You're able to do what hotels do: a hotel has to pay their mortgage on the property, but then they rent out each little unit to create cash flow. And the difference between what they pay on their property and what they bring in is their profit. This is no different, except that we're doing it with other people's property.

## Dealing with Owner Objections

People worry that when they talk to an owner, the owner's going to say, "No, no, that's too much wear and tear on the property—that's worse than having a regular tenant." But it's not worse; it's actually better. This always blows owners' minds, but there are several reasons: first of all, I'm going to take care of their property to a standard that no tenant ever would. Essentially, I'm running my own little hotel, so I have professional cleaning companies come in and clean the property every couple of days—every time a guest checks out.

So I tell the owner, "Mr. Owner, your property's going to be professionally cleaned spotless top-to-bottom at least two or three times a week. Not only that, I'm going to take care of any minor issues that come up with the property: if the toilet clogs, you're not going to get a call. I outsource that to somebody who'll take care of it. Not only that, I'm going to make sure your property's insured, so you can get insurance for about $50 a month—it's dirt cheap." I'll give them a completely separate insurance policy that covers anything that could go wrong with tenants or guests or anything. So I can ask, "When was the last time a tenant offered to insure your property?" The answer, of course, is *never*.

Then I explain to them that it's going to be less wear and tear on their property: my guests are coming into town to enjoy town and leave two days later. They're not going to have a dog that digs holes in the backyard—I don't allow pets. They're not going to have somebody in their family repaint the third bedroom pink, because they don't care. They're not going to have an ex-boyfriend or girlfriend show up at 2:00 AM and kick the front door in. Tenants cause *a lot* more damage than guests ever will; guests don't treat properties like that. They're in, they're out. They generally use utilities less; they're not using the stove, the fridge, the electricity, or the water as much, because they're only there one or two nights. Do you spend all your time in your hotel room when you travel?

When I explain this to them, owners usually say, "Oh, I get it." I demonstrate to them that this is the standard of cleanliness my property has to be kept to, because otherwise, how would I attract guests? The average hotel room is spotless, so this place *has to be*.

Then I break it down for them: I say, "I'm the best option you have for a tenant, and this is what I do for a living." I give them the whole thing, and they usually say, "Okay, let's do this." It gives me my pick of properties that are out there, and it's not taking advantage of owners because the owner is looking for a tenant. I'm giving them exactly what they want: I'm giving them the monthly rent they're looking for and I take great care of their property, so they win. I win because I make money, and the guests staying in my property win. It's a win-win-win for everybody. I know that's the only kind of deal Chris and his family team strive to do.

That's the kind of business I like to do. It's very exciting, because it's cool to be able to just take a property I don't own and immediately start earning cash flow on it. This kind of cash flow is far better than traditional real estate investing. It's just on a whole other exponentially higher level.

Great entrepreneurs hit roadblocks and challenges all the time, but they don't let that keep them down. They're back on their feet in no time; they don't stay in the fetal position. Like Chris, I have a real estate crash story—but I achieved success because of it. Let me explain what happened; I know you can learn a lot from it.

## Achieving Success through Failure

In my early twenties, I was looking for a way to build wealth. I heard that real estate was the fastest and most common way that people became wealthy, so I got into real estate. I found a couple of great mentors, I went through courses, I went through education—I spent an entire year absorbing everything I possibly could on real estate. I found that flipping houses was what I wanted to do, and I got into that: I flipped over 100 properties and made money on every single one of them. Everything was great—until it wasn't. When the market turned, I had just built a massive oceanfront home, a beautiful home, with seven bedrooms, seven baths. I was getting ready to sell it. I was going to make an incredible amount of money on that deal; it was going to be my biggest deal ever.

Just as I was finishing up the landscaping and the final touches, the market turned: there was all this crazy news about the banks that were having problems, and I couldn't sell it. I couldn't even *rent* it, because the vacation rental market was, of course, slowing down. I got to the point where I didn't know what to do, because I didn't have the money to pay for all the properties I had. I had *millions of dollars* of debt.

I had to walk away from everything, and that was when I lost not only my investment properties, but my personal residence. It was foreclosed on. So I was worse than broke, I was in the hole, over a million dollars in debt. It was an absolutely horrible time in my life.

For years after that, I didn't know what to do. In fact, I just gave up. I didn't believe there was any opportunity out there for me. I didn't know what I was going to do next. It wasn't until years later, when I was renting a two-bedroom apartment, that I thought, "Whoa, I've got this extra room here!" My roommate had moved out, so I thought, I'd try the Airbnb thing. My goal was only to make a few hundred bucks on that one room, but I ended up making enough to pay for my rent and utilities; I was just *pocketing* the money from my job every month. I was already in a whole different place, financially—it was amazing. That was when I thought, "This reminds me of the real estate business, but now I can start over again, without the sleepless nights, without all that money in debt."

---

**Chris:** This is precisely why we no longer sign on bank loans or use our own cash. Stick with that plan; you'll sleep better at night.

## Get in on the Ground Floor

I built my business differently this time, and it's a cool hybrid—it's real estate, but it's technology. For those of you who don't know, Airbnb is on an absolute *tear* right now. It just recently surpassed the largest hotel chains in number of rooms. In just six or seven years, Airbnb now has more rooms than the largest hotel chains in the world. And yet, if you add up all the hotel rooms in the world, Airbnb still represents less than 1% of those. It's growing at an exponential clip—more and more people are traveling this way instead of with hotels—but the opportunity is still early. You're still ahead of the curve here if you're hearing about this opportunity now.

Most people on Airbnb and VRBO and similar sites don't know how to do what I teach. Less than 0.5% have more than two listings. Most people have never cracked the code of how to do this across multiple properties.

After I had the idea to build this kind of business, I saw an article in *Forbes Magazine* that said there were 75 people making $1 million or more a year on Airbnb. I was floored: $1 million a year! I've now had the opportunity to interview people like that. I interviewed a guy two months ago who's bringing in over $2 million a year on Airbnb. It blew my mind that people are making six and seven figures, and that the number of people making over six figures is in the thousands. And then it came full circle, because *Forbes Magazine* reached out to me recently for an interview. Then *Inc. Magazine* contacted me and interviewed me. All of these companies are reaching out to me asking, "How did you do what you did? Can you tell us about Airbnb and what's going on?" Now I have this entire community of people like me who are BNB entrepreneurs. I like to create BNB entrepreneurs, help people out, and teach them how to do what I do.

## I Got to Fire My Boss

My biggest win was when I quit my job. I was working a job that I hated, one of those jobs that just pays the bills. Some of you know what I'm talking about; not many of us who work at jobs love what we do.

I was working at this job about 50 hours a week and dabbling in the Airbnb thing on the side, so I was just doing it on the weekends when I had time. But after I got my third or fourth listing, I was bringing in at least double what I took home from work every month. So I told my boss, "You're fired. I don't need you anymore." And I walked away from that job. That was the last time I ever wanted to be employed by someone else.

That was a huge win, because I didn't go from working 50 hours a week for my boss to working 50 hours a week for me. I was able to outsource my business and cut back to just a few hours a week on the Airbnb business—and that's when my entire life changed. Now I had the time to go do the things I wanted to do—I was able to start traveling. I've now visited 20 countries in the last 14 months. My wife is from Brazil, and we're getting ready to go live in Brazil for a little while and travel wherever we want to. It gives you that kind of freedom. I don't say that to brag. I just say it because that's what I wanted to do, that's what my dream was—to have the time and money to see the world, live around the world. That's what I'm able to do now because of this business. That's the biggest win for me. It's been just incredible.

## High-Payoff Habits: Self-Care, No Distractions, and *One Important Thing*

The first thing I do every day that's absolutely critical is my morning ritual. It doesn't take very long—a half hour or an hour. My morning ritual includes drinking a lot of water, because when you wake up, your body is dehydrated. I learned how to breathe deeply. I do some visualization, I do some meditation: I focus on where I want to be in the next five, ten, twenty years of my life. I spend some time just taking care of me, getting ready for my day, getting centered. I might read, I do some push-ups and some physical exercise. The only way I can have *all* of those habits is to group them all in one little chunk that I do in the morning, so I call it my "morning ritual."

I've found that all high achievers have a morning ritual, and mine is, to me, the most important thing I do all day. I do it first thing when

I wake up, then I go in the office. That's something I recommend people look into. There are some really good books out there on this; *The Miracle Morning* is one I recommend.

The second thing I do is turn off all distractions, and everything stays off for the first half of the day: I don't check email first thing in the morning, I don't have my phone on (it's on airplane mode). I don't have anything turned on in my house—no Messenger, nothing on my computer, everything is turned off. So the first part of my day, when I have the most energy available to me, is focused on my highest-level activities. I don't start my day in a frenzy, trying to figure out what I'm supposed to do by looking at everybody else's agendas. I don't do any of those things until later in the day.

Third, I spend the rest of the first half of my day focusing on my highest level activities. I look at my list of to-dos, all the things I could be doing, and I pick out *one thing*. I ask myself, "What is the one thing that, if it's all I accomplish, it would be a successful day?" Then I focus on that thing, even if it's not something I want to do.

I'm not doing busy work. I'm not doing something easy so I can check it off the list; it doesn't make sense to do 20 things that are easy but not meaningful, and leave the biggest thing for another day. I get into the habit of *executing on the most important activity*.

Those are the three things that I do. Then, in the second half of the day, I check my emails, my phone, all of that. Some of you might have a job where you *can't* do that—you *have* to answer the phone, and that makes sense. But if you have that luxury, that ability, maybe because you work for yourself, you need to be developing the habit of *focus*. That's how I do it. Those are my most important habits that I keep every day.

## Read, and Keep Reading

I'm obsessed with books. If you follow me on social media, you'll see pictures of books are my number-one thing. I read several books a week. There are many I could mention here, but the one I'm reading right now is *The Self-Made Billionaire Effect*, and I highly, highly recommend it. The author analyzes the top billionaires around the world and what they have in common. It's quite interesting, because it explains that there's a very clear path to wealth, but there's no very clear path to *super*-wealth, to becoming a billionaire. It tries, nevertheless, to dissect what makes these people different: How do they come up with these flashes of brilliance, these billion-dollar ideas?

I'm reading this book to figure out if I can put some of those things into my own mind, into the way I think. It talks about all the big billionaires you've heard of—Bill Gates, Mark Cuban, Elon Musk—and what makes them different. I'm learning so many things about the way they think. A lot of people think a billionaire is somebody who comes up with an idea no one's ever had before and launches a brand-new industry—but that's not really the case. A lot of times, they come up with something nobody's ever thought of *reimagining*.

One example is the woman who invented Spanx, Sara Blakely. She became a massive billionaire by looking at a market everybody said was dead: "You don't want to go into pantyhose—you don't want to go into that market." She went in there, created a product she thought she needed, and women went crazy over it. She basically reinvented an entire industry with just one product. So billionaires sometimes have the ability to look at something and think of it in a completely new way: they can look at it and see it not the way it is, but completely reimagined. They have amazing creative abilities. I love this book. The other book I'm going to read this week is Elon Musk's biography, which is really fascinating. It's just called *Elon Musk*. You should be spending a lot of time reading books, because they're the shortest path to success and mentorship from the greatest minds in the world.

## It's a Journey

If I could go back a few years, I would tell myself, "You haven't arrived yet." Some of you who are reading this may have had some successes in your life, and maybe you've had major failures, but regardless, *you haven't arrived yet*. I was young, and I thought I had arrived because I'd had some success. I thought, "Now I'm on top, and I'll always be on top." I was humbled very quickly to realize that you can lose your wealth; you can lose your success. As an entrepreneur, sometimes you do have to start over again. That's a common story among a lot of successful people: they have to start over from scratch.

I would tell myself, "You haven't arrived yet, and the journey is going to be mountaintops and valleys, and you're going to have to enjoy the wins along with the losses." I don't know what life will bring me in the upcoming years. Having some success again has been amazing, but I realize that I'm on a journey. I'm never going to stop; I'll continue, no matter what happens. I'm going to continue on that path, because I know that sometimes those huge setbacks are part of the journey we choose. If you want safety, you get a safe little job and work at it until you die—and that's what a lot of people do.

If you envision bigger things for yourself, if you have bigger dreams, then you're going to have to step out there, take some risks, and do some things. Sometimes that comes with wins, and sometimes it comes with losses. I have to tell myself, "Okay, Brian, as an older guy with some experience, I realize that I still haven't arrived, even now." That's exciting, because *no one wants to arrive*. If you arrive, then what are you going to do? Say, "I'm at the top. I'm done now, so what do I do? Just give up and retire?" That would be the advice I'd give my younger self, and that's what I'd say to you. Don't ever stop learning, growing, and searching. Life should be a never-ending quest to improve yourself. If you look at it that way, as an adventure, then you're never going to "arrive."

---

**Chris:** A lot of people think they could never read as much as Brian is telling you to, but you *can*: subscribe to Audible and get the app on your phone so you can listen while working out, driving, wherever. You'll be able to double or triple your reading. Listening to audiobooks on Audible has dramatically increased the number of books I get through.

I realize in hindsight that my toughest time was when I thought I was on top and didn't have a mentor. That's different, because at any given time, I've almost always had one or more, since back in the mid-1990s. Depending upon what you're personally working on at the time and what you're working on in your business, hire a mentor who has been there and can help. For example, 12–24 months ago I was seeking more help with lead generation and related funnels. Now I'm working with mentors about scaling, creating amazing culture, and things like that.

Visit the **New Rules resources page** at TheNewRulesBook.com for the property profits calculator Brian is offering for free. You can also find information there about his eight-week BNB Formula course—it's less than $1,000 to get trained!

# TAKEAWAYS FROM THIS CHAPTER

1 Learn from others' successes and mistakes:
educate yourself, get a mentor, and read.

2 Getting in on the real estate business doesn't require you to own
your own properties; it requires *very* little capital upfront.

3 Your competition is a hotel; if there's a hotel
in your town, this can work for you.

4 Learn how to talk to property owners
and show them how they stand to benefit.

5 Create a short morning ritual that centers
you and prepares you for the day.

6 Try to work with no distractions in the morning.
Save afternoons for correspondence and small tasks.

7 Accomplish *one important thing* a day.

8 Realize that you're on a journey. If you're going to dream
big, be prepared for both successes and failures.

# THE REAL ESTATE ROCK STAR

## Dan Schwartz

**Dan Schwartz is with InvestorFuse. He has a passion for helping the overwhelmed real estate investor and entrepreneur. He helps them work smarter and earn more by setting up effective systems. After launching InvestorFuse, a lead management automation platform for real estate investing, he helped bring the power of automation to hundreds if not thousands of happy investors. Dan has built a strong community around that technology. When not working or resting, you'll find Dan traveling, drumming, producing music, or helping other entrepreneurs grow their businesses.**

Rewind to around 2010: I had just graduated from school with a marketing degree from the University of Maryland. I was living at my parents' house after graduating, as millennials do these days. Lying on my bedroom floor, I saw two paths for my life and my career: I saw the limiting path, where you get a job with a fixed salary, and the *infinite* path, where you have the potential to make as much you want, with no ceiling—as well as the challenge of figuring out entrepreneurship and growing from that. I said to myself, "You know what? Let's do this! Let's find something that gives me the freedom to pursue the lifestyle I want." If you've listened to Chris's podcast or read his book or online materials, you know the idea of "designing your lifestyle" is something that comes up frequently. Well, that's what I wanted.

I had read *Rich Dad Poor Dad* earlier that year, which had planted the seed. I remember going to one of those free *Rich Dad Poor Dad* summits with my father and not opting into their coaching program, a $40,000 upsell. But I did some research online and met another young investor in Baltimore, Maryland. We did our first wholesale deal within a month or two of meeting, and we were off to the races! I had a couple of good coaches and mentors at the time. We flipped houses willy-nilly for a couple of years, living deal-to-deal as most people do, and brute-forcing our way into closing seven or eight deals a month at our peak. It was just the two of us and a lead manager.

I was also touring full-time, on the road playing music as a drummer in a band—music is my passion. But I was determined not to be a starving artist: I wanted to figure out how to be a touring musician and also have a business that would work without my direct involvement all the time.

## Becoming a Systems Guru

That set the stage for my interest in—and now obsession with—setting up systems. There were a lot of opportunities, a lot of moments when I realized *I* was the bottleneck to the growth of the company. I knew there was a way to resolve that bottleneck with effective delegation systems. I had a lot of time on the road to think about and work through that issue, and I wanted to use the technology available to us at the time to create a system that would automate your deal flow, assigns tasks to the right people on your team, and make sure you can sell the property in a timely fashion—at scale.

My circumstances forced me to get really good at that. I created some pretty cool solutions that other people then wanted me to help them out with. Eventually,I found that I was spending more time helping other people set up their business systems than I was spending on my own business: I was still doing deals, but most of my time was spent building infrastructure or helping to set people up on this platform called Podio, which helps you manage, view, and track all of your incoming leads. That parlayed into what I'm doing now with InvestorFuse. At this point, InvestorFuse is helping over 500 investment teams smartly execute their deals, capture all their leads, and follow up with all their leads automatically using Podio.

## Three Pillars of Real Estate Acquisitions

If you think about any real estate acquisitions operation, it comes down to three essential pillars:

1   **Lead generation:** creating opportunities to make money

2   **Lead management:** capturing those leads, working through and nurturing them to get the contract.

3   **Monetization:** What strategy are you using to take that contract and turn it into profit? You could wholesale it to another rehabber, flip it yourself, buy and hold it, do a lease option or owner financing—whatever strategy you decide.

## The Middle Pillar: Administration

I find that the middle pillar is the one most investors struggle with; it's the most administrative and *manual*. It's the most thankless act of this business: having to call people over and over and over again, constantly dealing with voice-mails and nos and people leading you on. It's hard to follow up with hundreds and hundreds of homeowner leads at scale, and most of the current systems out there aren't really built for that middle pillar.

We realized that we needed to optimize that middle pillar of lead management and all the little stages of the pipeline of a deal in between: if you can optimize how many leads you're capturing, you can optimize how many leads you're making offers on, increase the number of leads that turn into appointments, and finally, increase the number of appointments that turn into deals. You track all of these numbers through the process. If you do that, you can scale up your acquisitions funnel predictably.

When you don't have to close deals one at a time, then go hunting for that next deal, you can be confident building a predictable pipeline of deals. It all starts with thinking about your business as a funnel: *leads* come in, leads turn into *appointments*, appointments turn into *deals*, and then you have your monetization strategy in place.

So we only go all in on that middle pillar, which is the least sexy part of the business. All the fun stuff happens after you get it under contract; before that, it's all administrative tasks. We believe that by using technology and effective delegation to make sure you get as many contracts as possible, you can shave off a lot of time, and that's what InvestorFuse does.

## Who Are InvestorFuse's Customers?

Our clients come in all sizes, from single-person teams all the way up to teams of 20. Chris's son Nick and son-in-law Zach are fully immersed in our platforms, for example. Probably 20% of our users are rehabbers, 70% are wholesalers, and 10% are landlords, because no matter what exit strategy you're using, you've got to get a contract.

There are two modules, one for seller leads, and one for buyer leads. The modules interact with each other if there's a deal in which both buyers and sellers are involved. You can set tasks and automations for buyers and sellers.

Don't invest in lead management systems unless you have leads coming in. If you haven't done a deal yet or don't have a lot of opportunities coming your way, focus on *that* first. Close a deal or two; *then* you can reinvest in automating your system. This is not for folks who are just starting out and have no leads to manage. Experience also helps with the learning curve for using a new technology: if you're already familiar with the way leads generate contracts, your learning curve is drastically cut.

# Podio

Podio is a third-party platform that allows you to create structures for your business. "Structures" are data points around your leads: your offers, your appointments, all of the areas of your business. You create these structures in Podio, which wasn't built for real estate investors; it was built for marketing agencies. But we've repurposed and customized it to work for real estate investors, which shaves off a lot of the learning curve.

There are folks who try to figure out for themselves how to set up this kind of system. I was one of those poor people, and it's an enormous drag on your time. It's a huge technical time suck, and investors shouldn't be spending their time on it: they should be spending their time making offers and closing deals. InvestorFuse does away with all that wasted time. Once you're on the platform, you have to learn how you use it, but it's very much a "next action" system. You click the button corresponding to the action you want to happen *next*.

It's task-based, so you go into your tasks and do whatever tasks are due that day; you try to get the list to zero every single day. The task will tell you exactly what you need to do: when you click into the task, it shows you all relevant data about that lead. After your phone call with the lead, you just click on the next action that you want to happen: sending an offer, e.g., or going on an appointment. Usually, though, it's just a follow-up in two days. You can set a follow-up sequence, so there *is* some training, and you *do* have to learn where everything is.

Our biggest asset is our team. We have an amazing onboarding and support team to help with all the integrations. We'll get on the phone and make sure that you and your team are trained on how to use it. You get unlimited training until you're comfortable. There's a learning curve of a week to ten days to fully integrate our system into your business, but for something as important as creating predictable deal flow at scale, ten days really isn't too bad.

## The Importance of Leads

I know one guy who's a one-man show. He was doing six-figure months all last year before I finally convinced him to hire an assistant to help him with leads.

The system was built for the entrepreneur's peace of mind, to know that their team has something efficient that they can use and not have to worry about leads. It's what *I* wanted when I was on the road and worrying about all the leads that we were generating, and what might be falling through the cracks.

Once, a seller called my business partner late in the day. We had missed his first call, and he tried calling us back again later in the day. We just didn't have a system set up to notify us when a lead came in. We had to go in manually and look at our spreadsheet. "Man, I wish you guys had called me back earlier," the guy told Mike, my business partner. "I just locked up this deal in Canton." Canton is a high-end area in Baltimore, and this would have been a $50,000 wholesale piece. We completely missed out on that opportunity, and the seller was nice enough to call us and let us know about it. That lit a fire under us to figure it out, and that's when we hired our first lead manager whose full time job was to work the system, nurturing leads, answering the phones, and collecting all the data. That's an important first step for any investor who's looking to create a real business around real estate investing. You need someone focusing full-time just on lead management.

## Strategy vs. Details: Dan's Strength vs. His Kryptonite

Strategy comes naturally to me. I'm your classic entrepreneur personality type. I like to make moves and take action, and I'm very aware of actions I *shouldn't* be taking myself. I build systems around that insight so other people can execute on it.

My core strength is finding opportunities that have scale, and are higher-leverage. InvestorFuse is one of those: it's a company that has scale and that I know can help a lot of people. It's high-leverage and can make people a lot of money. We can create systems and have our own intellectual property that can be a massive lever for other people. I like to identify these opportunities, which is a trait I think a lot of real estate investors also have—What's the minimum amount I can spend to acquire a deal? What's the maximum amount I can make?—I build systems around that.

I'm a very systems-minded person, but working *inside* the system and getting into all of the details is not my forte. The more in the weeds I am, the more likely I am to *break* the system—and my whole team knows that. I think it's important for people to align themselves with others who understand what their core strengths are, accept them for who they are, and don't try to force them to do the things they're not good at or don't enjoy doing.

## Limiting Beliefs

Sometimes when people think about setting up businesses, they think they won't have to do *anything*, that they can create systems, hire people, and then just lounge on the beach all day.

On the opposite end of the spectrum, you encounter the limiting beliefs: "Oh, that sounds like so much work," or, "No one else can do this as well as I can," or "There are so many things I'd have to set up—this is going to take *forever!*" There are so many limiting beliefs that cluster around the idea that you can't escape the rat race you've created for yourself.

Here's a simple exercise: list all the tasks you currently do, high-light the tasks that you enjoy doing, and put those on a separate list. What you're left with is a job description for someone you need to hire. Take whatever little actions are necessary to get whatever's in your brain represented externally in a note, a system, or a step-by-step process. One process at a time, you'll start to see the power of delegation and of hiring people to do the things you don't like to do. I tell all our staff to do that: whenever they feel overwhelmed, I say, "Take a step back. Get a laptop, get a notepad, and just make a list of everything you do." It's super-helpful, and at the end of that list, you have a job description for *someone else*.

## Real Estate Rock Star

You can't have two careers at once. You can't try to do two things at the same time with equal ferocity: you end up half-assing both endeavors, and neither will work out. I'm speaking from my own experience touring full-time in a band while trying to run a real estate business. I thought for the longest time that I could be a real estate rock star. It took a moment of clarity to realize that my heart wasn't in *either of these*; it was split between the two. Finally, I asked myself, "What is my ideal lifestyle, and what career best aligns with that?" I chose entrepreneurship and left the band at the end of 2014. I left the rock star lifestyle, which just wasn't going to support the life I wanted for myself and my family.

Because of that decision, I made more money within six months than I ever had in my whole life; when you finally do make that decision, your mind's focus narrows down to that one thing. If you're reading this and find yourself in a similar situation, it's important to make that choice: What's going to give you the life you want for yourself and your family? The power of focusing on one thing is probably my biggest takeaway from that experience. Everyone on your team should be killer at *one thing*. They shouldn't be dealing with both buyers *and* sellers on a day-to-day basis. If you haven't read Gary Keller's book *The ONE Thing*, you should.

## Software that Builds Community

InvestorFuse is a win for all stakeholders. There are 520 or so companies on the platform, which is more than 3,000 team members across all those companies using the software. But the biggest win for me is the team and the community we built around it. Up until that point, there wasn't really an open community talking about how systems and technology can help you free up your time and your business, and help get you out of the rat race you've created for yourself. There wasn't any actionable advice around—just YouTube videos telling you, "You need to have systems!" but not giving you any sense of how to actually *do it*.

It started when I was setting up people's Podio workspaces in 2013. I had a 3,000-person Facebook group just about Podio, which some readers might not even know about. It struck a chord with people. It created an amazing network and community of investors who were actively doing deals, savvy about eliminating overwhelm, and were effectively creating teams around their business models.

## Buy Houses with My Bot

This year we released a little side project called SendFuse. It's a text bot that lets you text an address, then mail a sequence of postcards to the owner of that address. It isn't boots on the ground, in the field, driving for dollars. There's no app necessary. It's a bot, so you just send a text to SendFuse on your phone. You send the address, and the SendFuse service we've created will verify the address, search the owner, find the owner's name and mailing address, learn whether it's vacant or owner-occupied, make sure that it's a legit address, and queue up a sequence of eight postcards to go out to that owner. Two months out from launch, people were already closing deals and booking appointments from the campaigns the text bots sent out. This was one of those opportunities that I thought was high-leverage and very scalable.

Our postcards are the generic "we buy houses" type, but they're mixed-format: some look handwritten, some look like typed notices, but they're all postcards we've used and vetted. There's one sequence for owner-occupied properties, and a sequence for vacant properties. As we continue to see more use cases, we'll keep building them out. You'll be able to send out offers through the bot just by texting an address, with the offer price. It's the easiest thing in the world; the bot *tells you what to do*.

## The Year Ahead

There will be some massive improvements to InvestorFuse next year that a lot of folks will be able to enjoy. The next year is going to be a foot-on-the-gas year: we're perfecting lead management. The goal is to continue to push time off people's plates using technology like bots and artificial intelligence. We're going all in on the tech side of things because we know that when we create a killer app for real estate investors, it will be relevant to other niches in real estate too. We're scaling up, growing the team and the user base, and trying to help as many people as possible.

## Adam Grant, Author *du Jour*

I'm currently reading *Originals: How Non-Conformists Move the World*, by Adam Grant. He's the author of *Give and Take: Why Helping Others Drives Our Success*, which is also a great read. In *Originals*, the question is, "What makes an idea original and unique?" It's essentially a lesson in differentiation, but I think it's crucial for investors to understand.

## Advice to New Investors

Don't do it alone. Having a business partner, a mentor, a coach, or someone to bounce ideas off of really helps take the edge off this business. All of your anxiety can be eliminated with a simple conversation, or by listening to a podcast. It's important to surround yourself with folks who will support you through it. Don't try to do it all by yourself. Don't try to figure it out by yourself and reinvent the wheel. Whether that means having a business partner or hiring your first assistant, *don't do it alone*. As Chris always says, someone has already done exactly what you want to do. Go find them. Grab onto the shirttails of someone who's still in the trenches.

My real passion is helping the struggling entrepreneur. If you're reading this and you don't think you can grow a big business or do a deal, take note: this is the only life you get. This is a business where you *can* arrange it so you're only doing stuff that you *enjoy* doing. You *can* do things that excite you. You *can* work from wherever you want—it's truly possible to do that. I had the same limiting beliefs that you might have right now. Chip away at them, and *work smarter*.

**Here's the key takeaway:** the more time you spend *building* your engine versus working *inside* the engine, the more successful you'll be, the longer you'll be able to stay in business, the more fun you'll have, and the more freedom you'll have to do what you really want to do in life and spend time with the people you want to be with.

Know that it's 100% possible to achieve that. Focus on building your engine. I want to leave you with those words of encouragement: it *is* possible. Take a deep breath. Realize that right in front of you are all the resources you need to make this a successful business. Now all you need to do is *execute*.

## TAKEAWAYS FROM THIS CHAPTER

1   Focus on learning how to do deals before you invest in software.

2   You'll eventually need a full-time lead manager nurturing the leads, answering the phones, and collecting the data.

3   Identify your limiting beliefs and *get rid of them!*

4   When you feel overwhelmed, list the tasks you hate to do and *hire someone else* to do them.

5   Don't try to have two careers at the same time; you'll half-ass them both.

6   Find the one thing you excel at and do that. (Read *The ONE Thing*, by Gary Keller.)

7   Surround yourself with people who understand your strengths and support you.

8   Don't go into real estate by yourself—get a partner, mentor, coach, or at least an assistant!

# STILL DOING THE
# LITTLE THINGS
# THAT MATTER

## Todd Smith

Todd Smith of Sarasota, Florida, has been an entrepreneur for over 35 years and has enjoyed extraordinary personal and professional success. He owned his first business at the age of 18, became one of the youngest real estate agents ever inducted into RE/MAX's Hall of Fame at 28, and became an internationally recognized leader and trainer of Direct Selling Mastery, earning—get this—$27 million over the last 23 years in that industry.

I met Todd at an industry meeting way back in the early 1990s and we've stayed connected ever since. Todd has conducted over a thousand training sessions and seminars for audiences around the world. He's also developed numerous training manuals and audio-visual sales tools, teaching entrepreneurs how to achieve professional success and accomplish their personal goals.

His journey taught him that success comes from the compounding effect of doing the little things correctly and consistently. He's the author, quite appropriately, of *Little Things Matter*, a resource for all those who place a priority on being the best they can be. It's the first step in a comprehensive program designed to help people improve their business and personal lives.

I wrote *Little Things Matter* because my life's journey has taught me is that it's not the big things that separate "the best of the best" from the rest—it's the little things. Reflecting back on my real estate career, I got started selling real estate at the age of 23, and that was 32 years ago. I made a quarter of a million dollars, and within four years, I was, at 28, the second-highest-producing real estate agent in the state of Illinois. I did set goals for myself, but it wasn't that I had a dream of being a top-producing real estate agent; it was all the little things I did as an individual to stand out from the rest.

Here are some of the "little things" I made sure to do:

- **Arrive at all my appointments five minutes early**
- **Ring the doorbell at the exact time of the appointment**
- **Smile and greet the prospective seller**
- **Make equal eye contact with husband and wife**
- **Show an interest in the children**
- **Take time to kneel down and pet the cats and dogs**
- **Talk about things of interest to them**
- **Send a hand-written thank you note**
- **Always be smiling, upbeat, pleasant, and focused on them**
- **Never bring in your mobile phone (in those days, it was a large one, but I still wouldn't bring mine in today. I focus on the people in front of me.)**

One of the biggest things for me was discipline: every day, I pushed myself to do what most people weren't *willing* to do. My discipline combined with my focus on making sure I was doing every little thing allowed me to achieve that success. I remember listening to Anthony Robbins's audio program *Unlimited Power*, which I'd recommend for any of you reading this. I made sure I was mirroring and modeling. If they talked slow, I'd talk slow. If they talked faster, I talked faster. If they seemed like they just wanted to talk and build more of a relationship, I'd talk and build more of a relationship. If it seemed like they wanted to talk business, I talked business. If they leaned forward, I leaned forward. I was always dressed in a suit and tie, and my shoes were always shined. I did every little thing I could to build a relationship, to connect with them, have them like me, and have them respect me. As a result, my closing rate was 92% over my career.

"Why," I asked myself, "was I so successful?" I didn't really understand it at the time; I was intentional about the little things, but I had no way of comparing myself to anybody else. Then I moved into a career in direct sales, as Chris indicated, and I continued to implement that strategy of looking at every little thing I could do to be better. I believed in the global economic system, which is that *income follows value.*

If you want your income to grow, your value must grow first. Very seldom in life does anybody get paid more than their value. If they are getting paid more than their value, one of two things happens: either their income comes down to their value, or their value goes up to their income. Just because you're choosing the real estate market and flipping homes, or buying and selling on terms like Chris and his family—or you're considering doing that—understand that your success is still going to be determined by your value.

You're not just going to say, "Okay, I'm choosing to do something different with my life and I'll go from making $20 an hour to $100 an hour." Life doesn't work that way. Certainly, the vehicle makes a big difference, but it's who you become *within* that vehicle that makes the biggest difference. There are people who make big money in everything in life. It's all about choosing the right vehicle and pursuing that.

The point that I really focused on was continuing to grow myself and be the best that I could be. When I say "the best that I could be," I don't just mean "the best that I could be in business," I mean being the best *person* I can be. You can't just be a certain way in your business life, then be someone different in your personal life. I'm striving to be the best husband I can be, the best father I can be, the best friend I can be, the best contributor to our community that I can be, *and* the best that I can be in my business. These are all based upon my priorities: what they are, and how much time I allocate to each.

In business, you are a reflection of who you are as a person. You build a brand for yourself, and that's who you are. Your brand isn't just a "business brand" that's different from your personal brand. No, your brand is more than brand. I'm somebody who has striven for excellence at these little things throughout my career, as a result of which, my businesses have sold over $2 billion and I've learned that there aren't very many people at the top—because most people aren't willing to put in the effort it takes to *get* to the top.

When you're successful, you often don't know why at the time. As I began to analyze why I was successful, I eventually came to determine that it was because I strove for excellence at the little things. I felt I wanted to write a book—not so much to make money (and I haven't made money with the book, but you don't write a book to make money; I know very few people who have made money writing books). I wanted to write a book that taught what I believed was the key to success. I wanted to highlight the things that I felt would have the greatest application to the broadest audience of people.

It doesn't matter what profession you're in. It could be about professional football—it's that wide receiver who can catch the ball with a defensive player in his face on a corner of the end zone and get his feet in bounds. Those are the guys who make it to the NFL. It's not the guy who can catch a football. Anybody can catch a football. Anybody can run. Anybody can run fast. There are a lot of people who can run fast and catch a football, but can you run fast and catch a football in the right circumstances, and handle pressure the right way?

It's not the big things, and I could give you analogy after analogy. It's not the big things that make the difference. It's you becoming the best at what you are doing. You become the best at what you're doing by honing in and refining and becoming the best at the little things. If you become great at all of the little things, the compounding effect of your intentional efforts allows you to become the best at what you're doing.

## Five Steps to Success

I have trained hundreds of thousands of people, and I'll tell you that everybody wants a better life. Everybody wants a nicer car. Everybody wants a nicer house. Everybody wants more money. Everybody wants to travel the world. Everybody wants a better quality of life. Everybody wants to put together five deals in six months. It all boils down to this: What are you willing to do to achieve that goal?

But you've got to set realistic goals. Working with entrepreneurs all over the world, I've found that 90% of people set unrealistic goals: again, somebody's making $20 an hour, and just because they begin to do something else, they think they're going to make $100 an hour. It doesn't work that way. The world doesn't work that way. That's pie-in-the-sky thinking.

For anybody who wants to do something, it's most important to begin by asking yourself, "Why? Why do I want to do this? How strong is my desire?" If you don't have a burning desire to be successful at anything you pursue, you're not going to be successful. It's not easy to be successful in life. I believe you can be great at *anything*, but you can't be great at *everything*. You have to pick what you're going to focus on—what you're going to be successful at.

**The first thing is desire: You've got to have a strong, burning desire to be successful,** a desire so strong that it will push you every day to do what's required of you. If you're not willing to do what's required of you, then you might as well not even start. This is how I coach everybody. I'm not the kind of person who plays games. I say, "Hey, if you're not going to do what's required of you to be successful, don't waste your life on this project; find something else that's important to you."

**Second, build your knowledge.** How can you be successful at something of which you have no knowledge? So you say, "Okay, how do I build my knowledge? How do I educate myself on this subject?" Obviously, I admire all of you who are taking the time to read this, because it tells me that you want to learn. You want to get better.

I talked to a guy recently who's at the absolute top of his game. He's unbelievably successful, and he listens to all of Chris's podcasts at 1.7 speed, just looking for a little nugget here and there. He says, "Hey, 99% of the time I spend listening to something, I might not be learning anything, but it's that 1%, that one thing I learn, that makes a difference." You have to continue to build your knowledge. You have to start building your knowledge, and then you have to continue building your knowledge.

**Third: What's your plan?** "Okay, so now I know what I want to be successful at. I've built up my knowledge. Now, what's my plan going to be?" Your plan needs to be not just the big-picture plan, but a plan broken down into what you should do every day. A lot of people will set a goal to close six deals, but they don't build their knowledge. They don't have any plan. They're just saying, "I'm going to do it." Life doesn't work that way, and that's not the kind of thinking that comes out of the mouth or mind of anyone who's ever been successful, because people who have been successful know that success takes time.

Success doesn't happen overnight. Yes, there are a few people who will put together six deals in six months. Nobody would've thought that I would have the success I did, selling 68 homes in my first year in real estate and making a quarter of a million dollars. Yes, it can be done, but it can only be done if you build your knowledge and you have a plan.

**Fourth, it's time to execute.** Let me just say that most people don't have enough of a desire to push themselves, so most people fail at step one. Of those who do have the desire, very few people will say, "Okay, let me build my knowledge on something." Then there's a smaller number of people willing to put together a plan to execute in order to achieve what they've set forth. By the time you get to step four—executing the plan—you're down to less than 2% of the people who have gone through the first few steps, and are disciplined enough to execute that plan with excellence.

**Step five is to refine.** Based upon what you've learned, you're refining, tracking all your numbers, looking at all your data, and you're asking, "Where do I refine? How do I get better? What parts of things am I focusing on that *aren't* working? What parts should I focus on that *are* working?" I determined very early on in my real estate career that I was going to focus on for sale by owners. That was my target market. I was very clear on my target market, and I determined that I was going to be the best at targeting that market.

What's *your* target market? You're going to try different things and say, "Well, that didn't work." You don't want to say that after trying one or two times. You need enough statistical data to say that something doesn't work. I called my first for sale by owner, and they agreed to meet with me. If the first 10 people I called had said, "No, the reason we're selling 'for sale by owner' is because we hate real estate agents," what would *that* have done to my psyche? But overall, my numbers were what they were, regardless of 10 nos in a row or 10 yeses in a row.

Expectations begin with goal-setting, and goal-setting depends on your true desire. You can set goals until you're blue in the face. If your desire isn't strong enough, you're not going to do what's required of you to achieve those goals.

If you have big goals and big expectations, then I hope you've already been successful at something else in life. If this is the first thing you're hoping to be successful at, and successful at an extraordinary level, that's highly unlikely to happen, whether it's this or something else. How many times have you met somebody who began to do something new and was amazingly great at it right out of the gate? I can't think of even one person, and I know a lot of people. That's why I say the best of the best are the best at the little things, and the top achievers are an inch wide and a mile deep in a single category.

As Malcolm Gladwell said in *The Tipping Point*, it's when you've logged 10,000 hours at something: you've learned enough, you've refined enough, you've executed enough, and you're now dialed into exactly what it is that you should be doing for the optimal level of conversions and success. I've hung out with Chris, for example, and I know the level of discipline he has in all five of these areas; I know the hours he's invested since 1991 in real estate, so the level of success he and his family are experiencing is no surprise to me. Success leaves clues—follow the path.

## Build Your Influence: Be Likeable and Respectable

Let's begin at the beginning—the foundation. John Maxwell says that "leadership is one word: influence." If I were to ask, "What describes influence?" the answer would be respect. If you are respected, you have influence. When you have influence, everything in life goes better. Trust falls under respect. You can be trusted but not respected, but you can't be respected and not trusted. If you're not trusted, you're not respected either.

Whether you're leading people who work with you, around you, or alongside you, your success with them is determined by how these people view you. If you want the ultimate success, you want to be the kind of person people look at and think, "I like him/her," and "I respect him/her." You want to build a brand that people think of and say, "I like you and I respect you."

If people can say, "I like you and I respect you," they'll want to do business with you, they'll want to come to your birthday party, to the talk you're giving about what you're doing. Your ultimate goal is to be a person of influence. If you want to be a person of influence where doors of opportunity open, where people look at you and say, "I want to do business with you," where people refer others to you, you need to be somebody who is liked and respected.

When you look at being liked, it's all the obvious things: smiling, having a pleasant personality, being positive and upbeat, not talking about negative things, not talking negatively about people—being a source of positive, upbeat energy. Whether it's over the phone and you're smiling while you talk, or you're meeting with somebody and smiling, and you're greeting them, and you're repeating their name, all of this is what makes you likable.

There are hundreds of factors that influence people's respect for you. Are you on time? Do you get back to people when you say you will? Do you schedule firm appointments or do you leave them vague and open? What does your communication look like? Do you open your emails by saying, "Hi Dean, I hope you had a great weekend?" and then dive into your subject in a new paragraph, and you have white space between your paragraphs, no big monster paragraphs, and everything is proofed, and your communication is clear and concise. What do your text messages look like? How long does it take you to respond to email? How long does it take you to respond to a phone call? How long does it take you to respond to a text? What is the tone in your communications?

These are the hundreds of things that I talk about in my blog and in my book. When you're meeting with somebody, do you let them finish talking before you talk? Are you quick to interrupt? When you're listening to people, can they tell you're listening intently, or do they think you're waiting to say something? When you're listening and looking at them, are you looking off to the side? All of these things influence people's respect for you and influence whether they like you.

If you want to be somebody who is highly successful at working with people—sellers, buyers, owners—you need to build a brand for yourself such that when people think of you and when they look at you they think, "I like him. He's different," or "I like her. I like the way she accepted responsibility for that challenge rather than making an excuse for it." Or, "Even though this was a challenging situation, I respected that he was always on top of his communication with me. I would love to do another deal with him," or "I certainly would not hesitate to refer any of my investor friends to her because of the way she handled herself during this entire transaction."

It's not just about getting the deal put together, so to speak. It's about how you handle everything from front to finish, and whether they want to do more business with you, and have talked about you to their investment clubs, and talked about you to their friends. People hang around people like themselves. People who own apartment buildings hang around other people who own apartment buildings. People who own multiple pieces of residential real estate hang around other people who own multiple pieces of residential real estate.

If you want to be highly successful in this career over the long term, these are the kinds of things you want to do. And by the way, "the long term" is what I'd be looking at. This isn't a six-month or one-year thing. Don't waste your time if that's what you're thinking. You won't be successful in anything saying, "I'm going to do this for six months to a year." You have to say, "Hey, this is what I want to do. I would love to build this into my lifestyle. I would love to be a guy/gal who can put together deals and make an income and build a residual income through investment properties. I'm going to become the best that I can be at this. What can I do to become the best?"

You have to look at everything, including your social media posts. Who is going to refer you to some of these people? Maybe it's the people who are following you on Facebook. You're putting pictures of yourself partying on there. Let me tell you, that's not an image that will cause people to respect you or even like you, so you've got to be thinking about everything. Your brand is your brand. You don't separate it. It's not like your brand in business is *this* and your brand in your personal life is *that*. No, your brand is your brand, and people aren't stupid. If you think they're stupid, you're wrong. They're going to see it and they're going to determine whether or not you're some-body they want to do business with. Maybe somebody asks them, "Hey, do you know Eric Milander?" "Yeah, I know Eric." "What do you think of Eric? I'm thinking about doing a deal with him." "Well, I wouldn't do a deal with Eric if my life depended on it," or "Eric is somebody I really like. He's a great guy. I love his personality. He just always seems to show interest in me. He's a good listener. He's highly responsible. Everybody I know who knows him thinks highly of him." This is the brand that you want to build if you want to be successful in the world of business. And if you want people to trust you with their money and their real estate, it's especially important to build this kind of a brand.

## Plan, Prioritize, and Act—Daily

Have a to-do list. I know what I need to do so the day is spent doing *one thing*. While I could have 20 other things on my to-do-list checked off in the same amount of time, those 20 things weren't more important than the one thing I did. Returning to my five steps to success, step three is when you put together your plan. Your plan must be broken down into what you're supposed to do every day, and arranged in priority sequence. If you've got a plan, ask, "What are the things I need to work on first in this plan? What are the things I need to work on second?" Then you need to decide, "I'm going to work on things in priority sequence," not "I'm going to work on the things I want to work on." The things that you don't want to do are the things that make you the most money. That's how life works. That's why I say of the thousand little things on my list, not one has a higher value to the market than discipline. Discipline is pushing yourself each day to do what you know you should do even when you don't feel like doing it.

If you want to be successful—and this is number one on my list—you've got to put first things first. You have to make sure you're spending your time doing exactly what you predetermined you should be doing with your time today to be productive. It might mean that you're sitting there with your phone in your ear and you're making outgoing calls, because you determined that the most important thing for you to do right now to achieve your goals is to prospect. If that's the case, then you put that phone to your ear and you prospect.

I remember when I was getting started in my various careers, I would sit at the phone all day and prospect. I remember there were days I made up to 300 phone calls. Why? Because that was what I had to do that day. I didn't sit there and say, "I'm going to redesign my brochure," or "I'm going to make my website look better," or "I'm going to make my business card look better," or "I'm going to think through my presentation again," or "I'm going to work on my phone script." No, it was me picking up the phone with my heart beating out of my chest, making phone call after phone call after phone call after phone call. It was refining my approach. When people didn't do business with me, I always asked them why, and I learned a lot by asking them why.

Number two for being productive is working your to-do-list in priority sequence, and pushing yourself to do the things that you know you should do without excuses and without justifying those excuses. You could say to yourself, "Today's not a good day for me to make prospecting calls because it's cloudy," or "today isn't a good day for me to make prospecting calls because I'm a little tired. I'm going to wait until tomorrow." This is what everybody says. This is what 99.9% of people do. They make excuses for not doing what they know they should do, whether it's eating right, exercising, prospecting, whatever it is they know they should do, most people don't do it—and that's why most people aren't successful.

You have to have a plan. That plan needs to be broken down into what you should be doing each day. You need to be executing that plan each day *with excellence*. You need to be looking at everything you're doing each day and saying, "How can I do what I'm doing better?" and then making adjustments. As Chris indicated, it's the compounding effect of these little things.

The first time you're focused on making equal eye contact with each person in the room, you may not be great at it, but if you work on it every time you're in a room of people, you're going to get a little bit better every time. Each time you're in a room like that, you're saying to yourself, "Okay, I'm going to be very deliberate in making sure everybody in this room feels included in the conversation." We all know we should remember names, but how often do we remember people's names? It's about being in the present. It's about being intentional: "I'm meeting somebody. I need to make sure I remember their name. Oh shoot, I forgot their name. Well, I have to get better tomorrow." It's about every day, pushing yourself to get better at the things you know you should be doing.

## More Good Stuff Where This Came From

If you visit my blog, there are no advertisements. It's not a blog set up to sell anything. Just go there, learn, have fun, and click through the archives so you can see all the different categories. You can scan the list of lessons and see what you think can help you at this point in your life. These are timeless life lessons, and I'm confident that if you really want to get better and improve yourself, you can do it that way.

Also, I want you to know that I've known Chris for a long time and I can tell you I've never questioned his business ethics once. I've never questioned his integrity. He's somebody I have the highest level of respect for, which is why I've agreed to contribute to his podcast and this book. You're dealing the kind of guy who *is who he is*: you're not seeing one guy on his podcast or in his office or as an author of this book, and a different guy at home. He's the same guy. He cares about people and he's very good at what he does—as is his whole family. My respect for Chris is at the top.

---

**Chris:** Do you want to dramatically increase your knowledge in your given field? In addition to reading daily, listen to a book on Audible (or another app) in your car, at the gym, walking, at the beach, or wherever else you can. I tend to read physical books on the bike at the gym, and when I'm on the elliptical machine, I listen to Audible at 1.25–1.5X speed.

Todd talks about time commitment. In our *5 Rules* video, which is a required view for all of our new associates, I discuss the importance of a three-year minimum commitment, without which you're simply kidding yourself. Real estate is not a get-rich-quick enterprise. There's no question that it offers a larger return than anything else I could do, but it will still require you to follow Todd's 5 steps.

## TAKEAWAYS FROM THIS CHAPTER

1 The "little things" are the small, meaningful actions that make your clients like and respect you.

2 Income follows value: you have to create higher value before you can create higher income.

3 The Five Steps to Success are: 1. Have a burning desire, 2. Build your knowledge, 3. Create a plan, 4. Execute the plan, 5. Refine.

4 Success comes after *a lot* of hours!

5 Each day, make a to-do list with the *one important thing* you need to do.

6 Don't procrastinate; do it even if you don't want to. The things that you don't want to do are the ones that make you the most money.

# 30+ YEARS IN THE NOTES BUSINESS

## And Still Coming Up With New Ideas

## Eddie Speed

Since 1980, Eddie Speed has dedicated his professional life to the seller-financing and non-performing note industries. Over the years, he's introduced innovative ideas and strategies that have made a positive impact on the way the industry operates today. Eddie founded NoteSchool, a highly-recognized training company specialized in the teaching of buying both performing and non-performing discounted mortgage notes. He's the owner and president of Colonial Funding Group LLC, which acquires brokers' discounted real estate secured notes.

In addition, he's also a principal in a family of private equity funds that acquires both portfolios of notes. He's been a leader and innovator in the note business for over 30 years, and he'll tell you that those 30+ years have prepared him for the incredible opportunities that the current real estate market is bringing.

I started in 1980, and I just kind of fell into the business. I started dating a pretty blonde girl, and her dad was in this unique business of buying discounted seller-financed notes. That was crazy foreign to me; I was intrigued by the story. I started serving an apprenticeship with him and another guy. They brought seller financing as a defined business to most of the United States.

## We Teach Because We Know What We're Doing

Most people who get into the note business started as real estate investors, mortgage guys, or something similar. I started with no background: I was so clueless when I started, I thought "a loan" was being by myself. There's no possible way I could have made it without these guys when I was getting started (I want you to remember that I've mentioned how important my apprenticeship was to me, and how important mentoring is in general—for anyone.) That's why I didn't start NoteSchool until I'd been in the business for 20 years. I wanted to be confident in my knowledge of the business before I started trying to offer my services as a coach. Obviously, I didn't necessarily need 20 years, but I wanted to get it right. Chris and I both put a strong emphasis on making sure the person teaching a class really knows what they're talking about. But how do you *know* if they know what they're talking about? For starters, check and make sure they're still in the business of *doing* what they're teaching, not just teaching. We have a certain volume of notes under management—altogether, a $50 million portfolio—so we're not teaching something we aren't also doing. Likewise, Chris and his family are buying, selling, and constructing deals every week. We all have our fingers on the pulse of our respective markets.

## The Lost Art of Seller-Financed Notes

If you looked at my career, you'd say, "Eddie Speed is a seller-financed note guy." I started buying seller-financed notes in 1980. I developed the note system for HomeVestors in the early 1990s. HomeVestors was probably the first national real estate investor to embrace the idea of "We're going to create seller-financed notes, and then we're going to sell them to Eddie Speed."

I also did it for a lot of other investors, but along the way I developed a process so that, when you created a seller-financed note, you knew that it was salable in the secondary market for its greatest value. So seller financing has always been a theme with us, although we bought a lot of non-performing notes. We buy institutional notes that are called "re-performing notes." Citigroup or somebody like that gets the loan, it's paying again, now it's on track. Then we go buy those notes from the bank. So we do buy institutional notes, but among real estate investors, we'd be recognized as seller-finance guys.

Buying properties with seller financing is, as they say, "a lost art," or, as others say, "an art that was never really perfected." There are a few really seasoned people like Chris and me who regularly buy property with seller financing. So people don't consider me a real estate guy, but I am. People will generally object, saying, "No, I don't want to do that." Then, as Chris teaches, you get into their pain. You try to understand exactly what their issues or challenges are, and you offer to help with those things. If I say, "Sir, would you consider carrying financing for me?" Or, "Sir, what's the most important thing to you? Getting the highest dollar price for your property, or getting all the cash upfront? If you had to pick from those two, best price or most cash up front, which of the two would you pick?"

So now I'm starting to get into the seller's head and predict how they'd go about structuring the deal, if they were to do something. Let's say that the seller says, "Well, I don't know." And I say, "Well, let's talk about an option, sir. What if I could get you some cash up-front—maybe 30% of the price—*and* I could get you future income that would maximize what you could sell it for? Would that be something we could talk about?"

Then, all of a sudden, you can get it with seller financing. Readers may say, "Oh gosh, but I'd have to pay 30% down." No. What we might do is structure a first and a second, and have them sell the first to me and the seller keep the second.

## Build Your Own Bank with Good-Quality Notes

You have to think backwards and understand that if you're going to create notes, you're essentially building your own bank. Whether you're going to sell those notes (and hopefully you'd consider somebody like us to buy them) or whether you're going to keep the notes for yourself, you need to have that mentality: *I'm building a bank, and these are the people who are going to owe me money.* You also need to do your due diligence and make sure it's a win for you *and* a win for them; that's owning a portfolio.

Another caution is against creating notes that aren't good quality. You'll find yourself having to rework them and redo them all the time, or, catastrophically, you'll have to foreclose. That's owning a business, and it's not the same as owning a portfolio, which is something that lets you retire.

## The People Business

I'm a people person. I'm a communicator. And I have dyslexia. I've always considered it God's idea of a joke that I'm a guy in the paper business who struggles with reading.

Most of these business that have to do with buying real estate or buying notes are about *deal flow*. If you're in the deal flow business, you're in the people business, because people are making decisions about selling these assets. I'm buying notes *at a discount*. Guess what? When I give them the price, they're going to figure out that I'm offering less than the full amount of the note. Now the negotiation begins, because guess what they *don't* want? They don't want to sell their note at a discount; they want all the money. They want no discount at all, and here I am, trying to buy it as cheap as I can.

People think we're not in the paper business, that we hide behind a computer screen and just run numbers all day. And part of this business *is* running all the numbers. I'm not saying you can just skip that; you need to learn it. But equally important is that I bought 40,000 owner-financed notes at a discount. That's a whole bunch of notes, but I've heard a whole bunch of nos too.

## Making It Beyond Survival

My biggest win was when I crossed the bridge to where I wasn't chasing deals to survive every month and every quarter. When you have enough income every month to know that you could go three months, and if you bought no deals, you'd survive. That's the wealth everybody wants to achieve in the business. Of course, mine is more focused on owning notes, which means they're making payments every month. For some people in the terms business, it could be lease option income, or it could be rental income, or the three pay-days Chris and his team have brilliantly engineered and teach. But I think that's the win that anybody gets to when you've been at it long enough: when you don't have to chase the next deal to make sure you're going to survive, there's a freedom in that.

## Teaching Better Business

I'm really surprised at how much I love teaching, because I was a note guy for 20 years, and to be perfectly honest, I was sort of an anti-guru guy. I saw all those guys on late-night TV back in the 80s and 90s and thought, "I don't ever see *them* out in the trenches." So I was surprised that I ended up getting into the teaching business—and I was surprised at how much I loved it. I really was. I originally got into the business in order to teach my customers how to do it, so I could do business with them. That was the whole purpose: it was just customer training so that they could create better businesses and I could have more deal flow. Then I fell in love with training people.

Our executive team has bought about $3.5 million in discounted notes. We've got an executive team in the note space like no one else today. Many of these people came from other, bigger institutional investors that bought seller financing, and now they've joined up with us. But it's not Eddie: It's a team of people with experience. What we've learned overall is that we're not going to run out of things to teach. We've got classes and high-end training, and I do place a value on that. But NoteSchool's got plenty of good stuff for free: several days of training that we're happy to give to people.

## Know When to Quit

I've been through some cycles. I was living here in Texas in the late 80s, the "RTC days" (RTC for Resolution Trust Corporation). The most profitable business in Texas back then was the sign company changing names out in front of the banks. Then there was a pretty good speed bump in the late 90s, and Lord knows I lived through 2008. I've seen all these things.

My weakness as an entrepreneur is that I've given up *too slowly* on some things. There were times when I should have given up sooner, and I didn't. If you ask 200–300 people who know me well (some of whom Chris knows very well), "What is Eddie's number-one strength?" they'd say, "He's a tenacious soul. I mean, when that dude locks his horns on something, he won't give up."

## Get Ready to Roll Up Your Sleeves

I had a conversation with this guy the other day about somebody pursuing the business. We were talking about them getting all excited, wanting to pursue real estate investing or notes. And 90 days later, they were saying, "I don't know if this is going to work!" If you *don't* feel that way, I don't know what business you're in. This is part of being an entrepreneur. So you have to make sure you have a good plan, and then you need to know that there are going to be some speed bumps you'll have to ride out. But keep that desire in your heart and soul that says, "I want more for myself." That's it.

You have to realize that if you want what almost every American wants—to have a business for yourself, financial independence, time, and all the things that come with success—there's no other way but to work for it. There's a lot of gray area between here and the end of that story. It doesn't have to be 20 years, but you do have to be tenacious. Anything you can get good at—sports, music, or whatever—you have to work at it *obsessively* before you reach perfection—and this business is no different. Honestly, I was very lucky that I enjoyed the journey. It *is* fun. The more awareness people have of where they're going, where they're at, and how they're adjusting, that will take away some of the anxiety, and that makes a difference. But I look back and think, "I'd never have dreamed that I could be in a business for 37 years and love it this much." I can say that with integrity.

## Learn How to be a Deal Architect

I've worked with a lot of real estate investors, so if you're going to work at owner financing, and buying property with owner financing, learn how to structure it properly. And if you're going to owner finance property, or you're going to have a financial structure that involves future cash flow, learn how to structure that correctly.

For most of my early career, in the 1980s, I mainly bought notes from individuals who owner financed property—what I call "mom-and-pops." They owner financed one house, their personal home, and never created another note.

In the 90s, the way we grew our volume so much was by dealing with real estate investors. They created owner-financed notes and came to us to sell them. They'd show up with an owner-financed note, and it was structured wrong, it was poorly underwritten—just *wrong, wrong, wrong.* There are things they could have done, but they didn't know any better. Then they'd be frustrated when we offered them a substandard price. So I'd say, "Wait a minute, guys. Let me show you how to cook this pie before you start cooking it. Let's get the ingredients right so that, when you turn out, you got a perfect pie that's the highest value."

For most readers, let us help you with the formula of how to create financial structures. This is what I call being a "deal architect," so that you can do it in a way that gives you the highest and best results.

---

**Chris:** In my first book, *Real Estate on Your Terms*, I call the "deal architect" the "master transaction engineer." Eddie and I are both telling you: Arm yourself with this knowledge so you can walk into almost any deal in any format, at any price level and understand how to structure things.

## "Windshield Time" and Other Daily Disciplines

A very wise man told me many years ago, "Eddie, it's first things first, and second things not at all." For a long time, I've had more to do than I could get done on my to-do list every day. Theoretically, you make your to-do list every day, you click through it and get it all done with plenty of time to spare. You rub your hands together and say, "What a day! I'm going to start my list for tomorrow." But you and I know it never works that way. We constantly have to prioritize. So just know that prioritizing is number one. You're not going to get it all done; you have to be wise and focus on that priority.

Second, you must have good communication with the people who are key to your business. I have a number of different business entities that are run by very high-level people. I entrust the daily operations of the business to them, and they make the daily decisions. Nevertheless, I try to stay connected with them. The direction *they* see things are going is what we need to be talking about. So prioritize your key people and make sure you're spending enough time with them. I have some of the most seasoned people you'll ever meet in the notes business around me every day. And yet, we debrief about things that a beginner might look at and say, "Well, that's obvious." But there's so many strategic moves, it's *not* always obvious. That's why communication is so important.

Third is "windshield time." I live in Texas, and I don't work out of my house. I have an office, and I have staff. It's a drive to work every day for me. But even if you work from home, make your own "windshield time." It's quiet time to stop and reflect on your business, and make good notes to yourself. Think through what you're doing and don't let the everyday noise confuse you.

---

**Chris:** For me, it's two or three early mornings around 3:00–3:30 AM at Anytime Fitness, and it's not just about working out, even though that's super-important to me. It's also a great start of the day: it's "windshield time" for my mind, reading, reflecting, focusing for the day. Super-important. If this isn't already your routine , visit the **New Rules resources page** at TheNewRulesBook.com and grab the **Power of One Daily Discipline Chart** and **Explanation**.

## Rebuilding the Seller Finance Industry

I've put some components in place to rebuild the seller finance industry as I saw it in the 1990s and early 2000s. My managing director was originally at The Associates, and then he was at Bay View and ran their seller finance piece. They were buying between $200 and $400 million in owner-financed notes a year. But that market dried up because there was no institutional money to invest in these notes.

After studying the business for a long time, I figured out that what the industry lacked was reliable capital to fund these note transactions—if they were good notes. So what's our biggest resource in the marketplace today? The answer: dry cash from passive investors. The institutional money is probably not going to get back in the note space for different market conditions and reasons. It doesn't mean that it's a bad business, just that they've moved in a different direction. I don't see them necessarily coming back at that level. But there's a crazy amount of dry cash, particularly in self-directed retirement accounts. And this investor lacks deal flow.

So what we've focused on is bringing good deals into the marketplace, putting those deals in our capital fund, aging them over a certain period of time, then pushing them out the other end to a passive investor who just wants to own one note. We have a website called notesdirect.com, and that's its total focus. I've spent about three years gluing this together.

## Pitch Anything

I'm reading a great book—not a new book—called *Pitch Anything*. It gives you methods for presenting and persuading. What a lot of us entrepreneurs lack is the understanding that, at the end of the day, we're *selling* our businesses. We're *presenting* our businesses. If you're in the terms business, you're presenting the different financial deal structures, you're presenting *yourself* to the customers.

**Chris:** I've read it, as have my kids (our team), and it's one of many must-reads.

## Use Your Strengths

There are times when I've lost sight of my strengths. I was trying to emulate somebody else's business, and they were good at different things than I was. If I could go back, I'd sit down and counsel myself: *Eddie, you're unique. You have some unique skills, talents, and gifts.* Earlier, I mentioned my tenacity and my knack for communications. *Eddie, you need a business that focuses on those skills. You're not necessarily the accountant type. That doesn't mean you can't hire one, but you personally aren't one. And you need to build a business that lets you be good at what you're good at.* The roughest times for my business were when I wasn't clear about that.

## Strategies for Success

For most of us in the notes business, we're in some form of sales and negotiations. So if you're starting out, you have to be cognizant of that. Negotiation, really, is discovering people's needs and meeting them there. It's not necessarily a bartering price. It would be very hard to build an entrepreneurial business and not have sales and negotiation skills. So focus on them.

Don't paint yourself into a corner as a real estate investor. Think of yourself as a real estate entrepreneur, solving challenges and problems for people. The longer most people spend in real estate, the more they want to be the bank and the less they want to be the landlord. There are some things about this business that can help accelerate that, no matter what phase you think you're at.

---

**Chris:** If you're not sure whether to give up or grind it out in a particular situation, find someone who knows. Success leaves clues, and I promise there's someone who has experienced what you're going through.

After you settle in with the high-payoff strengths that you know you're great at, outsource the rest. I use Leverage, a high-level outsourcing company; you can find a link for them and get a free month on the **New Rules resources page** at TheNewRulesBook.com

## TAKEAWAYS FROM THIS CHAPTER

1   If you're in the real estate or notes business, you're in a *people* business—so learn some *people skills*. Learn how to communicate and how to negotiate.

2   Know when to quit. You'll avoid some major losses if you can admit you made a mistake and pull out. Also, know when to grind it out and make it work.

3   Expect to work hard—but learn to enjoy it!

4   Learn how to be a deal architect so that you can walk into any situation and structure an appropriate deal.

5   Daily disciplines: prioritize your to-dos, communicate with your key personnel, and make time for reflection.

6   Build a business that lets you really be good at *what you're good at*.

# YOUR "CLEANER" FOR ANY TAX ISSUE

## Gerry Delang

In 2001, Gerry had the opportunity to fill a huge need in the marketplace. He founded End Tax Problems to help taxpayers navigate and resolve their very painful tax issues. This company has successfully represented thousands of people over the years, restoring peace and sanity to their lives. I have personally done business with Gerry—years back—and you're going to see why what he and his team do is so incredibly effective. They've helped folks from all walks of life, from the long-term non-filer to the affluent businessperson facing payroll tax and personal tax issues. There's no single category that fits all their clients. Life events like health crises, divorces, business failures, accidents—all the things I deal with as an investor with homeowners—can often throw what was once an orderly financial life into disarray. Gerry has many seasoned agents and tax professionals on his team who have been working together for almost 20 years. If you have tax problems—big or small, business or personal—Gerry's team is here to serve you.

In 1998, Congress held a special session to deal with the IRS, which was out of control. We used to call the IRS agents the "black hats," because when they came to check on you, they could do just about anything they wanted to: they could put a lock on your door, take all of the money out of your bank accounts. So in 1998, Congress came up with the Taxpayer Bill of Rights, which created a whole new "tax resolution" industry.

As a result, a friend of mine started a company in Charleston, South Carolina. He knew I had an accounting background so he said, "Gerry, why don't you come up? We're doing something really special here. I'd like to lay it out for you and tell you what we're doing." Well, I get to Charleston, South Carolina, and there's a building, probably only 5,000 square feet, crammed with ex-IRS people: high-level commissioners, district commissioners, district directors, people with every possible area of expertise who had left the IRS because of the new rules and wanted to put their expertise to work on the outside. My friend had hunted them down, hired them, and created this business.

From 1999–2000, I immersed myself in that culture, learning from the best of the best what this new tax act meant, how to implement it, and how it benefited taxpayers. I had the opportunity to learn intensively about how to take care of the taxpayer: all the secrets, all the tricks, things that no one even *knew about* at the time. There were no books, no seminars, no webinars—everything was straight from the horse's mouth. So that's how I started—by helping *them* get started. After two years, in January of 2001, I left for Lake Mary, Florida, and eighteen years later, we're still here, in the same building.

## Personal tax issues that can cause huge stress

There's a whole spectrum of problems an individual or a business can have with the IRS. Let's begin with the individual: a personal tax issue can result from an early withdrawal from an IRA or 401k. It creates a cash crunch. Cash flow is an issue. Let's say you take the money out and don't have withholding. You forget to pay the tax, you forget to put it on the tax return. Two years later, the IRS sends you a notice that you owe $40,000 plus the penalty and interest. That's a very common personal IRS problem.

Another can be a result of a life event—divorce, illness, job loss—again, it's a cash crunch situation. You don't file your returns on time and they pile up: three, four, five years go by, and all of a sudden, five years of returns is a whole bunch of money to pay the IRS. What do you do? How do you start? How do you get back into the system without getting in trouble? At my firm, we do that all the time for folks—every year, all year round. We call it reentry. There are a host of life events that can cause upset in your tax life and we relieve stress by helping you.

Divorce can be a really big deal: whether it's a good divorce or a bad divorce, things get messy. Let's say the husband is a contractor, so he's a Schedule C. Maybe his wife's a schoolteacher or a nurse, so she's a W-2 and has withholding. When the marriage goes south, they get all tangled up. The lawyers get involved, and you hear, "Well, my refunds went to his taxes, and he still owes taxes." We sort out those kinds of issues with the divorce attorney or with the couple and determine the right path for taxes, for now and going forward. That's a common one—it's a life event you don't plan on. But when it happens, it can get complicated tax-wise too.

Ultimately, it's all about cash flow. When you've got plenty of money, you can just throw money at a problem. If the tax man comes and says you owe $130,000, and you have $5 million in the bank, what do you do? You write a check—you don't even think about it. It's over in eight seconds. But if he says you owe $130,000, and you have $30,000 in the bank, that's a problem. I know Chris talks about this, because people come to him in debt, or simply wanting (or needing) to produce income. As he always tells them, massive cash flow can solve a lot of problems, but it can also *help* you create a lifestyle that money *can't* buy (experiences with family, etc.)." So let's get you through your tax issues, but let's also make sure that you're generating massive cash flow with Chris's system or something like it. Get going on your cash generation—you'll be glad you did.

## Tax Issues for Small Business Owners and the Self-Employed

Let's move on to the small business: it's typically not a corporation, or if it is, it's an LLC, 100% owned, one owner, one member. All the income or loss generated by that LLC reverts to your personal tax return, so ultimately, it's your tax liability. You've got a Schedule C that you run your expenses through—and your business expenses—and that's how you minimize your taxable income. For most people who report that way, it takes a long time—years and years, even decades and decades—to gradually "tune-up" so they're getting the right expenses on the Schedule C, they're not putting them on the Schedule E, and they're building a nice tax return that

1 won't get them audited

2 optimizes their tax liability

3 gives them peace of mind (they know they're doing things right, and they know how to account for their expenses)

But the IRS is getting tougher and tougher now on Schedule C. Some things (like mileage), they won't allow you to claim without proof anymore. Maybe you're on the road a lot for your business. Here in Florida, we have a lot of reps who drive the state—300, 400, 500, maybe even 1,000 miles a week—and they've got to keep track of their miles. It's easy these days, with apps that plot your miles (you can print them or put them right into your QuickBooks. So if you're driving a lot, start keeping track of your miles with one of those apps. Otherwise, you might get a nasty letter from the IRS, asking you to prove your mileage—and if you don't prove it within 30 days, it's disallowed. If you want to get it approved, you go to appeals. Now you're talking about hours of headaches, penalties, and unnecessary disruption to your life.

Independent contractors, landscapers, pool maintenance technicians, photographers, and other Schedule C workers often have intermittent cash flow: a good month, then a bad month, a good quarter, then a bad quarter—but the IRS still expects you to make *estimated payments* based on what you paid in taxes the year prior. Something I see all the time is that people stop making their estimated payments, and when it's tax time, they get an extension. On October 1, they start getting everything together, and find out they owe $35,000—and they didn't make any estimated payments! Now what do they do? This is the most common problem I see for small businesses.

People who work on 1099s—real estate agents, mortgage brokers, any kind of salesperson—you feel like you make a few bucks, but you barely get by. You have your mileage deductions and so on. Come tax time, you still owe something, maybe your self-employment tax, but something. So you say to yourself, "I'll have a better year next year. I'll take care of it next year." I saw a lot of that in the crash. Real estate agents, mortgage brokers, anyone connected to construction or real estate who'd been a 1099 in the boom years, and suddenly... No job, no income, no money to pay taxes. What do you do? This is a very common IRS problem.

---

**Chris:**  Gerry is describing exactly what happened to me: when the crash happened in 2008, the end of the year came, and I said, "OK, we'll figure it out next year," but then it was too late. But talking to Gerry is like talking to a really good attorney—he relieves stress. I called him up (we'd met previously through a family connection), I signed off on some papers, Gerry called the IRS, structured the payment plan, and told me what to do. Done! I never looked back. It was that simple. I don't want readers who've gone through a major life event to think they're alone. These things happen all the time, and Gerry and his team can help you. Don't be embarrassed or nervous. Get Gerry's info from the **New Rules resources page** at **TheNewRulesBook.com** and give him a ring.

## Get Your Head Out of the Sand

Sometimes, a tax problem becomes an excuse for not going out and doing your best—doing whatever you can do, making as much money as you can make. Some people become like ostriches, burying their heads in the sand. They don't know what to do, so they just limp along in life. That's no way to solve a problem!

The value we bring to the table is to say, "Listen, we're going to identify the problem with the IRS, we're going to get accurate information from the IRS, and then I'm going to get some accurate information from *you*: What are you doing? What is your income? What are your expenses? Let's put it all in a snapshot and see where we are today, February 15, at 12:20 PM. Forget February 14 and before, forget February 16 and after. We're going to handle your situation today, February 15. Where are we? *We'll* call the IRS—you'll never have to talk to them. We know how to deal with them. We create a game plan based on what the IRS tells us and what you tell me. We get you back out on the playing field, back in the game of life—looking forward, not backward.

When you leave today, nothing about your situation has changed: you're not walking out with more money than you had before, because I don't loan money (in fact, you probably paid *me* some money), your IRS problem is still out there—but we've got a game plan now to get past it, whatever we have to do. And *we* handle it: you never have to worry about the IRS again as long as you do what we advise. When you signed those papers that allow us to contact the IRS on your behalf, you put this behind you; it's in your rear-view mirror.

Now you walk out of this office, you get back to work, and you forget about it. That's how you get your life moving again when you have an IRS problem. You don't dwell on it. You don't think about all the hypotheticals. You identify the facts, get accurate information, and then have someone who's done it before take care of the IRS while you get busy with your life again.

## How we provide the stress relief remedy

As soon as we're authorized to represent a client, we start gathering accurate information—first of all, from the taxpayer. So we might ask you for a copy of the last tax return you filed. Let's see what it looks like. If it's the one that incurred the liability, all the better. If not, no big deal. Then, with your authorization, we call the IRS. We have software that can download the last 20 years of your tax records directly from the IRS and put them in a readable format for our team. It red-flags everything that's a problem, whether it's a penalty, a late filed return, an unfiled return, a liability, assessed liabilities, or tax liens. It gives us a snapshot of what's going on in your tax life right now, as far as the IRS is concerned. We see everything that the IRS sees about you. Then, based on our experience, we can say, "This is what's going to happen next. Here's what we need to do. Here's how we can best resolve this for you." This is exactly what we did for Chris all those years ago: we set him up with a payment plan, we never discussed it again, and he never thought about it again. We've also helped many of his family's buyers who are doing rent-to-own and needed help with past liens, past tax problems, or other IRS-related challenges.

We keep the power of attorney for a year to make sure we get a copy of all the letters and see that everything cleared. Once we see that everything is cleared up, all the payments are done, and the accounts are zeroed out, we say, "You're on your own. Hopefully you'll never need us again, but you may know someone else who does"—and that case is over. We take it from start to finish, and you just take your marching orders from us. We tell you what to do, how to resolve it, and you never worry about it. You probably don't see a tenth of what we see.

## Are you in the crowd? Do you know someone who is?

In a crowd of 200 people, I guarantee you 60 of them have an IRS issue of some sort. I would say something like this to them: "If you're out there in the crowd today, you don't have to raise your hands. I've done this enough to know that 50 or 60 of you folks have an IRS issue of some sort. Maybe it's tiny, maybe it's huge, maybe it's been hanging over your head for six, seven, eight years. You don't know where to go. Maybe you called an 800 number you saw on TV and got less than favorable treatment. But I know you're out there. And here's what I want to tell you: if you haven't filed a return, whether it's a year late or 10 years late—I've even seen returns that were 30 years late!—get a hold of us. On a 10-minute phone call, we can tell you a little bit about what we can and can't do, and get you started on the road back to being a taxpayer in good standing. The longer you wait, the worse it gets. The IRS is not going away. So number one, if you haven't filed, give us a call."

"Number two, maybe you filed, but you haven't paid or made arrangements yet. I know there's a bunch of you out there with that problem right now, ducking the letters—maybe you've moved and they don't know where you are yet. You're on your way to becoming a non-filer, because if you owe, you're not going to file, because you don't want to talk to the IRS. So if you've filed and you owe, call us—before you become a non-filer. We can go in and look at your file with the IRS, see where your taxes are from and what they've assessed in penalties. Do you have liens yet? We might catch them before they file a lien, which would be a huge help to you. So don't wait; call us today and we'll get accurate information and give you a game plan."

"Number three, maybe you're already on a payment plan—the kind we call the 'payment plan for life,' because it seems like you'll be paying them *forever*. I've heard that a hundred times. But there's still a good reason to call us, even if you're under a payment plan: you may be paying *penalties* you're not aware of that we could get abated, reducing your liability. There may be a lien event coming up in which the lien is about to come off your credit. I can give you a little heads-up on the lien. There may be a way to settle your debt if it's substantial enough. If you owe $200-300,000, we might be able to get you settled up for less than what you owe pretty quickly. We can do that in the next six to nine months and get this behind you *now*—instead of six, seven, eight, or nine years from now. So if you owe and you're under agreement and you think you've got everything handled, there may still be a way for us to improve your situation, by eliminating some penalties, handling a lien situation, or in some cases, doing the analysis and saying, 'You know what? I think we can save you some dough.'"

"Last but not least is number four—and it's a big one. Let me tell you a story: I just got a veterinarian down here in Florida; he went through a divorce up in the Panhandle, moved down here and bought into a practice, and he's putting his life back together. He owes the IRS $300,000. He's got a new CPA, who calls me and says, 'Hey Gerry, we'd love to take this guy on, but he's got this *issue*. You've got to clean him up for us before we can handle him.' Not a problem. The CPA also says, 'The IRS just told us they want $85,000 by next month, or they'll levy everything he's got.'"

"We got involved, and we did exactly what we'd do with anybody: we got authorized, we downloaded his last 20 years, went through them with a fine-tooth comb, and learned that the $85,000 the IRS wanted was going to expire in six or seven months. That's why they were so hot to collect it. So the veterinarian (wisely) hired us, and we put the IRS on hold, sparred with them for the six or eight months, and the $85,000 fell off. He never had to pay it! That was a big win. Then we restructured the rest of the debt (I found a couple of penalties to get rid of), he paid that off in about 18 months, and then he was a happy, happy guy. We saved him that $85,000 plus probably about $40–50,000 in penalties—half of what he owed. He was three days away from writing them an $85,000 check for fear that he'd lose everything else. That's a good example of what divorce does, and what avoiding tax problems can do."

Back in the here and now, let me ask you this: If you knew with certainty that a free 10-minute phone call could set you on the path to resolving the IRS issue that's been with you for a month, 10 years, 20 years—however long it's been—wouldn't you make that call?

---

**Chris:**   When faced with a challenge like I was in 2008, it's best to do three things:

1   Find a mentor who will help guide you.

2   Work in "chambers." That means when you have an IRS issue, you hand it off to a specialist like Gerry. Then you go about your business and close that chamber door. You don't dwell on it.

3   Go create immediate cash flow with massive action. We can help you there!

You may think you're alone with your challenges, but others have been where you are now. Look for someone who's gone through similar circumstances—they can help you. Find them!

There's a great book I recommend to everyone: *Profit First*. Find out more about the author, Mike Michalowicz, on the **New Rules resources page** at **TheNewRulesBook.com**

My CFO is certified by him, and let me tell you, if you follow Mike's system, you'll never have a tax challenge. Regardless, *Profit First* is a must-read.

## TAKEAWAYS FROM THIS CHAPTER

1   Lots of people have tax problems—you're not alone. Speak up!

2   Don't run from the IRS. Get help and *do something* about it. The longer you wait, the worse it will get.

3   If you're a contractor filing a 1099 rather than a W-2, don't forget to make your estimated income tax payments every quarter.

4   If you deduct mileage, track it with an app designed for that purpose—the IRS now requires you to be able to prove it!

# CPA AND TAX WIZARD

## Paul Dion

**Paul Dion is my tax specialist—my CPA—and also assists many of our associates (students who have signed up for one of our Associate Levels to do deals) around the country, and Paul is meeting their tax and accounting needs. Paul operates a New England regional CPA practice specializing in proactive tax planning for business owners. He has offices in Millbury, Massachusetts and Newport, Rhode Island, right here in the same building as us. He has worked on my finances for years and recently came on board in one of our entities as CFO.**

I am a certified public accountant and a certified tax coach. I can work anywhere in the United States where there's a tax return to be done. If you're far away, obviously, we'd be interacting virtually—by phone, Zoom, or Skype, whatever you prefer—and I'm already doing that with many of the **Smart Real Estate Coach** students.

I've been in and out of corporate America, but I've had a tax practice since 1987. Some years, it was part-time while I was a corporate controller, and some years it was full-time. In 2006 I went completely full-time and changed the nature of the practice from just *tax preparation* to *tax planning* so I could save people money. I have more fun saving clients' money and helping them strategize than I do just filling in blanks on a form.

## The IRS will Find You

Talking to people, I've found that one of the biggest misconceptions they have is thinking they need to find an IRS-approved expense list to work from—but nothing like that exists. The rule is that if it's an *ordinary and necessary expense* to your business, then it's deductible. I try to tell people to talk to their tax advisor if they're not sure. It's better to hear no, and why, than never to ask.

Another issue is folks waiting until the last minute, or putting it off several years. Eventually, the IRS is going to find you. Trying to hide from them doesn't make a lot of sense. In fact, I've got a video going out this week with the line, "Are you hiding from the IRS for a very particular reason?" I try to show people the importance of getting their returns done.

If you owe money, it's better to get on a payment plan with the IRS than to do nothing, because the penalties are cut in half if you're on an installment agreement. The danger is if you haven't filed and they find you first: then, as far as they're concerned, you're very uncooperative; they get much more ruthless than if you volunteer to get it done first. There's a gentleman Chris has had on his podcast and on various conference calls who specializes in IRS negotiation on your behalf—Gerry Delang. I know he set up a payment plan for Chris years ago after the 2008 real estate crash, and not only was it very economical for him, it took away a lot of stress. He was able to go on with his life and his business. You can read his chapter in this book and get his information from the **New Rules resources page** at TheNewRulesBook.com.

The other problem with waiting is that sometimes people find that they have refunds they didn't even know they had. If you're owed a refund and you wait more than three years, it's gone. You can never get it. So it's better to get things done than to wait.

Finally, people in the real estate world sometimes don't see the difference between a *passive* activity (usually real estate rental), versus an *active* activity (property flips, being a real estate agent, or operating a business). They're two different worlds in terms of taxability and the structure you need to put in place in order to reduce your taxes as much as possible. It's very important to meet with an appropriate tax advisor who can tell you what the structures need to be and what the planning needs to be for either of those. There are different answers for the two worlds. I've been doing all the tax work and planning with Chris and his entities for several years, so I know all the nuances and how the terms business can and should be structured.

## Plan Ahead

In our practice, we prefer to sit with people and plan. If they have an emergency, we're going to deal with that first, but we prefer sitting with people and putting a plan together for them. That helps us determine where they need to go in different areas of their business or personal planning. Often it may involve setting up LLCs or corporations. Or it depends on other things in their personal lives that a tax return won't tell me. We may structure things differently for a short period of time to take care of those needs. This is not about a tax return; it's about proper overall planning.

For the real estate investors out there, I want to tell you that absent something else going on in your life, it probably makes sense to compartmentalize your risk from a legal perspective, whether it's an LLC or a corporation. If it's an operating business, I'm probably going to recommend an S corporation. But I've also had clients for whom an S corporation could get in the way of their exit strategy. That's why it's important to have a conversation first, to know not only what you're planning to do with your businesses, but *how you plan to get out of it* at the end, because that could change what we do with you and for you.

I'll give you an example from outside of real estate: somebody was building a business, and expected to sell it in five years for several million dollars. There's a strategy that only works with one kind of entity that allows you to avoid taxes on $10 million of gain. I'd probably give up this year's savings on an S corporation for the savings on $10 million and no taxes five years from now.

## This is Not a Do-It-Yourself Thing

One of the other big mistakes people make is that they start the business deciding to be do-it-yourselfers. You need an accountant, and you probably need a lawyer who knows what he's doing, and a good mentor—especially with real estate. All of us entrepreneurs are out there alone, so I think it's wise to think about joining a mastermind group, or a board of directors—even if it's virtual—to be able to get advice from people. Don't try to do it by yourself.

I happen to be Chris's CFO now, but before that we still met regularly and brainstormed. I'm going to come at this from an accounting standpoint and then you'll also want to do what Chris does and get the legal side handled—because the two affect each other. I know Chris uses Lee Phillips for all of that, and Lee and I communicate together as needed with different entities for clients.

I'm involved in more than one mastermind group right now. The real value is that I'm able to bounce ideas off of people who don't do taxes, because my mastermind is outside of my industry. (Although I do have a second mastermind in the Midwest that's tax-related.) In all of these cases I'm able to get ideas that I'd never have thought of. Sometimes it's just taking an idea I already have and tweaking it slightly when I hear what somebody else is doing. I can't overemphasize the value of having somebody else to talk to when you're dealing with these things. I think one of the really cool things Chris does as part of his Associates Level Program is to hold regular mastermind groups with them—just brilliant.

---

**Chris:** InfusionSoft has a mastermind group that has branched off as its own entity: Elite Forum. I attend the quarterly meetings, sometimes alone and sometimes with my team. The main focus is to take a business or an entrepreneur—doesn't have to be in real estate—from seven figures to eight figures. I'm part of that. I'm excited for it. I strongly recommend that you sit down and ask yourself, "Who or what can I associate with in the next quarter or the next year that could take me to the next level?" Visit the **New Rules resources page** at **TheNewRulesBook.com** for more info on this special group.

## You Do What You Do Best; We'll Handle the Rest

Over time, I've learned that if I'm going to do effective tax planning for clients, I need to be able to see their books on a regular basis. Too many of my clients were coming to me during tax season and either finally having the information—or not have it, and I would have to file an extension. This year, there were two instances where I didn't learn what the person was doing for 2016 until we did their 2016 return in October. I could have saved them in the range of $10–20,000 in 2017 had I known sooner what the numbers were.

We've put together a three-tier program. The whole thing is geared around getting people's books straight and reviewing them monthly or quarterly—on a much more frequent basis—because then we can capture issues and get them done right. The three-tier program is outlined in more detail for you on the **New Rules resources page** at TheNewRulesBook.com, but it's essentially a one-and-done-for-you program with the benefit of hindsight from all of Chris's entities.

More importantly, I'm dealing with real estate agents and investors who sometimes have to go to a bank or mortgage company, or even a private lender, for funding. If the books aren't ready, they're going to be in panic mode about being able to get information to the lenders. That's another reason why we've created these packages—to give people up-to-date financials, up-to-date tax planning. Our bundle package is a monthly fee, and it includes both personal and business tax returns. You pay a monthly fee for whatever package you choose, and then sit back and let us handle it all.

---

**Chris:** I love this monthly plan because years ago, I'd get this tax bill at the end of the year, and it was always a bit of a surprise. I'm sure you can relate. Most people are not planning properly, but this way you're on a set budget. You don't have to worry about it—and since Paul does it on automation it's even easier. I just can't overemphasize that. It warrants repeating for those readers who are not currently working with us: we never expose you to something we *don't* do or *haven't* done. There's no exceptions to that; we equip you with the tools that *we* find helpful, period.

## Big Wins for My Clients, and You're Next!

My biggest win so far is with a commercial real estate agent and contractor in the Boston area who was improperly structured, and was getting ready to pay some significant taxes. He refurbishes apartment complexes, and usually every one of his sales makes a profit of about $1 million. We made a change to his structure just in time, and now he consistently saves $45,000 in taxes with every sale. When we started, he was doing one sale a year, but now he's trying to get to two. So he's saving $45–90,000 every year just on his taxes.

The second big one is a real estate agent who's in the million-dollar range. He's saving about $35,000 on his next return. Based on his revenue, we're probably going to see that and a bigger number in the future.

One of the issues I'm playing with each year is I'm telling clients what they saved, *and then I'm not letting them off the hook*. I'm saying, "what are you doing with the money I just saved you?" I'm trying to make sure that they either invest it somewhere else, or enjoy a vacation with it (if appropriate). Otherwise, most people just see a lower tax bill and that's all they think about.

## Boost Productivity & Work from Anywhere with an Internet Connection and the Right Apps

I try to keep an eye on all the apps that are coming out. Will they help me? Will they make things faster, or more difficult? There's an awful lot of artificial intelligence starting to come out in software that we need to keep an eye on; it's probably going to help your business.

Several years ago, we put a project management software system in place, and it's gotten better over the years. We've eliminated all of the calls to clients for mundane things like signatures or missing information. We now automate almost all of those messages. Now when I want to deal with a client on something that's custom, I've got the time to do it because I'm not having to deal with all those crazy things.

We also linked our scheduling software to Zoom. If a client wants to meet with me through Zoom, we don't have to spend a lot of time getting it set up. They select the appointment, the appointment they select is for a video, Zoom gives them the entry code, and we're done. I know Chris and his team use the same software for their strategy calls and coaching calls.

Finally, for at least the last four or five years, I've been able to work from anywhere in the world where there's internet access, getting tax returns done and interacting with clients. Some of it is cloud-based, some of it isn't. I bounce between my Millbury office, the Newport office, my house, and from time to time other locations—and it works. A lot of what you do as a real estate investor can be done remotely, and I'll leave that to Chris and his team. I know one of the things they're teaching at this year's **QLS Live** event is doing deals without visiting the house. I don't want to give that one away—just get to the event.

## My Publications

The books I've already put out talk about operating businesses. Even though they're for real estate agents, the principles apply to any operating business. If somebody's dealing with property flips, the first book, *The Ten Most Expensive Tax Mistakes that Cost Real Estate Agents Thousands,* is good for them. I recently decided I didn't have a lot out there on real estate investors, and the ins and outs of the business, so I wrote a new book, still in manuscript as I'm writing of this chapter, but by the time this book is published, my book should be out too. You'll find all the info on the ***New Rules* resources page** at TheNewRulesBook.com. It's geared to the question, "What are the tax consequences in the real estate investing environment?" It covers sandwich leases, property flips, rent-to-own, and regular rentals.

## Be Different and Create Different Results

If you're in real estate investing, whether you're new or experienced, talk to a tax advisor before you go too far. You also need to have a good set of books. I strongly recommend QuickBooksOnline rather than QuickBooks Desktop, because you can share your data. There are also more AI features in the online version.

On the non-accounting side, surround yourself with people who have successfully made the transition to your new passion. Get yourself a mentor in that discipline, and learn from them so you can avoid the mistakes that others have already made—so you can grow faster. I mentioned masterminds earlier. I would tell you to join at least two kinds: one that's in your industry, and one that's a mix of people outside of your industry. I can't overemphasize the value of that.

Often, people don't even take the two simple suggestions I just gave you, so I'm just going to say this: *be different* and you'll get different results.

My last tip, if you're looking for a book to read that's going to help your business, seriously think reading *Profit First* by Michael Michalowicz. It's going to tell you how to keep money in your pocket after you've built the business. There's real value in that. I know Chris is working on having Mike on his podcast—and may very well have by the time you read this.

---

**Chris:** We share with you the systems and processes that work for us and will most certainly work for you. So here's the deal: I invite you to be one of our Associates who goes out and creates new deals and new income for yourself. You will then create enough of a mess (three different income streams per deal) that you'll want to have Paul online to handle it. Heck, you don't have to hire him as CFO like we did; you just grab one of his done-for-you packages and he's on board. You essentially have him on board as a quasi-CFO without the price tag.

It drives me crazy when people say things like, "Well, I can't do that much with deals; my taxes will go up." *C'mon, really?* If we can show you how to increase your income by $500,000 or $1 million over the next few years and Paul shows you how to minimize your taxes and plan properly, who gives a rat's ass if you need to set aside a percentage of that for the tax man?

Did you just catch yourself thinking, "OK, but not me—I couldn't do that"? Check these guys out— before coming on board with us, they thought that too:

## Bill R.

Bill came from a background of 30+ years in investment sales and leasing of commercial real estate. Nevertheless, he joined SREC because he admitted to knowing next to nothing when it came to acquiring investment properties using creative financing techniques. Since hooking up with SREC and working with us full-time, Bill has surpassed $700,000 in earnings. He is on track to hit over $1 million in earnings in his first full year.

## Claudia D.

Claudia, like many others, had wrestled with different programs. She was involved with us early on in the launch of our hands-on Associate program. She was able to focus her efforts, gather the support she needed from us, and is now averaging $45–50,000 per deal all three paydays. As I'm writing, she is working on her fifth deal.

## Don S.

As an electrical engineer, Don came to us having lost six figures on training without doing any deals. Unfortunately this is all too common in the real estate education space: (1) training, but no actual deals being done, and (2) even worse, trainers no longer in the field—without current experience. Don is also close to $1 million earned for all three paydays and one of these days, as soon as he actually works more than a few hours per week, he'll realize he could leave his job!

## Link E.

Link, already a successful entrepreneur with a weight-loss clinic he runs with his wife Ginger, was seeking diversification. He has put together about a half-dozen deals averaging around $70,000 each for all three paydays. Just like the others, calling him busy would be an understatement, especially with his large family. Link had no prior real estate experience.

## Mike M.

Despite Mike's crazy schedule of 12-hour days and a 1-hour commute each way, his fourth deal is on the books, and he's very close to making his full-time transition out of his J-O-B. Mike also has a eight-month-old son and finds time to dial in our systems to do deals. He's well on his way to his first $1 million with all three paydays. Mike had no prior real estate experience.

## TAKEAWAYS FROM THIS CHAPTER

1   When in doubt, talk to a tax advisor.

2   Don't delay getting your returns in. You may be missing out on a refund, or face stiffer penalties than if you work proactively with the IRS.

3   When it comes to taxes, plan ahead.

4   Join one mastermind in your industry and one mastermind outside of your industry.

5   Look out for apps and software that will streamline your business processes and save you time to be with clients.

6   Align yourself with Chris's Associate Program, and Paul will handle the accounting end when you start doing deals with him and his family.

# PARLAY YOUR IRA INTO MILLIONS

## Starting with $1,000—All Tax-Free

## Quincy Long

**Quincy Long is with Quest IRA, based in Houston, Texas. They administer client accounts from across the nation, with offices in Dallas and Austin. They opened their doors in early 2003, and since then, have become one of the leading self-directed IRA administrators in the nation, with over 12,000 satisfied clients. They pride themselves on their world-famous customer service, and I can attest to that personally. My whole family, all of our partners—everyone I know, in fact—uses Quest and they're all extremely pleased with them. I'll share a deal with you I recently completed in my IRA at the end of this chapter, plus a strategy for you to act on immediately.**

Quest administers IRAs that are for investing in alternative investments. Self-directed IRAs offer endless possibilities for investing: real estate, notes, oil and gas, private placements, just to name a few. All of Quest's offerings are self-directed: you get to make the decisions and their staff will provide expert account administration and transaction support services along the way. They like to say that the best client is an educated client.

In an effort to help clients make the best investment decisions, Quest offers classes weekly in their offices and streamed online. Quest also holds many presentations, workshops, and seminars across the US as part of their effort to educate clients.

Let me tell you how I got into this. Back in the 2000s I was a fee attorney for American Title Company, and I had a self-directed IRA. A self-directed IRA requires a network to make maximum use of it. So I decided to get a group together with people who had self-directed IRAs to come up with ideas to share, and to provide a space to do deals with each other. We started meeting about self-directed IRAs, just a few of us—but it grew and grew. Eventually, every time we'd have a meeting, I would come up with some crazy idea and chase it down to see if we could do it. That was my modus operandi. Through that process, I got to know my account administrator pretty well.

One day, I was sitting in my office, bored with the title company—having a bad day, I guess. The head of the company that administered my IRA at the time called and said, "We're thinking about opening affiliate offices and were wondering if you'd be interested." I said, "Sign me up—I'm bored!" and slammed the phone down. I had no idea that was my job interview! But a few months later I decided to join as an affiliate, which eventually turned into a franchise. After a while, we became independent—and have been for the last six years.

Quest is like a luxury car dealer, in the sense that we have the vehicle to invest in alternative investments, into promissory notes, real estate. We have a lot of private placements, meaning LLCs, limited partnerships, or joint ventures. These typically invest in real estate. For example, you might have a person loan money to an investor to buy and fix up a house. You might have a person buy real estate directly in their IRA, and you might have a limited partnership that was put together to buy an apartment complex. Real estate is not all that we do, but it's a good portion of it, either directly or indirectly.

As the "luxury car dealer," we give you the vehicle to allow you to make your investment. We do not provide investments, or invest-ment or structuring advice. We *do* provide education on what you can do, but then *you* decide what you want to do. We're facilitators. We don't teach you how to be an investor, but we share the stories of investors. We're there to provide you with the ability to handle alternative investments in your retirement account.

If you're thinking of transferring your current IRA to a self-directed IRA, the process is very simple. The first thing to understand is that even if it's a self-directed IRA, it's still an IRA, and all IRAs fall under the same rules. You might wonder why Fidelity doesn't handle real estate—because they're not set up to handle it. But it doesn't mean that you can't buy real estate in your IRA.

The first step is to open an IRA and transfer the money into the account, or contribute to the account—whichever one you want. It's no more complicated than moving money in Fidelity or Schwab, for example; it's just another IRA request to your IRA provider.

The next step is to locate some of the best investments. That can be done through networking, or you can simply follow your own ideas of what you want to do. I know Chris and his team work with IRA funds and provide some incredible returns for some of their private investors. You would be well served to take advantage of their expertise and 27+ years of experience. Once you've found the investment, you have to do some paperwork (everybody loves paperwork). Then we fund the transaction, and the asset belongs to your IRA. That's the process in brief.

In order to be successful in your self-directed IRA, there are some important factors to be aware of:

1   **You need to have knowledge of the rules.** There are some rules that you have to go to "deep in the street," or "between the white lines," as they say.

2   **You'll need some idea of investment *techniques*,** or you'll need somebody to hold your hand on the investment. Chris and I were recently discussing how he'll use his IRA-owned LLC and take, say $500, and turn that into tens of thousands if not hundreds of thousands. I think he'll share one of those

with you at the end of this chapter. His terms deals are incredible for your self-directed IRA. You could have them do it for you, but I'm sure he'd agree that you could also learn it for yourself through their coaching and mentoring.

3  You don't necessarily need to have money, but **you need to have *access* to money.** Likewise, **you need to have either deal flow or *access to deal flow*.**

4  **If you don't have the deal flow or the money yourself, you've got to have a strong network.**

Now let me elaborate on each of these points.

## Knowledge of the Rules

Quest's strong suit is answering clients' questions on rules or norms of paperwork. That's what we aim to do. *Our best client is an educated client.* We don't want you to guess. We're familiar with the rules, we can explain them, and you take it from there. The advisors you use are up to you. The fact is, we live and breathe these rules every day. Even a professional—if he or she doesn't live and breathe them every day—may not be able to appropriately guide you.

For example, you need to know about "prohibited transaction" rules. There are things that you can't do with certain people in your IRA, and you must learn those rules. If you're caught doing a prohibited transaction, it will destroy all the efforts you've made, so knowing and being educated on the rules gives you the advantage.

Although you can buy almost anything in an IRA, there *is* a list of people called "disqualified persons" with whom you cannot either directly or indirectly do business, or who cannot directly or indirectly benefit from your transaction, and at the top of the list is *you*. Everybody says, "What do you mean, I *can't benefit* from my IRA?" You are a fiduciary or a caretaker for your IRA, so your IRA cannot benefit you and you cannot benefit your IRA.

We refer to the IRA as "Mr. Ira" to help clarify. When Mr. Ira dies someday, he'll give you all of his money—but as long as he lives, you're a fiduciary for him. All of the actions are for the benefit of Mr. Ira, until the appropriate time. The money is distributed from the IRA.

The disqualified persons list is made up of the people that the IRS has determined to be too close to you to be on a transaction beyond arm's-length basis. This includes you, your spouse, your parents, your grandparents, your kids, their spouses, and grandchildren, and up and down the lineal line of descent. It includes any corporation, partnership, trust, or estate owned or controlled by any combination of the people who are disqualified from doing business in your IRA.

You can't buy or sell property or exchange property between the account and the disqualified person. You can't extend credit or loan money. You can't provide goods, services, or facilities; you can't directly or indirectly transfer or use the money for the benefit of a disqualified person.

I own some notes, for example, that are now at over a 16% return on my investment. I would love to contribute those to my IRA, but I can't. If an IRA has a house with a roof that needs to be fixed, I can't expend my own personal money to fix that roof. I'm a disqualified person. I can't extend credit. If you have a piece of land in your IRA and you want to build a house on it, you can't provide the materials and labor to build the house yourself, because you're a disqualified person. If you have a beach house in Belize, and you need to go down and check on the beach house, that's a prohibited transaction because you're benefiting from an asset owned by your IRA.

## Investment Techniques

You can buy almost anything in an IRA with the exception of collectibles and life insurance—those two are off-limits. Everything else, in theory, can be handled administratively.

Let's say you found an investment that you want to buy. Let's just say it's a piece of real estate. First of all, you need to understand that the purchaser is *not you*. It's your IRA. The contract is going to say something like **Quest IRA Inc. FBO** (for the benefit of), then your name and your IRA number. That's who's making the offer, not you. It's assigning the contract to your IRA (Mr. Ira, as we called him before) Who handles your IRA? Quest IRA. So Quest IRA has to sign the contract and do the closing. To do that, you send us the money. You fill out a *Direction of Investment form*. Say, "Hey Quincy, remember that money I sent you?" Once you send it to So-and-so Closing Attorney or Such-and-Such LLC, for an asset in my IRA, we exchange the cash in your IRA for that asset, and continue to hold that asset for you. Once you have the asset in your IRA, the revenue that comes from that asset belongs to the IRA—because *it* is the owner. Expenses belong to the IRA as well, so make sure you have enough money to cover expenses.

Let's say someone puts a $100 deposit on a lease purchase, and ends up cashing out at, let's say, $10,000. That $10,000 then shoots back into the IRA when it's done properly. So it doesn't have to be a purchase—it can be an option as well. This is what I meant earlier when I said "some of Chris's techniques" and "...on TERMS." Chris's owner financing and lease purchase deals are incredible for this.

## Access to Money and Access to Deal Flow

You don't need to have a large amount of money to open a self-directed IRA. In the accounts Quest manages, we have anything from very small amounts to very large amounts. It's pretty common to have a small amount. There's no restriction on how much or how little money it can be. Case in point: Check out how Chris grew $500 to $126,000 in his notes at the end of this chapter.

## Networking

If you don't have a lot of money or a lot of deal flow, how do you get it? By networking. That's what we do very well at Quest IRA. We provide networking opportunities for people to get together and learn from each other. We can't *put* people directly *into* an investment—that would be a violation of securities laws. When you are the account holder, that's where the "self" part comes in, and where you've got to have a strong network.

For example, I have a little deal flow independently, but most of my investments come through my networking—and I'm inherently lazy. I like for somebody else to do the work and I just make some money and everybody's happy. It's all about education, networking, and access to deal flow in money.

## The Coverdell ESA

All of the information for self-directed IRAs can apply to other accounts. One of my favorite investment vehicles, the Coverdell Education Savings Account (ESA). I call Coverdells the Roth IRAs for education. You can contribute after-tax money, in very tiny amounts, if you wish. You can put in only $2,000 a year for each child, but all the money you make is tax-free as long as you pull it out for qualified education expenses. Qualified education expenses include anything from kindergarten through college, tutoring, school fees and tuition, books, materials, computers. So if you make a decent amount of profit in a Coverdell from a deal, you can pull it out for college or even for private school tuition—or whatever it is that you need.

When you make a transaction in your Coverdell ESA it's the same as with your Roth. It's **Quest IRA FBO** [your name] doing the deal. It goes through the attorney. You're not involved, nor is the beneficiary—that future student. You're like the puppet master, if you will. You're making Quest IRA do whatever you want. You're not directly involved in the process except for reading and approving contracts and finding the investment.

## The Inherited Roth IRA

The king of kings is the inherited Roth IRA. It's worth a whole chapter by itself, because no matter what age you are, with an inherited Roth IRA, you can make all the money tax-free. And it can pass to succeeding generations. Often I'll see people set up an IRA and name their grandchild as beneficiary. Whatever was in that IRA goes to their grandson, and now he has a tax-free account with which to make money for the rest of his life. Our record youngest right now was 10 months old when he inherited a Roth IRA with a few hundred bucks in it. Can you imagine having an account for the rest of your life in which you can do deals, and out of which you can take money tax free? Is that a legacy to leave to your family? I think so.

There's a rule to be aware of, however: for either the person who died or the person who inherited it, you must wait five tax years before you're completely tax-free. Those rules do not prevent you from contributing to an inherited Roth IRA or traditional IRA. Our Facebook classes walk you through this.

## Contribution vs. Profit

The difference between contribution and profit is a point of confusion for many. A *contribution* means you're taking money out of your pocket and you're putting it into the Coverdell or the IRA. A *profit* comes from an investment. Think of it like the stock market. If you purchase a stock or a mutual fund, that's an asset. Later on that asset might be sold for a greater price than the one at which you bought it. Just substitute real estate, a note, or whatever, for a stock. Sometimes the stocks or the mutual funds produce income, and sometimes they don't. Sometimes you buy real estate that doesn't produce income. Sometimes it's rental property. It seems so foreign to people, but it's so simple. It's just a different type of investment. You're not removing money from your IRA to buy a house and later putting the money back in your IRA—it never left your IRA in the first place! You exchanged cash for an asset and later sold that asset back for cash. This is the same thing as buying and selling stock—there's no limit to how much profit you can make. That's not a contribution. That's just profit on your investment.

## Invest in What You Know

It's always best to *invest in what you know best*. The people who lose money with their self-directed IRA have often been led down a path to invest in something they don't truly understand. Every time I've lost money, it's because I invested in something other than real es-tate, which I do really understand. So invest in what you know about.

## Do the Due

The other mistake I see people make is that they don't "do the due." *You've got to do your due diligence.* It doesn't involve just the *buildings* of the property you're buying. It's also critical to do due diligence on the *people* you're dealing with, no matter what type of investment it is. Those are the questions people don't ask, but they should. "Do the due" and invest in you, but you know best. That's the best way to use self-directed IRA.

## A Tax-Free Life

The bottom line about being an investor is that it's all about leading a tax-free life. There's plenty more to discuss: line-inherited IRAs and the complete freedom from taxes, the differences between Roth and traditional IRAs, how quickly you can accumulate wealth with them when you don't have to pay taxes. You'll find our contact info on the **New Rules resources page** at TheNewRulesBook.com. We look forward to hearing from you.

---

**Chris:**  I started with $1,000 in my wife's IRA and $1,000 in mine. We then directed Quest to invest those funds in an LLC, so now the two IRAs (Quest IRA, FBO [our IRA names]) own the LLC. We're not the managers of that LLC—that's against the rules. The manager is a trusted accountant I know.

I then directed the LLC to use $500 for a down payment on a six-unit building that the LLC bought on TERMS (owner-financing with monthly principle payments—no interest). Approximately 24 months later, after some improvements to the units and increasing rents, the building was sold for a $126,000 profit. Our two most recent deals in the same

LLC were lease purchase acquisitions with the same down payment. One returned $38,000; the other, $51,000.

As soon as your personal cash flow is where you need it to be, you can do the rest of your deals in your self-directed IRA or IRA-owned LLC, and enjoy tax-free income.

## TAKEAWAYS FROM THIS CHAPTER

1   Educate yourself on both the IRA *rules* and the best investing *techniques*. See Quest for IRA *rules* and Smart Real Estate Coach for *techniques*

2   You don't need money or deal flow, but you do need *access* to both money and deal flow, which you get through *networking*.

3   When deciding how to allocate monies in your self-directed IRA, *invest in what you know best.*

4   When weighing an investment, *do your due diligence* and investigate both your potential investment and the people involved.

# USE YOUR LLC AND REAL ESTATE

To Protect Against Taxes and Protect Your Ass(ets)

## Lee Phillips

Attorney Lee Phillips is a counsel of the United States Supreme Court. He has three university degrees. He's held licenses in real estate, mortgage broking, securities, life insurance, and he's a registered investment advisor. Lee is nationally recognized in the fields of business structure, asset protection, financial planning, and estate planning. He's also the founder of LegaLees Corporation, a company specializing in solving asset protection and tax problems for the high net worth individual. His passion is asset protection—and a very large part of that is protection from the IRS.

## The Impact of Taxes

For the past 30 years, I've been helping some of the wealthier people in the US try to control their taxes. The fact of the matter is the doctor can't see 20% more patients. You can't do—or you may not *want* to do—20% more rehabs or whatever it is you're doing, but if we can cut your taxes by 20%, that's a big deal. People don't really understand that taxes are one of the major asset protection threats out there. If I say "asset protection," you think lawsuits, right?

It's the IRS—that's probably your biggest asset protection threat. I'm going to make a statement, to which you might say, "That's ridiculous," but *they're taking half of what you make*. There's the income tax. There's the state tax. There's the sales tax. There's the airport tax.

I rented a car about a year ago in Tampa and I guess they needed the car in Orlando because my rental fee was $1 a day and I had the car for a week. That's only $7, but get this—it was a little over $63 when I got to Orlando because of the taxes—but they don't call them taxes anymore. They call them "fees." What did they call Obamacare? They called it a fee, and eventually the Supreme Court said, "No, it's not a fee. That's a tax."

So let me demonstrate to you what taxes do. I'm going to take a dollar and I'm going to double it 20 times: $1, $2, $4, $8, $16, $32. If you do that 20 times, you end up with $1,048,000 and change—about $1 million. There's no tax on that sequence, just simple doubling. But everything you do is taxed.

So let's take a 40% tax—federal and state—and see what it does. If I've got $1, that doubles to $2. I've got a dollar in profit, until I *tax that dollar of profit*. Let's tax the dollar of profit and see what happens: If I tax that dollar, I no longer have $2, I've got $1.60. If I double the $1.60, and get to $3.20, I've got to take the 40% tax again, so I don't get $3.20, I get $2.56. If I double the $2.56, I get $5.12, but I have to tax it so instead I get $4.10.

So on the one side, with no taxes, I've got $1,048,000 and change. If I tax it 20 times and double it, but take a 40% tax each time, I've got $600,000, right? Nope. You end up with a grand total of $12,089 This is because taxes are compound interest in reverse. It's a big deal—it's a huge deal. What taxes do to your money is the bottom line.

## Control Your Taxes

Traditionally, there are three ways to control your taxes. The first is to postpone the tax, with something like a 1031 exchange, a standard IRA, or a 401k; I don't pay the tax today, I pay it later. But you can't find me anybody who'll say, "Wow, my broker made me rich."

I can't find people who will say, "I have made money in my 401k or my IRA." Why? Your broker isn't any smarter managing your general account than your 401k account. The tax benefit of the 401k growing without the tax outruns the stupidity of your broker. That's why you make money in those accounts and you don't make money in your standard account.

Another way to control your taxes is to change the nature of the tax. For example, if I hold a property for 13 months, that's a different tax consequence than if I only hold it for eight months, because of capital gains taxes. Short-term capital gains and long-term capital gains are different taxes: I've changed the nature of the tax.

The other way you can control taxes is to shift the tax—you can shift income. I can make my kid pay the tax instead of me. You can't do that outright; you have to use a legal tool. We use an LLC or a family limited partnership or corporation. This means that if I run my rental money through an LLC and my children are all owners of the LLC, I can be an owner too, but I get to direct where that rent goes and who pays the tax. I'm shifting the burden of the tax to someone else. If my kids are in a lower tax bracket than I am, then the family as a whole saves money.

So you can *postpone* the tax, *change the nature* of the tax, or *shift* the tax. That's about all you can do in tax planning.

## Control Your AGI

The problem is that your tax planners never think "tax planning." They think about a deduction or two. If you're going to understand how to cut your taxes, how to lower your tax burden, you have to understand how to control your AGI, your Adjusted Gross Income. That's the magic number. Adjusted gross income controls everything. It controls whether you can do your IRA or not. It used to control whether you could convert your standard IRA to a Roth IRA. It controls your tax bracket.

All the accountants reading this are going berserk because it's not really AGI—but yes, basically it's adjusted gross income that controls your tax bracket. It controls whether you get your itemized deductions and whether exemptions phase out, and whether you get child care credits. It also controls AMT, the Alternative Minimum Tax, passed around 1968 to make sure that the rich paid their fair share of earnings.

For 75 years, they've been saying that the AMT is to make sure the rich pay their fair share. The problem is that the alternative minimum tax is now based upon your adjusted gross income. How much money do you have to make in your AGI to have the alternative minimum tax kick in? There's no precise number, it depends on how you make your income and several other factors, but it's about $80,000.

So if you're above $80,000 in AGI, give or take, then you're paying the alternative minimum tax. That means the IRS uses a different formula to calculate your tax—an alternative tax calculation. But wait a minute—$80,000 isn't exactly rich, in my book. They've taken this concept and applied it to the middle class. Once the camel gets his nose in the tent, we're dead!

So right now, AGI determines whether you pay the Obamacare taxes and everything else. *How do you lower your adjusted gross income?*

## The Advanced Tax Tactics Course

About 10 years ago, I wanted to figure out this AGI stuff, how to control taxes. I went on the internet, and I looked to see what I could find on "how to lower your AGI." There were a number of sites on the internet that—in all seriousness—said, "The way you lower your AGI is to adopt a kid." These people have never raised a child. You do not raise children as tax deductions.

In our office now, we have someone who was a special auditor for the IRS for seven years. He did the big criminal cases. He taught the auditors how to do the audits, and I'm amazed at what he can do with taxes. So he and I together have created what we call the Advanced

Tax Tactics Course. It includes a 100-page workbook and five hours of audio CDs, and we teach you about taxes and how to control them.

If I can give you what it effectively a 20% raise, might that not be worth five or six hours of your time to figure out? Our goal in the Advanced Tax Tactics Course is to cut your taxes by 20–30%, and it works really well. In order to do it, you've got to understand the concept of "above the line" and "below the line." These are accounting terms and the "line" is the last line on page 1 of your 1040. That line reads "adjusted gross income." Anything above that line either raises or lowers your adjusted gross income.

Anything below that line has no effect on your AGI. Your home deduction and your mortgage are below the line. Your charitable deductions are below the line. All the things that your CPA tells you to control your taxes are below the line.

The only thing you as an *individual* can do above the line is to make a contribution to a standard IRA. So that $5,000 (or whatever it is this week) is above the line. If you make your standard IRA deduction, that lowers your AGI. If you're a teacher, you can buy supplies on the third Sunday of the fourth month if it's a full moon, and that's deductible above the line. Moving expenses associated with your business, that's above the line.

But there are two things that you can do above the line. Your business is above the line: your LLC, your corporation, your S corporation, those are above the line. If you file a Schedule C on your small business, that's above the line. The other thing above the line—and this will blow your mind—is real estate.

All of the depreciation, all of the rents, everything in real estate is above the line. Most folks know that people who do real estate investing somehow get wealthy. They think, "There's the appreciation and everything else that goes along with the property. The tenants pay the rent and the rent pays the mortgage." But do you realize that that's really a *tax-free* dollar that you're paying the mortgage with? Because the real estate *depreciates*. You can take the depreciation.

Your real estate is a tax shelter. Your real estate or terms business is a tax shelter. They're above the line. This is one of the many reasons that what Chris and his team are doing is changing lives and changing finances for so many people.

No accountant, no financial advisor ever sits you or any other real estate investor down, puts his or her arm around you and says, "Look, we need to put your AGI on a diet." They never do that. They don't even *think* this way. They've never taught you how to maximize the tax benefits of your real estate, how to maximize the tax benefits of your terms business.

## Lower Your AGI with Two Weeks of Tax-Free Rent

The LLC business and real estate are your keys to reducing taxes. For example, let's take the IRS code section 280A(g). This says that if I have a residence, and I rent it out for no more than fourteen days per year, that rent is tax-free. It's not income. It's not reported.

I have two residences, one in Utah and one on Siesta Key in Florida. The law says I can rent the residence and get tax-free income for 14 days a year, so when I go on vacation for two weeks, I put an ad on Craigslist and charge $2,000 a day to rent my house. I will always get someone who'll come in and rent the house for $2,000 a day, and that $2,000 a day is tax free. It's not income. It's not reported.

My business pays $2,000 a day to rent my house in Florida for me to entertain Chris Prefontaine, Al Lowry, Robin Thompson—I've had a lot of people down to the house. I make a bill and submit it to the business and the business pays the bill. It looks just like a hotel bill, but look at what happened: that money came out of my business tax-free. The business got a deduction. I don't report it. It's not on a 1099, nothing. On my accounting sheets it says "rental, residence, 280A(g)."

Now, your CPA is going to say, "Hey, buddy, you've got to have a reasonable rent." That's fine. Go down the street to the Hyatt. I think the back of each room door says it's $1,400 a day at the Hyatt. That's the only other hotel on the island. I feed you lunch and dinner. Am I pushing it with $2,000? Probably. Can they throw me in jail for doing that? No. The most the auditor can do is say, "That's an unreasonable rent. I'm only going to give you $1,400 a day."

You could do the same thing. You could hold your office meeting at your house. Go down and see what the Marriott charges to rent a conference room for the afternoon and serve lunch or dinner, and that's the price you charge your company. For 10 people or so, you'll pay the Marriott $800 or $900. This is absolutely, perfectly okay.

You can do $1,000 a day for a half-day of conferences or meetings. As long as you don't do it more than 14 times a year, any rent that you get is tax-free. Why would the IRS do that? Well, have you ever heard of High Point, North Carolina? High Point is the furniture capital of the world. Once a year, they have the furniture market in High Point, North Carolina. Now it's in Vegas and half a million people come, but they still have a furniture market every year in High Point. High Point has maybe a Motel 6 or two. You can't house 300,000 people in High Point, North Carolina for two weeks in hotels. People have to open their homes. The way they got the people to open their homes was to pass a law that if you rent your house for no more than 14 days a year, any rent that you get, you don't have to report." It's just water under the bridge.

That's how the law came about, and it's been around for decades. Your accountant will know about it. He'll say, "Well, it's risky. You have to charge a reasonable rent." Okay. What happens if I charge more than a reasonable rent? "Well, the IRS could audit you and they'd say that's too much, and you'd have to pay a back tax on it." Okay. What's my chance of being audited, 1%? Okay, I might have to pay a little extra money if I get audited. Other than that, I'm fine. *Nothing happens.* But keep it reasonable. We don't want to do anything shady by any means. But if you do that 14 times a year, even if you're only charging $500, that's $7,000 out of business and into my pocket tax-free. Didn't that help the bottom line?

So, if that came out of your business, anything that happens in your business ends up coming in above the line. If you make a profit in your business, that adds to your AGI. This is a deduction from the business, but I've moved the money around the block and got it into your wallet tax-free. It lowered your AGI by $7,000 or $10,000. If I can lower your AGI, maybe I can drop you into a lower tax bracket. Maybe I can make it so you still get your itemized deductions. If I can lower your AGI, I can control your taxes.

If we can cut your AGI by 20–30%, that's our goal. Yes, you do have to study a 100-page workbook and you've got to listen to five hours of audio CDs. They're all indexed. You can listen to whatever you want, but you can go through them and learn 10 ways to lower your adjusted gross income—and that's huge.

## Use Your Business to Lower Your AGI

If you've got a company, we teach you how to use the company to lower your AGI. There are many other things we can do in the company besides using the 280A(g) code section. We can lower it with the company or we can lower it with the real estate. We've both been real estate investors. We know how to do it and we teach a lot of the pitfalls. There are some pretty bad things lurking in the IRS code.

For example, you've got your office. Your office needs a place to stay. So you think, "Okay, I'll buy a building, then I'll rent it to my company and they can have their office there." If you do that, the IRS has a little surprise for you: they reallocate your rental income. It's not passive income, it's non-passive income, which means it doesn't offset your depreciation on the office building.

Once you know what to do and how to work with it, using your business and real estate above the line to control your taxes can be pretty cool. Readers can get a deal on my Advanced Tax Tactics course, which normally goes for $399. For details, see the **New Rules resources page** at TheNewRulesBook.com.

## Legal Pockets

People don't really understand how big of a deal taxes are for their bottom line. Your employer takes the money out of your paycheck, and you never see it. If people didn't have the money taken out of their paychecks—"withheld" is what they call it—and actually had to *write a check* at the end of the year to pay their taxes, they'd go nuts. That's exactly why they have the money withheld. You never see it, so you just don't think about what taxes do to you, but it's the difference between $1,048,000 in profit and $12,089! That's a big difference.

If you take my course, we also go through asset protection. Taxes are a good chunk of it, but there are also lawsuits. There are all kinds of things that enter in to what I call "asset protection," because today, *making it* isn't enough. You've got to *keep it*, too. If the IRS doesn't take it away from you, the lawyers will get it, the tenant is going to get it—*somebody* is going to get it. The whole attitude of the nation today seems to be, "If you're rich, that's bad, and we're going to take it away from you."

You've got to watch your wallet. My company is going to create what I call "legal pockets" for you. If you're walking down the street and you get your wallet stolen, you're through, aren't you? But if you've taken some of the money *out* of your wallet and put it in your front pocket, the wallet gets stolen out of your back pocket, but you don't lose all of your money.

We create legal pockets and we isolate those legal pockets from each other so if a thief gets into one of your pockets—and that thief might be in the form of a lawyer or even the IRS—you've moved your assets out and behind some sort of a shield. Then when the IRS is barreling down the road at you, you're standing behind the shield and you just watch the IRS go right on by. They can't take your property.

---

**Chris:**  I've worked with Lee and his staff now since 2014, and the education, tax savings, and asset protection are everything I wish I'd had before the 2008 crash for a myriad of reasons. I highly recommend that you go through his course and get your butt to his boot camp so you'll be able to protect your ass-ets. Check out the **New Rules resources page** at **TheNewRulesBook.com** for contact info.

## TAKEAWAYS FROM THIS CHAPTER

1   The IRS is your biggest asset protection threat.

2   There are three ways to control your taxes:
    *postpone* them, *change the nature* of the tax, or *shift* it.

3   Lower your AGI, and you lower your tax burden.

4   Both your LLC and real estate investing
    can help you lower your AGI.

5   You can lower Your AGI by renting out
    your property 14 days a year tax-free.

6   Lee's "legal pockets" can protect portions
    of your assets from the IRS or lawsuits.

# FROM POVERTY TO
# ON FIRE

## Dr. Joe Vitale

Dr. Joe Vitale is a globally famous author, musician, marketing expert; movie, TV, and radio personality; and also one of the top motivational speakers in the world. His many bestselling books include *The Attractor Factor*, *The Key, Attract Money Now,* and *Zero Limits*. His latest releases are *The Awakened Millionaire* and *The Miracle: Six Steps to Enlightenment.* A popular expert on the law of attraction, and an actor in several movies including *The Secret*, Joe has also appeared on all of the top TV networks and written for *The New York Times* and *Newsweek*. His most recent accomplishments include being the world's first self-help singer-songwriter, as seen in *Rolling Stone*. To date, Joe has released 17 albums. Several of his songs were recognized and nominated for the Posse Award, the Grammys of positive music.

Dr. Vitale also created the Miracles Coaching program, which you're going to hear more about, to help people achieve their dreams. This man, once homeless, is today a bestselling author who believes in magic and miracles and has spent the last four decades learning how to master the powers that allow us to channel the pure creative energy of life without resistance.

## The Awakened Millionaire

*The Awakened Millionaire* book and project is my latest mission. What I'm trying to do is to help people overcome their own hidden, unconscious beliefs that are causing them to have a lack in sales, a lack in income, or a lack of more money coming in. What people don't know is that they are unconsciously blocking their own success. This is the cornerstone message of all my work. It's why I write my books. It's why I started Miracles Coaching. It's to help people become what I call an Awakened Millionaire.

An Awakened Millionaire is somebody who has made peace with money internally and even spiritually, and is also enjoying the material side of life. That's the awakened part, and that's the millionaire part. My mission with the book—the book is a manifesto—is to set people on fire to help them realize that if they love what they're doing and they go out and express that passion, they will make a profit from it, but it all takes place *inside*. This is what I'm so excited about.

I've done so many things in my life. I could talk about marketing, copywriting, and publicity. I could talk about all the different books I've written, all the different things I've done from music to movies, but what's really important is to help people come to this important realization. Once they remove their own internal limiting beliefs about money, they can have more sales, and they can close more deals. Not only that, but they can even be happier and healthier when they follow their passion and turn it into profit. It's a big concept, but The Awakened Millionaire is a movement.

## Follow Your Passion

It doesn't matter what business you're in. What matters is that you follow your unique passion. Hopefully, everybody who's in real estate loves real estate, and they're passionate about the business. That's where I want them to be, but that passion could be for anything: it could be for running a bakery. I'm primarily an author: I'm passionate about my books, I love books, I'm a book nerd, I'm a book addict, so writing my books and talking about my books is a form of passion for me.

I think that's the secret. You want to look within and ask, "What am I excited about? What do I care about? What is my passion? What is my purpose? What is my calling?" When you pursue that, you will tend to make more profit. You still have to work on your beliefs about money, your beliefs about deserving it, and so forth, but as you work on those beliefs and follow your passion, no matter what profession it is, you will tend to do fantastically better. It doesn't matter if it's real estate or a coffee shop.

## Interrogate and Dismantle Your Roadblocks

You may be saying, "I'm passionate about X, but..." Those "buts" are *excuses*, which are based on beliefs, and all of those beliefs need to be looked at very closely. You want to ask, "Is it true? Am I really too old to go into business? Am I really too young to go into business? Do I not have enough experience to go into business?" Look at all of these objections like you're selling yourself, and you are also doing the "close" with yourself—and get to the point where you can dismantle these objections and release them. Then you can go out there and do it.

## Living Your Dream, Step 1: Love Where You Are

One way to start is, first, to love where you are. Love where you are. This goes all the way back to Napoleon Hill and his famous book, *Think and Grow Rich*. If you haven't read it, that should be number two on your list. Go read *Think and Grow Rich*. If you've already read it, go back and reread it. Napoleon Hill talked about "loving where you are."

Love your job as it is. Fighting with it, resisting it, complaining about it, these are all low-energy complaining mentalities and vibrations that won't help you fix it or help you be happy now. It's so important to love where you are and appreciate where you are, because if you're in a job, there are *millions* of people who wish they had that job. There are lots of people out there struggling, even starving, so what you want to do first is to love where you are, *be grateful* where you are. Just relish the fact that you've got work—you've got employment. I know Chris writes daily in his gratitude journal, because we discussed it recently at dinner. This is a life-changing idea for you—write daily in a gratitude journal.

## Living Your Dream, Step 2: Identify Your First Baby Step

Second, ask yourself, "How do I get started in real estate? What do I do to open my business or get my business going? What baby step can I take right now?" People who don't take action are overwhelmed with their own "big ideas": They want to have the largest real estate business in the state, and maybe they haven't even made their first sale—maybe they haven't even made their business cards.

Alternatively, you may already have a business, but you want to change niches and perhaps jump into what Chris and his family do. I have a bias because I know and respect Chris, but if you tear apart what he and his family are doing—I mean, really do your due diligence—the chance to create three streams of income with each deal is quite amazing and definitely unique.

The very first step, then, either way, is to take a baby step in the direction of that big dream. When you have a big dream, you can suffocate under it, unless you realize, "Wait a minute, let me do something right here where my shoes are, right here in this moment. What is that first obvious step?" Maybe it's making the business cards, maybe it's looking for the office property. Maybe it's pivoting from what you're doing now and contacting **Smart Real Estate Coach**. I don't know what it is—that's unique to you—but here's the key: once you take that first baby step, the next step becomes apparent. Then you take that next obvious step, and when you've taken it, the next step becomes apparent. Now you're moving forward!

Instead of sitting there and being overwhelmed by the idea of being an entrepreneur or opening a business, bring it all the way down to what's doable, what the baby step is in this moment. Then do that.

## Living Your Dream, Step 3: Get Support

The third thing to do is to get support, and what I mean by that is a kind of "mastermind." Napoleon Hill wrote about masterminds in *Think and Grow Rich*—and also in a bunch of his other material. A mastermind is where two or three or more people—about six, usually—are in a group to support each other. They don't have to be in the same business. Very often, it's better if they're *not* in the same business, but these are people who support each other with resources, with energy, with mentality, and with encouragement.

They're kind of like cheerleaders. You want to get into a mastermind where people will say, "You can do it." They believe in you as much as you believe in yourself, and they can bring you up on those days when you *don't* believe in yourself. A mastermind is a pool of resources. Napoleon Hill also said that when you're in a mastermind, even if there's only one other person, but if two or more are gathered, there's a kind of a third mind there. That's almost metaphysical, but you're tapping into this world consciousness, almost like a collective unconscious, and when two or more people are gathered, they can support each other to achieve those dreams of entrepreneurship or real estate business, or whatever it happens to be, even faster.

A phenomenal example is how Chris and his family team include mastermind sessions with their Associate Levels. I think it's brilliant and, more importantly, effective. His students are doing deals at a level that other educators (who, frankly, appear to be more focused on selling product) can't match.

## Your First Mentor should be a Book

It's absolutely *brilliant* to look for mentors. My first mentors were always authors. So way back, when I lived in Houston and my first book was coming out, in 1984, I think, it was a cause for celebration because I was finally *published*. But it was also a cause for disappointment because I realized publishers don't know how to promote books. It was up to the author to learn marketing, so I decided to learn marketing way back in the early 1980s.

Where did I go? I went to the library. I found authors who had written books on copywriting, advertising, publicity, marketing. That was my first level, my first resource for finding mentors. These people who had already lived it, who had already figured it out, put their ideas and their philosophies and their strategies and their to-dos right there in books.

That has been the case throughout my life. When I wanted to be a musician about five years ago (I was nearing the age of 60 and it was on my bucket list), I thought, "Well, how do you write music? How do you record in a studio? How do you learn how to play the guitar? How do you do what you need to do to be a good musician?" The first places I go are books. Those are my mentors, but I'm notorious for never stopping there, because if the authors of those books are alive, I often reach out to them, and I did that even when I was a kid.

When I was a kid, I thought at one point that I was going to be a boxer. I had big dreams, and I was interested in boxing. Jack Dempsey was still alive, so I wrote to him. I still have an autographed photo of that early heavyweight boxing champion of the world. A few years later, I thought that I was going to be a magician. I remember being about 15 or 16 years old and wondering about my life and how you become a Houdini today. I wrote to John Mulholland, a man who had known Houdini, and asked for his advice. I still have that two-page, typewritten letter from 1970 or 1972. Chris shared with me that he's been doing the same thing since high school. It's really, really cool that most of the people you reach out to are flattered and happy to help.

I do that today. When I decided that I was going to be a musician, I was thinking, "Man, I'm going to read all the books, but where are the stars of music, and how do I reach them?" I managed to find my way to the home of Melissa Etheridge, one of the greatest female rock stars of all time. I studied songwriting with her at her feet, in her home studio, just the two of us.

I could go on with all these delicious stories because I love it, but what I'm saying is that finding mentors is a brilliant clue to success, and it's not as hard as you might think. There's no reason to be intimidated because first of all, when I didn't have money, I went to the public library. Today, I go to Amazon every single day, and UPS or FedEx or the mail arrives every single day with more books written by mentors. I also know that today, because of the internet, you can reach virtually anyone alive by email or just by going to their websites.

I'm a big believer in mentors. I'm a big believer in having coaches and getting into coaching, because we don't know it all. No individual knows it all. We have got to keep reaching out if we want to grow and if we want to succeed. Chris and I met specifically because he reached out to me. Then we had dinner together here in Texas. Now we have a business relationship. See how that plays out!

## Reaching Out for Help: Make it Short, Sweet, Direct, and Complimentary!

Forget intimidation entirely because people are people, and they want to respond to people who sincerely want help. What I was taught decades ago is to consider how *you* feel when somebody asks for help from *you*. You probably feel flattered, and if you can do it, you probably will.

The vast majority of people, famous or infamous, are the same way. I've told stories throughout my life in which, even as a kid, I'd reach out to mentors, to famous people, and I would tell them sincerely who I was and what I was trying to do. I'd be short, I'd be sweet, and I'd be complimentary. I've learned that if you want to reach somebody, you simply find their contact info, and you write them a sincere, short letter or email that begins with some sort of compliment.

I love it when somebody writes to me and says, "I'm a fan. I read your books," or, "I saw you in *The Secret*," or even better, "I listen to your music, and I really love your songs and your vocals," and then go into who they are: "I'm a beginner, I'm this or I'm that, I'm starting a real estate office, I'm going to open my business," and then tell me what they want: "I'm looking for a suggestion on the best book on copywriting" or, "the best book on publicity," or whatever they're looking for.

I've found that if it's flattering, short, sweet, with a direct call for action, your question or your request, more often than not, you're going to get your request because people are people, and they want to help sincere people.

Even better today is that, because of the internet, you're only a click away from anybody. Google anyone alive, anyone you want to reach, and you're going to find their website, possibly with their contact info right there, or you'll find their manager, their booking agent, somebody who can get you to that person. Don't be intimidated. You have every right to ask, and more often than not, people will say yes.

## Keep Marketing

Don't stop marketing. Because I've written so many different books on so many different subjects, including a book on P.T. Barnum called *There's a Customer Born Every Minute*, I had to research America in the nineteenth century. Because I wrote a book about Bruce Barton, the founder of BBDO, one of the largest advertising agencies in the world at one point, I had to research the 1920s. That means I have more of a historic overview of business unlike some people, who just look at the now.

What I've seen is that the businesses that keep marketing, even in the hard times, and even in the successful times, are the ones that last. It's really easy for people to stop marketing when they can say, "Business is good! I'm closing sales or deals all over the place—I'll stop running my ads." That's one of the biggest mistakes of all time. You want to keep your promotion going through the great times and the slow times. You have got to keep it going, so don't stop marketing.

## Never-Ending Learning

Don't stop growing, stretching, learning, educating yourself, and inspiring yourself. This is one of the secrets to business: you've got to keep learning; you've got to keep up. Today, one of the things that I feel like I'm sprinting to keep up with is the whole world of social media: Facebook, Twitter, Instagram, and all the other things that I don't know anything about, seem like they're for the youngsters of the world. Well, the youngsters of the world are buying houses, they're buying real estate, they're investing, and they're entrepreneurs too, so I can't dismiss them or overlook them. I don't want to stop learning. I've got to keep expanding my mind, my awareness, my consciousness, my techniques—and I'd suggest that everyone does the same. It doesn't matter what business you're in, but it's certainly it's true for real estate.

## Try Everything

Don't stop trying *everything*. What do I mean by that? Well, a big problem in business is people want to do *one thing*. They say, "I'll just do Facebook," or "I'll just do Facebook Advertising." That's a big mistake. You want to do everything you possibly can.

When people used to ask me, "Hey Joe, you were homeless in Dallas, and you were in poverty in Houston. What's the *one thing* you did to get out of it?" it used to frustrate the hell out of me: everybody's looking for the one pill, they're looking for the one secret, they're looking for the one book.

But I finally decided that I do have an answer. There's one thing I did: *everything*. I did everything. I read the books, tried advertising, tried direct mail, and when the internet came along, I tried that. But I kept doing *everything* because you don't know which part of the everything is going to work, so I wouldn't stop doing everything. I'd keep pursuing it. Whatever niche you're in, there's someone who can show you how to make sure you're maximizing your efforts. Chris and his team do that with their students.

## Don't Surrender the Goal

Don't give up on having a goal. I always want to have a goal. It may be a financial goal, a certain amount of money, it might be for a certain level of success, but I don't want to give up on the goal. I may try different things to get to that goal, and along the way there will be different ideas that I'll pursue.

If some idea doesn't seem to be working, again, I have to look at the bottom line and ask, "Is this nudging me in the direction of the goal?" If it doesn't seem to be, then I'll have to ask, "Do I need to tweak the idea, do I need to drop the idea, do I need to get somebody else to do the idea, or do I simply let it go?" That's going to be very subjective. I'll do my best to be objective by asking, "Does this seem to be moving me in the direction of the goal?"

What I don't want is to give up on the goal. I may fine-tune the goal, I may tweak the goal, but I won't surrender the goal. I may surrender the *idea*, but not until after I've pursued it enough to get a sense of whether it might work.

## Not Failure, *Feedback*

I've changed the word "failure" to "feedback." It's feedback. Where somebody else would say they tried to do something, and it didn't work, I would say that they tried to do something, and got some very useful information as a result. Hopefully, that useful information caused them to rethink the direction and rethink the process to the goal so they can now take a different route to getting there, or perhaps a different way to attempt it.

Let's go back to my first book, published in 1984. So I'm finally published, and I've got the book in my hand. It's a proud moment. Then, shortly afterwards, I realized the publisher isn't selling this book at all. The publisher doesn't know anything about marketing. I'm holding a book that, in other people's eyes, would be considered a failure: it's not selling. At that point in time, nobody knew how to market it, including me.

Is that a failure? No, because I got the feedback that publishers are printers. They may be prestigious printers, glorified printers, but they're *printers*. They don't necessarily know anything about marketing. That propelled me to learn about marketing, copywriting, publicity, to reach out to the greats of advertising and study their works—again, mentors and books. I devoured it all, and so I became a marketer.

Because I became a marketer and started to promote my first book in the early 1980s, people in Houston noticed it, and then they'd ask me, "What are you doing to sell your book?" That moved me into becoming a consultant. I became what I called a "book specialist" back then, because people who wanted to write books or had written a book and didn't know how to promote it were now hiring Joe Vitale to write their ad copy, or their news releases, or their publicity. It moved me in a whole new direction.

Then I became more and more of a marketing consultant, more and more of a copywriter, and more and more prestige came my way. Then of course, as the internet came along in the early 1990s, everything I was doing offline in Houston to build my career, I put online, and the world began to notice me, and I was considered one of the first internet marketers. I wrote one of the first books on internet marketing. I made my presence known, started getting clients from all over the world, from countries I never even heard of, didn't even know existed. I could go on and on, but where did it start? With a "failure," with a book that wasn't selling, but I don't call it a failure, because that was a *gold mine* of feedback.

*Publishers don't know how to market books. Okay, I'll learn how to market books.* That line of thought changed my life. It could've been called a failure, but as you can see, it wasn't a failure at all. That was a golden moment; it gave me feedback that changed my life forever.

## Biggest Wins

I've had a lot of "wins" in my life. I'm a very lucky guy. I'm going to be speaking at a seminar soon for which I had to create a graph of my life showing the highlights, the ups and downs. When I first made the graph, it was a little intimidating because I was homeless at one point. So at the beginning, the line is down at the bottom, even off the page. It's a "life was miserable" kind of a graph.

Then as I get closer to the age of 50 on the graph, more and more successes show up. Now I'm going off the chart, upwards, not even the sky is the limit. We're just going into orbit with all kind of successes. So when I reflect on my life, all kind of wonderful things come to mind.

My most recent success is as a singer-songwriter. I performed in Austin, Texas, with my Band of Legends, and got a standing ovation.

That's a huge success for me. My most recent album is called *The Great Something*. I dedicated it to Melissa Etheridge, and I wrote a song for her on it. I think the songs are better than anything I've ever done before. *The Great Something* is a big success.

I think about books I've written. My most recent book was called *The Miracle*, and it has been a bestseller repeatedly on Amazon. There are 35 five-star reviews of it, the last I peeked at it, so I'm very, very proud of that. Of course, I've been in a bunch of movies, the biggest being the movie *The Secret*. If people haven't seen it, it's well worth seeing. It's inspiring—not because I'm in it, but because there's a message for all of us. That was a very life-changing moment for me.

I have to admit, my first audio program with Nightingale-Conant, which was called "The Power of Outrageous Marketing," was a defining moment in my life because I had been a customer of Nightingale-Conant. I had bought their cassettes early on and borrowed them from the library. I had listened to Wayne Dyer and all these wonderful people who helped me when I had nothing and was nobody, and there was no evidence around me that I'd ever be a success. So I had listened to Nightingale-Conant, and was just so grateful for the material they were putting out, and then around 1998 I created my first program with them. That was a huge moment, and I went on to create other audios including "The Missing Secret." "The Missing Secret" that I recorded with Nightingale-Conant is their all-time bestselling audio program. It beat "Lead the Field" and Earl Nightingale and everything else they'd ever done. I have a note from the president of Nightingale-Conant telling me this. Talk about a moment that is still burned in my mind as this golden trophy. I could go on. I'm very fortunate, but I've been working at it and am still working at it—still going for it.

## My Top Three Productive Habits

### 1    Read

I read every day. I'm a bookaholic, as I mentioned earlier. I love books. I'm always eagerly looking for new materials. I read about marketing, I read about psychology, I read about neuroscience, I read about success, I read about other people, and I read the classics. I go back and reread *Psycho-Cybernetics* and *Think and Grow Rich* and *The Power of Your Subconscious Mind*. These are classics of success literature. I read every day. I'm reading biographies, I'm reading how-tos, I have books open in different places, all around the house and office. Even right now, I'm sitting in one of my offices, and I see stacks of books waiting for me to continue reading them. I will make time every day.

## 2  Write

The second thing I do every day is write. I am an author. I think of myself as that, first and foremost. I write blog posts. I write articles. I have five different books that I'm pursuing, that I'm writing right now. Some I'm focusing on pretty intensely, and others are on the back burners, but I'm writing every day. I think this is a big ticket to my success, and it's my passion and life calling, so I'm going to pursue that. I'm going to keep after it with all the gusto I have in me.

This is a discipline that also works me continuously toward my goals. For others, it may be a discipline other than writing—define what yours might be. Chris has a great chart called **The Power of One Daily Discipline**, which you should get your hands on and use every month.

## 3  Make Time for Silence

The third thing I do every day is to make time to allow for silence. I make time for relaxation, meditation, or simply gratitude. That is an essential missing step for virtually everybody in business; they're so driven to achieve goals, so driven to make more money, so driven to succeed. I certainly understand the drive. I certainly have it myself, but I've learned that if I make time every day to *receive* ideas, to be available for inspiration, to make time for meditation or relaxation or silence, I rejuvenate myself so I can have that drive to continue toward success.

## [4]  Bonus Tip: Move

I've listed my top three daily productive habits, but I want to give you one more, a bonus tip. I've learned that there's a fundamental need for movement. I work out almost every day—five days a week, not *every* day. I've got my own gym. Three days a week, I do high-intensity cardio; two days a week, I do strength training; one day, I do lower body; one day, I do upper body. I've found that this is an important ingredient to success. For the longest time, I did my best never to exercise—I thought it was a waste of time and I could "get away with it." But you can't get away with it. Life is movement. You have to keep moving. That's a bonus tip.

## Role Models

I wrote a book on P. T. Barnum—yes, the circus promoter, but people need to know he was far more than that. He was an entrepreneur, a politician, a writer, a speaker, a negotiator. He was very spiritual. Barnum is still a mentor to me in my life. I will very often think, "What would P. T. Barnum do in this situation? How would P. T. Barnum promote today?" I think most people in business today (and I include myself) don't think big enough. Most of us are taking very conservative steps to increase our business, and I look at P. T. Barnum, and at the Barnum-like characters who have lived throughout history.

In my book *There's a Customer Born Every Minute*, I talk about the ten things he did then that we can still do today. I talk about all the people like Sir Richard Branson who are doing many of those things today. P.T. Barnum, Richard Branson—people of that "big-thinking" caliber are my mentors today.

## Miracles Coaching

I started Miracles Coaching well over a decade ago because I realized that the times in my own life when I had the biggest breakthroughs were when I had a coach. We can all change and grow on our own, but we do better with a coach. If you listen to shows like Chris's, which provides so much information, when you act on this information, you're going to grow, you're going to change, you're going to get more of the results that you want in life. If you read the books I'm talking about and go back to the great success literature, whether it's *Think and Grow Rich* or my own books—*The Attractor Factor* or *The Awakened Millionaire, There's a Customer Born Every Minute*—and keep working on yourself, you're going to grow, you're going to change, you're going to go in the direction of your dreams.

I can't imagine, for example, someone being in the real estate space and not devouring Chris's best-selling first book, *Real Estate on Your Terms.* It's an absolute must, and you can and should be listening to the audiobook over and over. But if you want to *accelerate* everything, you need a coach. A coach is somebody who can look at you and your life objectively, who can listen to you and *reflect back to you* your limiting beliefs, who can reveal to you all the little snags that are holding you back, but which you won't necessarily see.

Working on yourself is a little bit like trying to play chess with yourself. You know your own moves. You can't outsmart yourself because you're working within your own system of beliefs, you're working within your own state of consciousness. You need somebody on the outside who can objectively reflect back to you what you're thinking even when you don't know you're thinking it. You can't possibly know it without intense, ruthless scrutiny of yourself, because it's your own belief system. You're living out of your beliefs, so it's difficult to see them.

Chris and I had this very conversation about several of his students who had bought programs from various real estate educators but never were able to do a deal. Then they join his special **Associate Level** programs and immediately start producing deals. Why? Coaching.

I created Miracles Coaching and trained all the Miracles coaches to be that outside ally, the person who can be your mirror, who can point out these beliefs and help you release them and remove them. This is a person who can believe in you, which is what you really need as you're going through the efforts to achieve more in your life.

Miracles Coaching has been profound. I did it over 10 years ago, and you can find more information on the **New Rules resources page** at TheNewRulesBook.com. Everybody there has been trained by me. You'll see a video of me there describing it. There's a form you can fill out to apply for a free consultation. You can get a sense of whether it's for you or not, but in my opinion, anybody who wants to have a breakthrough, who wants accelerated results, needs a coach, whether it's through Miracles Coaching or something else that you believe in.

I still use coaches today because *I'm not done*. I'm still growing, and I still find limiting beliefs within me. The only reason I was able to leave homelessness and poverty and achieve some modest—and later, phenomenal—success is that I found coaches along the way. In the early days, I was fortunate enough to find people who saw something in me and donated their time. Today I willingly pay people to coach me because I know the power of having a great coach. That's the essence of Miracles Coaching: somebody who believes in you and can help you.

## Strategies for Success

### Write Down Your Goal

The very first thing to do when starting anything is to write down your goal. What is your goal? What do you want out of being in real estate, or being an entrepreneur? Spell it out as vividly as possible so you can say, for example, that your goal is to make six figures—or maybe seven or eight figures; *dream big*. Go ahead and make it something that seems like a stretch—it's possible! I have a quote that people have been circulating all over the internet—all over Twitter and everywhere: "The goal should scare you a little bit and excite you a lot."

When you write down your goal, it should make you a little nervous, a little shaky, but it should also make you really excited, like, "Boy, when this one comes through, I'm going to dance in the streets and sing in the rain." *That* exciting.

I once saw a documentary about billionaires, and this one billionaire said that if you're at a party and tell somebody, some stranger, what your goal is, and they don't think you're crazy, then you haven't thought big enough. Have that fear, excitement, and boldness in mind as you write down your goal.

## Do Something Every Day in the Direction of that Goal

Next, do something every day in the direction of that goal. Again, baby steps. You don't have to do something overwhelming, you don't have to do something terrifying, but you do have to do *something*. Some of the baby steps will be obvious and unique to the business, whether it's real estate or some sort of entrepreneurship, opening a restaurant or whatever it happens to be.

Also, you should be reading success literature every day. Read *Think and Grow Rich*, read *Psycho-Cybernetics*, read *The Power of Your Subconscious Mind*, by Joseph Murphy. Read these classics. You don't have to read the whole book in a day. Read a little bit every day. Almost anything you want to go after, anything you want to accomplish, can be found in a book.

## Visualize Your Goal as Having Already Occurred

Third, visualize your goal as having already occurred. Most people, if they know about visualization and mental imagery, know that you sit and imagine having your result. Most people imagine it down the road, like six months or a year from now (you've got your business, and it's flourishing—you're driving the hot-rod car, whatever's on your bucket list). But I'm suggesting something a little different: visualize it as *already done*. You *already* have the successful business. You're *already* driving the hot-rod car. You're *already* living in the mansion or the beach house, or whatever it is that you were longing for.

Instead of visualizing it down the road, off in the distance, in the future, *embody the completion of it in this moment.* Spend a little time every day, especially at night when you're getting ready to go to sleep, and do this little exercise in self-hypnosis, this trance-like experience where you pretend that you accomplished your goal today. Imagine what it felt like to accomplish it, because this will accelerate the manifestation and the attainment of the goal you want. You'll tell your mind this is what you want. Your body will feel like it's already true. Your unconscious mind can't tell the difference between what's real and what's imagined, so when you imagine it with this feeling of reality, it will go forth to make things happen to create it for you.

---

**Chris:** Joe's chapter is a great one because you can download the **Power of One Daily Discipline** chart, write down some of his action items, some of his suggestions, and start with them this month.

That one dinner I had with Joe opened many opportunities for me, for my family and my businesses. I cannot emphasize enough the importance of coaching, mentors, and mastermind groups. Finish this sentence for yourself:

> **If I could just meet _____, I know it would profoundly affect my business (life, cash flow, whatever it is for you).**

Then reach out and find that person via the internet, by phone, or however you can, and get some time scheduled with them. Don't even read the next chapter until you do this.

## TAKEAWAYS FROM THIS CHAPTER

1 Figure out the secret beliefs that are keeping you from your dreams, and dismantle them.

2 Get help—employ a coach or join a mastermind group.

3 Identify your first baby step.

4 Visualize your life as if you'd already achieved your goals—*right now*, not down the road.

5 Never stop marketing.

6 Read, write, and make time for silence *every day*.

7 Move your body: work out several times a week.

8 Do something every day, however small, to move you toward your goal.

# ARE YOU
# A REAL ESTATE
# PROFESSIONAL?

In this chapter, I am going to revisit some of the points that we addressed at one of our annual **QLS Live** events. I want to get you thinking with some questions about being a real estate professional—truly a professional, operating at the Olympic level versus the high school level:

1  **How long do you think it takes** to become a professional real estate entrepreneur?

2  **What does it cost** to become a professional real estate entrepreneur?

3  **How much will you earn** as a professional real estate entrepreneur?

When we look at the different associates (students we do deals with and revenue-share with) around the country and start to consider what the different paydays are—**Payday #1, Payday #2,** and **Payday #3**—the numbers are rather large. Below, I am going to give you our actual numbers from 2017, which change monthly, because I want you to wrap your hands around what you can actually earn when you create three paydays.

Now just as a disclosure, your results may vary, but I am going to give you our actual averages. Now, if I mention different associates around the country and their averages, you can weigh that and decide whether you can beat it, or aim a little lower. You do whatever you want to figure out your business plan—I'm just giving you the results we've seen. That's number one.

Number two, when I ask, "What does it cost to become a professional real estate entrepreneur?" realize that some people come to us brand-new. Take Mike in California, who is having success because he is coachable and he diligently studies the material. He happens to be a **High 6** associate (for the different levels, see the ***New Rules resources page*** at TheNewRulesBook.com) and he is on his third deal, but I'm sure by the time this book is out, he'll have more completed. When you start to do the averages, you do the math, take the average deal with all three paydays that I'll review below, depending upon the area, and then multiply by three. It's rather large.

That's a little different than someone like Bill (who has a chapter in this book) or Don, who were both featured on my podcast. Each of them took six or seven months to do their first deal, but now they're at six and seven figures. Everyone's going to get started a little bit differently. Before meeting me, Don and Bill happened to spend a whole bunch of money on programs that didn't work for theme. They're not happy about that, but so be it. When I ask the question, "What are the costs to become a professional real estate entrepreneur?" I don't know what it will be for you. Just be open-minded and open to managing your expectations about how quickly this gets going.

## How Long Does This Take?

Since I began coaching around 2000, the most common question I get is, "How long does it take?" I could write a whole chapter about managing your expectations, but let me say this. What we teach is not a push-button get-rich-quick plan. What we teach is not a "just do this online and everything will happen" kind of thing. It's not. If you're looking for that kind of quick fix, then maybe this isn't for you.

I just want you to manage your expectations. I don't want you to get too caught up in it. At our **QLS Live** annual events, we take a very close look at all the things that you are going to have to learn in terms of skill sets. These are your game plan or your money-producing activities. In other words, what are you going to do every day? When my team or I work with you, we help you with that, among other things.

Mindset is a big piece of this. Dr. Joe Vitale addressed this at our **QLS Live** 2018 event, for an hour and a half. Whether you realize it or not, all of us let mindset get in the way, and it's a big issue. So I invite you to honestly evaluate where you are today versus where you want to be when it comes to your skill set, your game plan, and the money-producing activities you do every day. Evaluate your mindset and your expectations around earning a profit.

Once you start looking at where you are today versus where you want to be, you will quickly realize that no matter how much time you spent learning, it's still going to take a lot of time. But I want to try to shorten that cycle with you. If you decide to work with my team, or if you have another mentor, make sure that they help you shorten the cycle.

Frank Williams, in his book *If You Must Speculate, Learn the Rules*, says, "If you are intelligent, the market will teach you caution and fortitude, sharpen your wits, and reduce your pride. If you are foolish and refuse to learn a lesson, it will ridicule you, laugh you to scorn, break you, and toss you to the rubbish heap."

Why do I want to share that? In our office, our family team acts on everything. In other words, if we have a curve ball thrown at us—and that goes for our education and coaching business as well as our own deals—not only do we change whatever it was that brought about that challenge or curve ball, we also make changes to the programs that we offer. We change any forms, checklists, or legal things that need to be changed. Then we immediately share the updates with students and associates around the country. By the way, this is why it's essential that your mentor or teacher is still in the field and not someone who did deals 5, 10, or 15 or more years ago—that's a recipe for a major headache for you. Things move quickly in real estate, and you have to be on the leading edge and stay educated. That's just to remind you that we're in the trenches too. We learn just like you, and as things come up, we adjust as needed.

## Profit Expectations

Let me give you what you can expect for profits if you are in line with our averages.

As of now, **Payday #1** is averaging $26,503 for us. Now, for those of you who have read the Amazon bestseller *Real Estate on Your Terms*, and/or the **Instant Real Estate Investor Blueprint**, you understand that the $26,503 average for **Payday #1** is not necessarily all up-front. Plenty of times it is, but when my son Nick, our buyer specialist, sits down with the buyers, for the majority he structures that average of $26,503 *over time*.

What might that look like? Depending on the price of the house, they might put down $10,000 with the signing of the buyer's "letter of intent" with the attorney. (All of our current forms are on smartrealestatecoach.com, where we house our **QLS** video program and more.) The additional $16,500 might be next February's tax refund plus the following year's tax refund. Those three might total $26,503. Understand that it is not always up-front. **Payday #2** can be anywhere from $300 to $500. We've had it as high as $1,000, but **Payday #2** is the spread *every month* that you get between what you are taking in from your buyer and what you are sending out to your seller or your mortgage company. Our average right now is at $313.

If I look at that over time, **Payday #1** has increased. **Payday #3** has increased. **Payday #2** has settled, if not gone down. Why is that? You run your business however you choose to, but we put more weight on the total package. We put a lot of weight on **Payday #1**. I want skin in the game before they get the house. Our biggest headaches have been when we didn't do that. **Payday #2** is important, but it's not critical. It's not the crux of the deal.

**Payday** #3 runs $25,000 to $50,000. So if you add up all of those, depending on the term (12, 24, 48, 60 months), we are now averaging around $73,000 for all paydays. As of this writing, Mike is doing three deals, Don has done nine, and Bill has done eight or nine. You figure that times $73,000 (everyone's average varies by market) if we are creating three paydays in every deal.

Now you start to see how my three opening questions are all related: How long do you think it takes to become a professional, what do you think it costs, and what will you earn? Those things have to be in alignment.

If someone tells me they're not sure they can afford one of my Associate Levels, my answer (in my head, if I don't say it outright) is, "Relative to *what*?" You have a chance to make $73,000 per deal, hypothetically (we don't guarantee anything—this gives you only our average) if you use our averages over time. Maybe you want to dumb that down to $50,000. If you think you'll get $50,000 per deal, and you can do one deal every other month this year, which is very realistic for anyone—that's 12 deals times $50,000. You do the math. It's a pretty impressive number!

I hope that gets the wheels turning in your head. If you look at our Associate levels—**90 Day Jump Start, Starter Level, Immersion**, and **High 6**, the cost to participate ranges around $5,000–100,000 We have a **90 Day Jump Start** membership that's only $5,000, and that's an easy way to get an introduction to what we do. Is that a lot of money? Relative to what? Let me give you some examples:

A doctor is going to spend a minimum of nine years in school. Once their practice is set up, for the first few years—depending on the specialty—they'll earn $150–200,000. These numbers are from an old internet survey, so they might be a little conservative.

An attorney is going to spend about eight years in school, and once their practice is set up—depending upon their specialty—they might earn $120–170,000 at first.

A judge is going to spend eight years in school, then must practice for 15 years as an attorney...to get a job that pays $10–110,000. Go figure.

A CEO spends 4–7 years in school and maybe 20 years in business learning the skills required, and will then earn $150–350,000. I'm keeping that very broad because a lot of CEOs are on the road. We used to have a neighbor who was super, super-successful—sold a

$2 million sailboat, traveled the world. But when he's working, he doesn't see his family *at all*.

An interior designer spends about four years in school, minimum, and earns about $50,000 a year.

A commercial pilot may spend eight years between school and military training to get a job starting at around $60,000, and eventually earning up to about $180,000 a year.

I love our CPA, but how do they do it? I don't know. They spend four years in school and an additional two years studying to take the CPA exam so they can go out and average a crushing $60–80,000 to start out.

A schoolteacher, sadly enough, spends a minimum of five years in school, and in many cases, six, seven, or sometimes eight, and start at $45,000 a year, on average! Even if it were $100,000 a year, look back at our numbers: If our team right now is running $73,00 for all paydays, can you do the math?

In each case, I think you'll agree that these people are prepared to do two things: first, invest a tremendous amount of personal time in order to have a career, and second, spend a tremendous amount of money preparing to earn whatever their income will be.

Sometimes I say to our associates, "I don't know what's stopping you from just doing six deals a year and getting out of your J-O-B. It's got to be driving you nuts." They just chuckle, and say, "Yeah." Some of them do, in fact, make that transition after an office visit here with us (which comes with the Associate levels). They leave here with a tremendous game plan. But some don't have a plan to exit their job. Some like to juggle both, and that's okay. They like what they do.

## How Much Time and Money Are You Prepared to Spend?

How much time and money are you prepared to spend to create the income flow you'd like to have for the rest of your life? Now, go ahead and answer that. How many months are you going to spend? Jot that down in a journal. How much money are you willing to spend?

Let's take a conservative approach and expect a learning curve of 90–180 days. What if you had the wherewithal to sit through it and manage your expectations, but then you cranked out 12 deals after six months? It took you 18 months to crank out 12 deals, but then let's say that your market happens to be like ours, and you hire us to help you and you do about the same average of $73,000, or maybe only $70,000. What's 70 times 12? How many months, and how much money, would you spend if that effort produced $840,000?

Now, because it comes in three paydays, it won't be $840,000 all in the same year. But you create that much income. You receive all or most of your **Payday #1s**, you receive all of your **Payday #2s,** and you're waiting for your **Payday #3s**. That's a pretty cool little business.

At our **QLS Live** 2017 event, I announced our numbers as a team. We had done 19 deals at that point, and these were the averages: from **Payday #1s**, we averaged $481,000; **Payday #1s** increased with these 19 deals so that our net spread monthly was $5,198.31. **Payday #3s** brought in exactly $726,658.06. So with 19 deals, in about 10 months, with this particular profit center, we created $1,395,249.66.

If you could make 19 deals that would bring in $1.39 million of income over the next 12–48 or maybe 60 months, would that be worth your time?

After 26 years or so in the business—our team has 50 years combined experience—we can look back and can say that we've determined for sure what the biggest obstacles are that real estate professionals face in building successful businesses. We've concluded that any one of the following could get in the way, and these are the things we are going to help you with. I'll go into more detail on some of them below:

- **Inability to set specific goals**

- **Difficulty maintaining a positive attitude in a sometimes-negative environment**

- **Inefficient use of time**

- **Soft skills**
- **Lack of commitment to the business or expectations not in line**
- **Bad mentors or coaches**
- **Lack of a proven and simple system**

## Inefficient Use of Time

For time blocking, go check out Dan Kennedy. He's one of my mentors and friends. Look at his *No B.S.* book series, and find the one on time management. He's updated it several times. I suggest you read it at least three times a year for the next three years. That's how much I think you're going to enjoy it.

## Soft Skills

I think you'll agree that this one is overwhelming, because if you knew exactly what to say and when to say it, you'd be champing at the bit to get on the phone with a seller or a buyer and let them ask you questions. You wouldn't be able to wait. But over time, that's where you'll be if you let us coach you. It's pretty interesting to hear some of the live calls that associates do around the country. It's absolutely astounding to hear the progress they go through from day one to month three, for example. It's exactly the same way my son-in-law Zach and my son Nick built their niche roles in our company—they studied scripts. They are very well-scripted, and that gets the results that we get on a daily basis. Even so, we're constantly trying to improve.

If you want, you can immerse yourself in exactly the same path that my son-in-law Zach took. He went from not knowing anything about the business to eventually duplicating me, going out and doing all of our buying. Then you want to get your hands on the **Seller Specialist Program**. If you package it with something else or if you're an associate, you typically get a discount. It goes through hours of video—every form, every script, everything that he did and we do—

so you can do it yourself and then hand off that manual to someone you train. These are the skills you need.

## Lack of Commitment to the Business, or Expectations Not in Line

It's extremely important to balance your commitment with managing your expectations. If you have never done any deals, and you need to get one done in the next 30 days, is it reasonable to expect it with 100% certainty? I don't think so. Can you do it? Sure. Sean comes to mind. He's a police officer in Pennsylvania. In his first 30 days, he did a deal, then got busy with life and didn't do many after that. Then he came back to our event with his wife. They're both fantastic, and they'll probably do a bunch more deals. Does that mean you'll do a deal in 30 days? I don't know. I don't know you well enough, but you could.

## Bad Mentors or Coaches

If you can't find a coach on the **Smart Real Estate Coach Podcast**, something is wrong. There are some phenomenal coaches on there. It doesn't have to be us, but for goodness sake, pick someone from the podcast, and once you do, don't look left, don't look right, and don't look back, and put the blinders on for *three years*. You're starting a business, as Mike in California so eloquently said at our live event.

Do it for at least 12 months. I need you to commit to me—and, more importantly, to yourself—and say, "I can do this with you for 12 months. I will put the blinders on. I won't do anything but what you tell me." If you can do that for 12 months, you will love the experience. If you think doing that will be a challenge for you, *don't do it*— as much as I'd love to have you as a client.

## Lack of a Proven and Simple System

Success leaves clues. If you listen to my podcast, you've probably heard some of the interviewees say this. It means someone has done what you want to do. If my style or my kid's style matches where you want to be, if our numbers match what you want to create, then by all means, get on it! Get after it and let's get you into the *proven, simple system that we have.*

The list of obstacles and challenges goes on and on, but we've come to the conclusion that the biggest ones are skills and commitment to systems, so tackle those first.

## Conclusion

When I finish a book, I don't like to get caught up in long conclusions that lead me nowhere, so I'll be as blunt and to the point as I can be. First, I've asked my good friend and accountability partner to add an epilogue that's very meaningful, so I'm certain you'll enjoy that.

Second, I hope my opinion and suggested courses of action are clear to you now. This is not rocket science. If you don't implement after reading this, *stop reading books*—you're just wasting time. It's not a matter of how many books you go through, and how fast —you have to keep your rate of implementation up. Here's your path to success:

1  Pick a niche in this lovely, life-changing business of real estate.

2  Pick a mentor to work with who is currently in the space you want to crush it in.

3  Commit to three years without getting distracted by any shiny objects or other people.

Once you decide, you can email me personally at chris@smartrealestatecoach.com. I check email twice weekly, on Tuesdays and Fridays, so don't stress if you don't get a reply right away. I will personally reply on my email days. If you're interested in the niche we specialize in, get your butt over to **Smart Real Estate Coach** immediately; start with the **Quantum Leap System (QLS)**. You'll find it on the *New Rules* **resources page** at TheNewRulesBook.com.

# EPILOGUE

## Don't Quit—Win The Oscar Instead

## Stephen Woessner

Stephen is the founder and CEO of Predictive ROI, a media company, and the host of *Onward Nation*, a top-rated daily podcast for learning how today's top business owners think, act, and achieve. *Onward Nation* is listened to in 105 countries around the world. He is also the author of three books, including the #1 best seller, *Profitable Podcasting* (this chapter is an excerpt). His digital marketing insights have been featured in *Forbes.com*, *Entrepreneur.com*, *The Washington Post*, and *Inc. Magazine*.

Congratulations on making it to the end of this book. It wasn't easy. But now you have to keep building on that momentum: get out there and grow your real estate empire by applying the insights and wisdom generously shared by the experts in this book.

But the only way you can do that is to push yourself, to think past the thoughts of quitting or taking it slow that will soon be assailing you—if they haven't already started. If you're feeling that right now, rest assured, that's the impostor syndrome trying to steal your destiny from you. Instead of quitting, my hope for you is that you'll win the Oscar. I'll illustrate the tenacity you're going to need with a lesson I learned from Tony Robbins. It's a story you may already know—a story about grit, perseverance, and being so committed to what you want to do, what you believe in, that you work desperately to create it.

327

The story is about Sylvester Stallone — one of Hollywood's most successful actors. But Stallone didn't have success handed to him; he had to earn it. He had to knock down obstacles and barriers to prove he was worthy. He had to starve, he had to endure hardship, he had to freeze in his New York City apartment and find warmth in the public library. He had to go without everything, He faced more than 1,500 brutal and cruel rejections from talent scouts and agents. But he didn't quit.

Sylvester Stallone had been listening to some of Tony's audio programs and really liked them. So Stallone did what any of us would do: he invited Tony over for dinner so they could talk things over.

Before dinner, Tony said to Stallone, "You know, I've heard your story from other people but I'd really love to hear it from the horse's mouth. I don't know how much is mythology and how much is true."

Stallone agreed to share his life story with Tony. He had always known what he wanted to do, ever since he was very young. He wanted to be in the movie business. Period. Not TV, but the movies. Being in the movies was an opportunity to help others escape the realities of their daily life. But more than that, it was an opportunity to inspire audiences.

Stallone's drive and passion are what make his movies inspiring. He helps audiences see how they can overcome unbelievable obstacles, because in his own life, he's done just that. When he was born, Stallone told Tony, he was pulled out of his mother's womb with forceps—that's why he looks and talks the way he does. "I really wanted to do this," he told Tony, with resolve in his voice. "I know why I wanted to do it, and I wasn't going to settle for anything else."

Stallone went out to try and get acting jobs, but it's not like he showed up, went, "Yo, Adrian," and the casting directors said, "Oh, wait, you're a star." In fact, the early years of Stallone's career didn't work out too well. He was alone, hungry, and grinding it out just to survive.

Casting directors looked at Stallone and said things like, "You're stupid-looking; do something else." They made fun of the way Stallone talked, and told him that there was no place for him in the movies. They said, "You're never going to be a star. You're insane. No one is going to want to listen to someone who looks and sounds dopey, and talks out of the side of his mouth." Imagine hearing that. How would you feel? What would you do? Would you quit?

Stallone was told no—not once or twice, but over and over, relentlessly. He told Tony he'd been thrown out of agents' offices in New York more than 1,500 times. "Hey, wait a minute," Tony pointed out. "There aren't even that many agents *in* New York." Stallone said, "Yeah, I know. I've been to them all—five, six, seven, eight, or nine times."

Then he told Tony about the time he'd made it to an agent's office at 4:00 PM and the agent wouldn't agree to see him. Stallone refused to leave. He stayed there all night until the agent came back the next morning.

His persistence paid off, and he landed his first movie role. "Oh really," said Tony. "I thought *Rocky* was your first movie?" No, this other movie that Tony had never heard of was his first. "Oh, well, I was in it for about 20 seconds and I was a thug that somebody beat up. They made me feel like, people hate your guts, so maybe getting beat up will be a good thing." He did three movies like that, but didn't get any more. But he kept going out to look, only to take rejection, rejection, and more rejection. But did he give up? Did he quit?

Finally Stallone realized that it wasn't working. So he changed his approach. He was desperate, starving, he couldn't afford to heat his apartment. His wife was screaming at him every day to go get a job. "Well, why didn't you?" asked Tony. "Because I knew that if I got a job, I would get seduced back, and I would lose my hunger. And the only way that I could do this was if it was the only choice and I'd burned all my bridges. Because if I got a normal job, pretty soon, I'd be caught up in that rhythm and I'd start to feel okay about my life—and my dream would just gradually disappear. So I wanted to keep that hunger, keep that hunger burning. Because hunger was my only advantage."

Stallone said his wife didn't understand it at all. They had vicious fights. It was freezing, and they had no money. One day, he went to the New York Public Library, because it was warm. He didn't plan on actually reading anything, but he sat down near a book someone had left there, the poems and stories of Edgar Allan Poe.

Stallone started reading it and totally got into it. How Poe had lived, how he died, what really happened—Stallone studied all of the details. "Well, what did Poe do for you?" Tony asked him. "Poe got me out of myself." Stallone said. He got me to think about how I could touch other people—not worry about myself so much. And that made me want to become a writer."

Stallone began to write screenplays, but nothing worked, and he and his wife were still broke. He didn't even have $50 to his name. But finally, he sold a script called *Paradise Alley*. Big success! He told Tony he sold it for a $100, and that felt like a ton of money. Stallone was thrilled; he thought he was on his way. Selling that script never led to anything (although he did produce *Paradise Alley* many years later), and Stallone just kept going and going and going. Finally, he was so broke he sold his wife's jewelry. "Tony," he said, "there are some things in life you should never do—that was basically the end of our relationship."

Now his wife hated his guts, and they were still broke. This is where the story gets really good—it's painful, but it's a great illustration of why you should never quit.

Stallone was now so broke that he couldn't even feed his dog, and he loved that dog more than anything else in the world. It was the lowest day in his life. He stood outside a liquor store and tried to sell his dog to strangers for $50. Finally, someone bargained him down, and bought Stallone's dog—his best friend in the whole world—for $25. Stallone walked away crying. But he still wouldn't quit.

Then providence lent a hand: two weeks later, he was watching a fight between Muhammad Ali and Chuck Wepner, who was getting bludgeoned, but kept coming back for more; he wouldn't give up. Stallone had an idea. He started writing as soon as the fight ended, and he didn't stop. He didn't sleep. In 20 hours, he wrote the entire movie script. He saw the fight. He wrote the movie. Done. When he finished, Stallone told Tony, he was so excited that he was shaking. He really knew what he wanted, knew why he wanted it—and he took massive action to get it. But now that he had the script for *Rocky*, he still had to sell it. Some people read it and found it predictable, stupid, sappy. He kept going, trying to sell it. No one would buy it— and he was still broke. (Stallone wrote down everything those early critics said, and read it at the Oscars when *Rocky* won Best Picture. Massive success can be the greatest revenge.)

Finally, he met two agents who read the script and believed in it. They loved it, and they offered Stallone $125,000 for it. "My word," said Tony, "you must have been out of your mind." And he was. But he had enough presence of mind to tell the agents they had a deal on one condition: Stallone had to star in the movie. They were in-credulous: "What? What are you talking about? You're a writer!" But Stallone pushed back: "No, I'm an actor." They went back and forth like this, but Stallone held firm. This was *his* story. *He* was Rocky.

They said, "Look, there's no way we're going to pay $125,000 for a script, shove some no-name actor into the starring role, and just throw our money away. To make this movie, we need a star. Take it or leave it." So as Stallone left, he told them, "If that's what you believe, then you don't get my script."

Again, here's a man who's hopelessly broke. $125,000 was more money than he'd seen in his lifetime. But he walked away, because he knew his destiny and why he was committed to it. The agents called Stallone a few weeks later, brought him back to their office, and doubled their offer for the script, but Stallone still couldn't star in his own movie, so he turned it down. The agents came back with their final offer: $325,000. They *really* wanted this script. But Stallone said, "Not without me in it." They said no.

Finally, they reached a compromise: Stallone would get $35,000, plus a revenue share in the movie so he would share in the risk with them. The bottom line for the agents was that they didn't think the movie would work, so they weren't going to spend much money on it. They only invested $1 million to produce *Rocky*. It grossed $200 million.

But here's where it gets really interesting: "So what did you do?" Tony asked Stallone. "$35,000 is a far cry from $250,000 or $325,000, but it's still a lot of money when you don't have two nickels to rub together. What's the first thing you did?"

He went straight to that liquor store where he'd sold his dog and stood there for *three days straight,* hoping he'd see the dog's new owner. Stallone wanted to buy back his dog.

On the third day, he spotted him. Stallone couldn't believe it. And there was his dog! "Do you remember me, sir?" Stallone asked him. It had been about a month and a half since he'd sold him his dog.

"Yeah, yeah, I remember," said the guy.

Stallone said, "Look, I was broke, I was starving. He's my best friend in the world. I'm sure you love him too, but I just have to have him back. Please—I'll give you $100 for the dog. I know you only paid me $25, but I'll give you $100."

"Absolutely not," said the man. "No way. That's *my* dog now, and he's not for sale."

"You know how you say you have to 'know your outcome'?" Stallone asked Robbins. "Well, I knew mine, so I kept changing my approach."

Stallone offered him $500 for the dog.

The man categorically refused.

Stallone offered him $1,000.

"*No amount of money* will get you this dog."

"So what did you do?" Tony asked. "I knew my outcome," repeated Stallone, "so I decided to take massive action. I just kept changing my approach until I got my dog back."

"So what did it cost you, in the end?" asked Tony.

"$15,000 and a part in the movie!"

Butkus, the bull mastiff with a supporting role in *Rocky*, was Stallone's real-life dog, the dog he bought back for $15,000.

If you're committed, there's always a way. You just have to keep changing your approach. You were meant for greatness. You are instilled with an abundance of talent and gifts. Don't let something as small as fear—or your circumstances—limit all you were meant to be. Find a mentor, apply the lessons you learn from this book, and *don't ever quit!*

# ABOUT THE AUTHORS

## Chris Prefontaine

Chris is the best-selling author of *Real Estate on Your Terms: Create Continuous Cash Flow Now, Without Using Your Cash or Credit*. He's also the founder of **Smart Real Estate Coach** and the **Smart Real Estate Coach Podcast**. Chris has been in real estate for over 25 years. His experience includes the construction of over 100 single-family and duplex homes and ownership of a Realty Executives franchise, which he eventually sold to Coldwell Banker in 2000. He has also participated (and still does, selectively) in condo conversions and "raise the roof" projects.

Chris has always been an advocate of constant education; he regularly participates in high-end mastermind groups and consults with personal mentors. With his family team, he runs his own buying and selling business, buying two to five properties a month, and helping his students all around the country do the same. Chris and his family team have done over $80 million in real estate transactions. They mentor, coach, consult, and partner with students around the country, teaching their students to do exactly what they do.

## Nick Prefontaine

Nick grew up in the real estate industry, and got his start at an early age. By the age of 16, he was going door-to-door to pre-foreclosure homes, knocking on up to 50 doors per day.

In 2003, Nick was in a snowboarding accident that left him in a coma for over three weeks. The doctors told his parents that he'd probably never walk, talk, or eat on his own again. Less than three months later, he *ran* out of Franciscan Children's hospital. Now a Certified Infinite Possibilities Trainer, Nick speaks to groups that can benefit from his message about overcoming adversity.

Nick now specializes in working with lease purchasers to get them on the path to home ownership. Regardless of a buyer's credit situation, he looks at their complete financial picture and comes up with a plan to get them into a home.

## Zach Beach

Zach has been around the real estate business for over seven years, coaching and mentoring throughout the industry. He graduated from UMass Dartmouth with a degree in marketing and a minor in finance.

Zach currently helps **Smart Real Estate Coach associates** who are looking to start or continue a real estate investing business. He specializes in speaking with sellers to find the best options for them, and he also helps to acquire between five and ten properties per month between the family business and Associates. Zach has been able to thrive in this business after only a short period of time thanks to his skills in marketing and finance. He is a problem solver, a people person, and he's always educating himself. He constantly strives to be the best he can be, sharpening his skill sets in order to educate others.

## Don't miss out...

**Stay connected with the Smart Real Estate Team!** Follow us on social media to stay up to date on the latest real estate tips and insights:

 facebook.com/smartrealestatecoach

 youtube.com/smartrealestatecoach

 linkedin.com/company/smart-real-estate-coach/

 **@SmartRECoach** (twitter.com/smartrecoach)

And to hear from leading experts in the real estate space—just like the ones in this book—be sure to subscribe to the **Smart Real Estate Podcast** for weekly episodes packed with lessons, stories, and nuggets of wisdom.

Find it on iTunes, Stitcher, or at

 SmartRealEstateCoachPodcast.com

# YOUR FREE BONUS

We've loaded this book up with advice and insights from the 24 leading experts we interviewed and from our own team members. But we didn't want to stop there, so we created a **resources page** including everything referenced in this book—links, PDFs, videos, and more—to accommodate your learning style and help you put the advice from this book into action.

The great news is that you can access this site completely free of charge. Just fill out our simple form and we'll give you access to the entire vault of resources—and you might even find a few free gifts in your mailbox! You can find it at:

## TheNewRulesBook.com

And if you have any questions, you can always contact our team at

## Support@SmartRealEstateCoach.com

## Hiring the Smart Real Estate Coach Family Team

One of the fastest ways to grow your business or launch a new business is by getting advice from someone who has been there and done that. We've exposed you to many different experts and related niches. If our TERMS niche is one that resonates with you, be sure to check out our Consulting and Associate levels on the free *New Rules* **resources page** at TheNewRulesBook.com.

We're on a mission to close the "gap." The gap is the enormous space between students taking a course or seminar and then going out and completing deals. There are too many incomplete and ineffective programs and seminars in the real estate field.

Our **QLS** video program equips you with everything you need. *Everything.* And our Associate Levels enable you to do deals because *we do them with you!*

If someone else in this book got your attention, be sure to visit their links on the *New Rules* **resources page** at TheNewRulesBook.com and see what they have to offer.

Made in the USA
Lexington, KY
31 October 2019